HEXACHORDS IN LATE-RENAISSANCE MUSIC

For Ellena and Rosalie

Hexachords in
Late-Renaissance Music

Lionel Pike

Ashgate

Aldershot • Brookfield USA • Singapore • Sydney

Published by
Ashgate Publishing Limited
Gower House
Croft Road
Aldershot
Hants GU11 3HR
England

Ashgate Publishing Company
Old Post Road
Brookfield
Vermont 05036–9704
USA

British Library Cataloguing-in-Publication data

Pike, Lionel
  Hexachords in late-renaissance music
  1. Music – 16th century 2. Scales (Music)
  I. Title
  780.9'031

Library of Congress Cataloging-in-Publication data

Pike, Lionel.
  Hexachords in late-renaissance music / Lionel Pike.
  Includes bibliographical references and index.
  ISBN 1–85928–455–8 (hardcover)
  1. Music—Theory—16th century.   2. Music—Theory—16th century.
  I. Title.
  ML174.P55   1997
  781.2'52—dc21   97-20327
                                                                            CIP
                                                                            MN

ISBN 1 85928 455 8

Printed on acid-free paper

Music typeset by Andrews of Harrogate

Text typeset in Sabon by Photoprint, Torquay, Devon
and printed in Great Britain by Biddles Limited, Guildford.

Contents

Preface

In this study I presuppose that the reader has a basic knowledge of the techniques of Renaissance composition. To have included a discussion of this would have greatly added to the cost of the book without improving it, for expositions of the basic tenets of the style are plentiful and easy to come by, even if we still lack a theoretical work that attempts to take in the whole spectrum of sixteenth-century composers rather than concentrate on just one man. Those wishing to study the basic techniques should read one of the classic works on the subject: among these are the books by H.K. Andrews, Jeppessen, Merritt, and Rubio.[1] I have nevertheless included such historical background as I think is warranted by the pieces I have examined and the conclusions I have drawn.

I have referred in the main to music that is available in secondary sources, for in analytical discussions it is vital that every reader should be able – if he or she so wishes – to check an author's conclusions against the complete musical work which is the subject of the investigation. Nearly all the works discussed in this book are thus readily available in good music libraries. The examples may differ from the secondary sources, since I have given quotations at their original pitch and in their original note-values. The reasons for this, especially as far as pitch is concerned, will emerge during the course of the book. I have barred the examples regularly, and (since they are not aimed at performers) tacitly omitted to indicate where textual repeat marks and ligatures occur. To avoid confusion with the description of vocal strands as 'parts' I refer (except in quotations) to a piece written in more than one section as being in a number of '*partes*'. I refer to a theme used in imitation as a 'point of imitation', or simply a 'point'.

In general the book starts by investigating small-scale examples of the use of hexachords and solmization syllables, moves on to discuss larger-scale applications and complete pieces, and continues with case studies of the streams of emulative settings of two poems – settings containing an element of parody (a term used here in the Renaissance sense of 'building upon a model' rather than the modern sense of 'imitation with an intent to denigrate') in which the use of the hexachord is part of the barometer that measures progress within a stream of inter-linked settings. It concludes by investigating English examples of the use of the hexachord in both vocal and instrumental music.

I am greatly indebted to many friends, colleagues and pupils. My lifelong love of Renaissance music was born of my experiences as a cathedral chorister: I owe much to the incomparable training under a devoted cathedral organist, Clifford Harker. I am also deeply indebted to those who tutored me when I was a university student – to the late Dr H.K. Andrews and to Sir David Lumsden for their expert guidance, highly intelligent insights into the craft of composition, and encyclopaedic knowledge. I am grateful to Royal Holloway College for granting me sabbatical leave in which to work on this book: and to Professor Ian Spink for his continued help and encouragement. This book started life as lecture notes: thus many students have helped me. In particular I am grateful to the many who did not mind my lectures being turned into choir practices, and my choir practices being turned into lectures. Many thanks, finally, to David Andrews (of Andrews of Harrogate) for his care and attention in typesetting the music examples.

My first book was dedicated to my wife: she has again borne the brunt of editorial work, and has never minded acting as a sounding-board for my ideas. She deserves no less than that all my work should be dedicated to her. My children, however, have other ideas, and have asked for a book to be dedicated to them. This was not the reason for writing this book; but it is nevertheless inscribed to them with all their father's love, and in the knowledge that they have both helped in its construction in various ways that they will not yet understand.

Lionel Pike

Note

1. Andrews 1958, Jeppesen 1946, Merritt 1939, and Rubio 1972.

Introduction

The period I have set myself for discussion in this book is roughly defined by the earliest and latest composers discussed in detail in it – Willaert and Tomkins. The music of this period – roughly the last two-thirds of the sixteenth century, though going slightly beyond it in both directions – is generally of an astonishingly high quality: some would go so far as to argue that it has never been surpassed. Part of its fascination stems from its position at one of the greatest cross-roads in the history of music; part derives from the fact that it is a period full of paradoxes. The evolution of the language of music during this era is not in question; yet some of the terms used to describe this development call for explanation, if not for apology. Let us start with the word 'language'.

Language is fundamental to civilization:[1] without it there can be no preparation for the future, no displacement (that is, no discussion of persons or elements 'in the third person', those not present at the discussion), no religion: abstract ideas are an impossibility without it. Language presupposes both an encoder and a decoder: the speaker or writer on the one hand, the listener or reader on the other. For the act of communication to be effective the decoder must have the same understanding of the language as the encoder. It is a truism that music is itself a language; and no less than in other languages, encoder (composer) and decoder (performer or listener) must have the same understanding if communication is to be effective. The present-day listener has lost touch with some of the important elements of the language of late-Renaissance music: changing patterns of education and changes in musical style have led to the disappearance of at least two fundamental elements – rhetoric and the hexachord – which are essential to a true understanding of this music. The present book is concerned with the second of these elements.

Some will object to the Darwinism implicit in my use of the word 'evolution':[2] yet it is undeniable that, during the late sixteenth century, music

1

grew in intensity and expressiveness as composers sought to achieve ever more vivid means of illustrating their chosen texts. For a time such new procedures remained within the frame that defined the bounds of the classical polyphony; but inevitably there appeared composers who edged beyond that frame, and they were followed by those who leaped out of it. It is in the nature of such evolution, perhaps, that the upward graph of progress is not steady; and some present-day observers will argue that music went into decline, at least for a time, after the great period of classical polyphony. Moreover, some would argue that the ever-more-powerful word-illustration (often referred to as 'madrigalisms' since they were a particular mark of the madrigal) was not the only means of communication which music had at its disposal. A Gothic cathedral may say more to us than a Classical façade – or, at least, it may say something different and equally valid: similarly an Eton Choirbook antiphon communicates in a different way from a Monteverdi madrigal – but what it has to say to those with ears to hear is equally valid.

Having made these caveats, I stand by the word 'evolution': but evolution has necessarily distanced us from late sixteenth-century music, and has hindered our understanding of it. The changing patterns of education and the changes in musical language have, as mentioned above, taken away from the present-day listener all knowledge of rhetoric and most knowledge of the hexachord system. It is 'most' rather than 'all' knowledge of hexachords that has vanished, only because certain elements survived (tonic sol-fa and French pitch-names are examples): but the detailed workings of the system at its height – when it was the fundamental ABC of musical training – are no longer a part of every musician's make-up. If late-Renaissance music is to be fully understood, both encoder and decoder must have the same understanding of the basic vocabulary of its language: it is for this reason that I devote this book to a study of the ways in which the hexachord was used in the composition of music.

There is copious evidence to suggest that a re-assessment of music by taking solmization syllables into account is overdue, and I present some of this evidence below. But it would only be fair at the outset to point out that the music of the late Renaissance coincides with the final flowering of that system; we shall see that there are good reasons why composers continued to invoke solmization and the hexachords, yet the changes in musical style that led from Renaissance to Baroque called for a more flexible system, one more readily able to deal with the new chromaticism and new range of modulations and tonalities. We shall see that much music of the late Renaissance invoked some property or other of the hexachord system: but it is equally clear that other music did not, and it is a paradox that the same composer (indeed, the same piece) can on some occasions invoke the hexachord system and on others ignore it.[3] At a time when all the elements of musical composition – tonal workings, melodic design, text illustration, the concept of rhythm, dissonance treatment, even the manner in which music was actually composed (horizontal writing changing to vertical) – were changing it is no surprise that this is the case.

Although this book is not primarily concerned with modality, it will be necessary to refer to the modal system from time to time: thus it is necessary to present an outline of the system, however brief. The simplest way of describing the modes is to imagine that they are scales consisting of the white notes of the keyboard. The scale on D is known as dorian, that on E is phrygian; the others in order are lydian (on F), mixolydian (G), aeolian (A), and ionian (C); the locrian mode (on B) is avoided in polyphony. By adding one flat to the key signature each mode can be transposed up a fourth, so that dorian becomes 'G dorian' and ionian 'F ionian'. The addition of two flats similarly transposes each mode up a further fourth, making, for instance, 'C dorian'. Each mode was considered to consist of two elements, a fifth (*diapente*) and a fourth (*diatessaron*). In the authentic modes the diapente was placed below the diatessaron, a situation that was reversed in the plagal modes. Each mode was considered to have its own particular quality; its 'aria'.[4] A composer therefore chose the mode whose *aria* most closely fitted the nature of the text he was setting; only extremely rarely did music move into other modes, for to do so would be to invoke a different *aria*.

The factor that really distinguishes modal from tonal writing is the concept of modulation.[5] Modal music might, and did, cadence on various degrees of the mode: but it did not then treat that degree on which it had cadenced as a new tonic – or, at least, it only did so in exceptional circumstances. To have changed from one mode to another would have meant changing from one kind of expression to another.[6] This would be a positive advantage in some kinds of music, since the character of the text might itself change. The poetry so often set in Italian madrigals – that of Petrarch and his followers – often called for contrasts of feeling; and subsequent chapters will show how composers reacted to these shades of expression by their handling of modality or tonality. But a Lenten motet, for example, was much less likely to call for contrasts of expression: even so, one occasionally encounters pieces in mixed modes, or pieces that modulate in a modern fashion between modes or tonalities, without the text calling for extreme contrasts. As I will show in Chapter 5, Tallis, in his *Incipit lamentatio Ieremiae Prophetae* and in *In ieiunio et fletu* (1575) moves to a very much flatter area than his basic mode in order to illustrate weeping: in neither piece is this idea at all far removed from the remainder of the text in character, yet the flat areas are embryonic new tonal areas created in a more or less modern fashion. Only with major/minor tonality did a technique of modulation for structural purposes evolve: but this new system involved also the reduction of the number of scales to two (one major, one minor), though each was available at any pitch. The colour of the modes was lost, but the possibility of long-range tonal planning and dynamic contrast of key areas that was eventually to result in 'first-movement form' or 'sonata form' was born.

External factors had considerable influence on composition during the late Renaissance. A rising tide of humanism[7] encouraged composers to seek for a more direct means of communicating with the listener: it is a paradox that, while religious humanism repudiated much sacred medieval thought in favour of a revival of 'human' learning, we still find elements of medieval scholasticism in the symbolism of church music. But, in either case, there is a fast-growing desire to communicate vividly through music: musical expression began to develop; and once the process had begun, it mushroomed apace. At the end of the fifteenth century music was still decorative. The antiphons in the Eton Choirbook and the Masses of Taverner were still decorative rather than expressive. Vocal lines were added to one another (often around a *cantus firmus*) to build an impressive edifice of sound: the parallel with the upward-soaring arches and the interweaving strands of a high vault in the late Gothic styles is close. But the music, starting from the basic three-voice medieval polyphonic nucleus, stretches that ideal by adding layer upon layer of additional counterpoint. The words are largely immaterial to the construction of the music: but just occasionally, as in the *Nesciens Mater* of Walter Lambe, a particular chord progression seems to draw specific attention to an idea in the text, and sometimes certain numerical means of symbolizing words are used.

Throughout the sixteenth century this idea of music changed. Just as in church the *word* – the authority of the Bible – attained central significance for many, sweeping away the medieval liturgical and theological accretions which had been built up over the centuries, so the word (secular as well as Christian) became of greater significance to composers. The expression of the word – the bringing out of its meaning by illustrative devices, sometimes in a naively 'surface' manner, sometimes in a deeper way which might involve the overall design of a piece rather than the illustration of single words or ideas – became paramount. Every facet of a composition played its part in this growth of expression: it follows, therefore, that music must be conceived by the composer in a different way. 'Successive' composition – the addition of contrapuntal lines to a pre-existing basis, a procedure that owes much to the medieval love of reference back to authority (especially where the *cantus prius factus* is a plainsong) – could no longer give the composer sufficient control over his material. Harmony could be a potent force for expression; but only by conceiving all the parts together could he maintain strict control over it. One of the most fundamental changes in the art of composition, then, is traceable to the desire for text expression.

It follows from this that the language of any music which successfully sets a text forms a close parallel to that of the text itself: indeed, it would be possible to argue that the closer and more obvious the parallel, the more successful the musical setting. Does this mean that music has nothing of substance to add to a text? Obviously it adds emotional depth and colour not available in a recited poem: but, as Denis Arnold has pointed out, the eventual result of this was a type of

> music which makes no kind of sense divorced from the words. Whereas the earlier madrigals (and indeed later madrigals written in the older manner) would make sense played on instruments – the title pages of English madrigals often contained the phrase 'apt for voices or viols' . . . these avant-garde pieces would lose their whole raison d'être if so performed.[8]

But for some composers there was an underlying logic quite apart from that which illustrated the text: as Arnold goes on to say of Marenzio, ". . . he accepts the obligation to bring out the intensity. But he sticks to his fundamental view that music must make sense on its own terms". The position is similar to that taken by Mendelssohn when he declared that if composers could say all that they wished to say in words, they would not need to write music. In the best composers there is, then, a logic beyond that which merely translates the text into notes: the best vocal pieces are written 'in music' as well as in translations into sound. It is a paradox that it was at this very time when the word was so important that purely instrumental music began to take over centre stage.

The fundamental changes which resulted from text expression led to other changes. The old successive method of composition had resulted in a series of contrapuntal strands with a freedom from the constraints of a regular beat. This *tactus* (as the regular alternation of strong and weak pulses was called) does not have the strength that we find in later music, but the feel for such a beat is evident in the fact that the placing of suspensions was governed by it: in classical polyphony dissonances occurred on strong pulses and were prepared and resolved on the surrounding weak beats. It was natural that, with a vertical conception of music, there should be a stronger feel for harmony and a consequent move towards bar-line music for all the strands. The growth of bar-line music leads eventually to the effect of hammering on the strong beat which we find in so many Baroque concertos, though the feeling for dissonance treatment changed little, except that in certain types of music (in much Corelli, and in Lotti's *Crucifixus* settings, for instance) the density of suspensions is increased and dissonances are inclined to grow more pungent. Nevertheless, there were still composers who, though they conceived their music in a basically vertical and 'bar-line' fashion, continued to apply contrapuntal strands which, by their occasional movement across (rather than with) the strong beats, maintained an impression of polyphony. Many early works in the new style seem to recognize the clear tonal (major/minor) scheme and the clear bar-line nature of the music by insisting on cadential ostinati such as I–III–IV–V–I; harmonic ostinati had been used in the old style, too – witness the *Romanesca* and *Passamezzo* basses: but in the new music the more tonal nature of the patterns and their tendency to move in shorter phrases towards cadence points is a completely new effect. Such a ready-made formal scheme as the ostinato was, in addition, an obvious help to composers in the new style, particularly those who wished to abandon the old contrapuntal schemes and needed formal props to replace them.

There is another paradox here: it has often been maintained that the rise of the madrigal was in some measure the result of a desire to treat Petrarchan texts in a more expressive manner than could be achieved by the mere prettiness of a tune – as was found, for example, in the frottola.[9] Counterpoint seemed a more passionate and fitting handmaid to more serious and passionate texts: yet this position was not maintained to the end of our period, as the search for expression ultimately led back to a concentration on a single line, for counterpoint was thought to neutralize the message.[10] A solo voice can be more direct in its expression of a text than can a vocal consort: it is hardly surprising, therefore, that the search for expression goes hand-in-hand with a tendency towards the solo vocal line.[11] This is seen at first in a concentration upon the upper voice of a composition, sometimes resulting in the feeling of tune with accompaniment, a texture that replaces the old one of counterpoint built around a tenor. Such a texture leads naturally on to the conception of the accompaniment as a series of chords, and to the eventual reduction of those chords to a *basso continuo*. The further step of solo voice (or perhaps duet) with continuo is the next logical move.

Counterpoint becomes an irrelevance for many writers of such music. There is no place for points of imitation in monodies, though it is true that some composers nevertheless wrote solo voice pieces which are in effect full choir music reduced in forces so that the continuo part replaces the 'missing' choir. Yet despite all the claims made for monody, counterpoint would not be put down, but kept bobbing up like a cork in water. The metrical psalm tune in England, for example, was at first puritanically white-washed of all polyphony, as the churches themselves were stripped of ornament; but the old techniques, which lived on in such things as the *In nomine* settings, soon invaded even the psalm tunes themselves, and they began to be harmonized polyphonically. The recercars of Frescobaldi, coming at a time after the 'new music' had taken a firm hold, show a virtuoso handling of polyphony as astonishing as anything in the *prima prattica*. In what seems on the surface like a negation of the trend towards monody, some composers eventually made contrapuntal arrangements of works that had at first been solo songs or monodies.[12] Far from turning their backs permanently on polyphony, some composers began to acknowledge that inner (contrapuntal) voices in a composition could provide a particularly expressive quality.[13] Granted the general move towards vividness of text illustration and clarity of expression, one might expect that some kind of facial or dramatic gesture might be employed to emphasize the meaning of the text: the development of dramatic presentations through *Intermedi* into opera and oratorio, then, is part of this same trend.

The growth of chromaticism was partially a response to a desire to set expressive texts with due expression (the semitone is the most expressive of intervals, and a wide use of it naturally resulted in chromaticism) and partially a response to a belief that chromatic and enharmonic styles would help music to regain the power which ancient Greek music was supposed to possess. Such a process was bound to destroy both the modal system and the hexachord system in due course. *Musica ficta*, too, if applied whole-scale, may break down modal purity, though the normal application of semitone inflections does not do this. There are basically two reasons for applying *musica ficta*: to avoid forbidden intervals (the tritone and augmented fourth, the diminished octave, and so on) whether these are harmonic or melodic; and to make a part more grateful to hear or to sing. Normally, A, B, D and E could be flattened, and C, D, F and G could be sharpened (as well as B♭ being made into B natural) by *musica ficta*.[14]

Mention of *musica ficta*, however, must be amplified by reference to *musica recta*: the latter refers to the introduction of pitches which, while they may not be indicated by the key signature, are nevertheless 'understood' by virtue of the use of a particular hexachord or the 'Una nota supra / La semper est canendum fa' rule. With the 'open' key signature (that is, one without flats, since sharps were not used in the period under discussion) a passage suggesting the use of the F hexachord would involve B being sung as *fa* (B♭) rather than B natural; and an ascending passage on the notes C–G–A–B–[A] would also use B♭ on the understanding that 'Una nota supra la / Semper est canendum fa' (meaning 'when only one note above the top of the hexachord is sounded, it is a semitone rather than a tone higher').[15] But – as we shall see – any semitone is normally called 'mi–fa' in the hexachord system (Morley, in *A Plaine and Easie Introduction to Practicall Musicke*,[16] shows that this was not invariably so, since F♯–G for him was still 'fa–sol', with F♯ taken as merely a chromatic inflection of the ordinary solmization name, and not requiring a change of hexachord). 'Mi–fa' does not always result in an interval chromatic to the mode in use; a mixolydian piece will use B–C 'diatonically', for example: but if the same piece in the same mode were to use B♭–B natural, the result would be 'chromatic' to the prevailing mode (though, of course, such an interval might result from *musica recta* rather than *musica ficta*).

'Mi–fa', then, plays an important part in the writing of expressive music, and the density of semitones in a piece might almost be taken as a barometer of its expressiveness. Clearly, though, this cannot be a general rule, since present-day listeners, no less than sixteenth-century ones, will be apt to find some relatively non-chromatic works more expressive than very chromatic ones. Yet the increase in the density of the use of 'mi–fa' is a rough indicator of the amount of effort expended in being expressive. Equally clearly, there comes a point beyond which it is no longer feasible for the performer to think of every semitone as being 'mi–fa', for the density of chromatic semitones in some works is such that changes of hexachord would be virtually continuous if the singers attempted to force each semitone into its own hexachord.[17]

'Mi–fa', however, did not only refer to the semitone. By assuming that the notes belong to two different hexachords it could also refer to a tritone (indeed, by taking 'fa' as C in durum and 'mi' as E in naturale, it could be a major third – or minor sixth – as well): the old saying 'mi contra fa diabolus est in musica' refers to the tritone (mi = B, fa = F, for example) rather than to any of the other intervals suggested by those two hexachord sounds. It is clear that the use of 'mi–fa' for expression was extended to the use of the 'mi–fa' tritone for expression of a certain type. Since the tritone is not an easy interval to sing melodically, its appearance in melodic form is rather rare; it is more likely to appear as a cross-relation or as part of the harmony. We should, however, remember that all harmonies were calculated above the bass: a chord with a bass note of D and with F natural and B above it was not regarded as containing a tritone, but as one containing a minor third above the bass alongside a major sixth above the bass.[18] The relationship between the upper voices is not usually a matter of concern, though care had clearly to be exercised about the sounding together of certain notes which, while being consonant with the bass, create dissonances among themselves: such combinations as the major with the minor third, the minor sixth with the major third, or the sixth with the fifth above the bass were treated with care, or in some cases, avoided.

If 'mi–fa' can mean the tritone as well as the semitone, it can, by extension, be used to indicate a confrontation between the molle hexachord (which contains F and B♭) and the durum (with its B natural): both the tritone and the (chromatic) semitone are thrown up by this confrontation: for this reason the combination of molle and durum was discouraged by theorists, though they made an exception for chromatic music. We shall see that this combination became a potent force for expression, and a logical extension of the diatonic 'mi–fa' used for expressive purposes. Changes between major and minor and tritonal relationships are thus part of the trend: both grow ultimately from the idea that 'mi–fa' is an expressive device.

From Josquin onwards the methods used in text expression became more and more powerful and increasingly abstruse. In certain areas – in the Italian madrigal, for instance, where the most brilliant developments took place, and where musical language evolved fastest – the techniques were clearly aimed at the *cognoscenti*: such rapid progress would have been beyond the understanding of those not 'in the know'. The passion for academies where the *cognoscenti* met to hear and discuss music helped in producing a spiral of self-perpetuating evolution which, by the end of the sixteenth century, had become a fast spin, and out of which came the 'new music' and the new forms (opera, oratorio, etc.).

The music discussed in this book illuminates the no-man's-land between the Renaissance and Baroque eras. The difficulties raised by the changes in musical style can readily be seen in the treatment of Monteverdi by musical scholars, for he is variously described as 'the end of the Renaissance' and the 'creator of Modern Music'.[19] In a sense both descriptions are apt, for Monteverdi straddles the two great periods, building upon and extending the old techniques as well as pointing the way forward to new ones. Palestrina, too, has been regarded both as the high priest of the classical polyphonic style and also as one of the leaders in the move towards the new major/minor tonality. With such disagreements between honourable men about fundamental facets, it is scarcely to be wondered at that the period can seem like a minefield to the unwary. The idea that major/minor tonality was a natural outcome of modal writing has been questioned: indeed, some deny the concept of evolution altogether:

> . . . there is simply no plausible concept of natural evolution in music or any other art. New devices appear to fulfill new and often unpredictable needs.[20]

The change from modal to tonal writing still awaits its chronicler: basically, the music of the early sixteenth century (and music before that time) was modal, whereas music from the second half of the seventeenth century onwards was tonal. The time has come to restate this basic proposition, for some recent theorists have seen fit to question it. Saul Novack, for instance, has doubted the straight change from the one system to the other by saying

> Most general music histories tell us that the Baroque era ushers in the major–minor system of *tonality*, in contrast to the preceding practice of *modality*. This dichotomy, modality vs. tonality, is misleading and unfortunate.[21]

And David Fanning makes a valuable point when he comments

> Thus tonality and modality may converge towards a middle ground where one may suspect that the terms are more a convenience for analysts than separate musical realities.[22]

It would be foolish to deny that there is a no-man's-land – as I have just called it – between modality and tonality: but it is nevertheless a fact that the basic musical style eventually changed from a reliance on modes to a reliance on major/minor tonality. This is a profound and fundamental change, and one that goes hand-in-hand with a move towards the vertical conception of music and new methods of organizing rhythm and structure. We shall encounter evidence of these developments, and evidence of resistance to them; yet this cannot be the whole story, for much of the music examined here is of the highest quality, and is aimed at the *cognoscenti*. Such music represents only a small proportion of the music of its day. Nevertheless, we may recall that the academies where the thinking musicians gathered played no small part in musical progress, and that, as Michael Levy, puts it, 'Few arts at any time . . . have advanced by respecting the rules'.[23] But not all music for the *cognoscenti* was forward-looking: Victoria's, while including much religious symbolism, was certainly not.

Herein lies another paradox. Those who advocated a change to a new style of music, the *seconda prattica* – and we would number most of them among the *cognoscenti* – pressed for a new way of composing, taking as their authority the marvellous effects of music reported by classical authors. They agreed that, since the *prima prattica* (as we now call the classic polyphonic style of the sixteenth century) could not match this supposed power of ancient music, the current style must be inferior. The theorist Vicentino concluded that music makes its greatest effect only when new, and that its power wanes with repeated hearings.[24] This is certainly not in keeping with the ideas expressed in this book, for the structural purpose behind many of the works examined here is more likely to be appreciated only after several hearings. Even the *cognoscenti* themselves must have realized this, for Artusi says that Monteverdi's *Cruda Amarilli*, when he first heard it in Ferrara in company with several knowledgeable musicians, was sung and repeated.[25] Vicentino advocates chromatic music, basing his view on the assumption that the Greeks used diatonic music 'during public festivals in common places for vulgar ears' and chromatic and enharmonic music for 'the private amusements of gentlemen and princes for refined ears . . .' We know this music advocated by Vicentino as *Musica reservata* – the area reserved for those with particularly refined ears and intellects.[26] In fact, much of the music which appeals to the *cognoscenti* is not enharmonic, and much is not particularly chromatic either. It is not *Musica reservata* in the normal sense. I do not treat much chromatic and enharmonic writing in this book because the ideas of Vicentino produced little music of real value, a fact which did not go unnoticed by later theorists of the period. Galilei, though, makes a slightly different point when he says that the marvellous effects of ancient music are reported by men of high intelligence: this, he maintains, is part of its excellence. Nevertheless, he goes on, sixteenth-century music is practised by the lowly born and illiterate: since it must therefore be inferior, he advocates a return to the supposed practices of old. Both Vicentino and Galilei seem to us almost intolerably class-conscious: both value highly what appeals to the *cognoscenti*. But each of them has a different view of what this actually is.

Bottrigari, taking yet another view, maintains that contrapuntal skill is appreciated by professional musicians, but is not enjoyed by everyone. This is also not the whole story, for many of the works examined here contain elements of construction which go beyond the purely musical. It may be that Mei had this in mind when he wrote to Galilei:

> I believe that the proposed goal . . . was not the sweetness of the consonances to satisfy the ear . . . but the complete and efficacious expression of everything he

wanted to make understood . . . by means and through the aid of high and low sounds . . . accompanied with the regulated temperament of the fast and slow, articulating the sections of his works according to the one and the other quality so that each one by itself through its proper nature was accommodated to some determinate affection.[27]

This could easily be taken simply to emphasize the generally current view that music should carefully illustrate the text, and that this text should be clearly audible: but it could also be taken as implying that the in-depth expression of the text could be part of the overall structure. That music should be more than mere notes is suggested by several theorists: some maintain that the true goal of the composer is to express moral precepts in an endeavour to 'improve' his listeners. Such music is clearly reckoned to be of more value than music which does not express such a purpose. However, some maintain that this moral message cannot be conveyed through the medium of counterpoint.[28] It is another paradox that many of the works examined in this book are highly contrapuntal, and yet express ideas beyond the mere notes. We think of the Renaissance as being that time when classical antiquity acted upon the arts to produce a fresh impetus in music; this new impetus is the *seconda prattica* (a style which is rather more 'Baroque' than 'Renaissance'). Yet it is a further paradox that *prima prattica* theorists also appealed to the writings of classical antiquity.

There are two general streams in the music of the late Renaissance: on the one hand there are those who advocated purity of harmony, and on the other there are those who advocated the expression of emotion. Even though they may be opposed, their basic tenets are not so very different. Many objected to the loss of classical balance when composers moved over from the *prima* to the *seconda prattica*: yet we shall see how the best composers of the new music could still write perfectly formed, marvellously balanced works – though the nature of such balance is utterly different from that of the classical Renaissance school.[29] As we have seen, the vivid expression of the text was one of the main spurs to progress at the end of the Renaissance: much progress in musical language can be traced back to this search for vivid word illustration. The ideas of emulation and parody in the Italian madrigal show how this exploration forwarded the language of music: a portion of this book is therefore devoted to these procedures, illustrating the part played by the hexachord in the stream of compositions making up a series of related works. But clarity and audibility of the words and accurate expression of the text were not only sought by the *avant-garde* composers: all those caught up in any way in the humanistic trends and religious movements of the period also had similar aims. The conservatives, too, used parody, and – although it is beyond the scope of this monograph – church music of the *prima prattica* was imbued with symbolism that deeply enhanced the meaning of the text. Indeed, it is a further paradox that some of those who followed the *prima prattica* style seem to have gone even further along the road towards clarity and accuracy of text illustration and towards the preaching of moral precepts than did those who advocated the overthrow of counterpoint: Palestrina is a prime example.

These views may well make the reader question the use of the word 'Renaissance' to describe the music of the period covered in this book: indeed, very little of the music discussed below owes its style to a conscious attempt to recreate the glories of the ancient world. Nevertheless, as an accepted term for the period (and one which is generally understood by all) it has an obvious usefulness. To have called the period 'Mannerist' on the basis that there is a certain school of more-or-less experimental composition leading eventually to the *seconda prattica* would have been to ignore the equally valid claims on the intelligent listener put forward by the *prima prattica* composers. The complex musical structures analysed in this book perhaps suggest why this 'Renaissance' happened so much later in music than in the other art forms. Galilei recognized that music lagged behind the other arts, and his explanation was that his contemporaries were ignorant of ancient music and its theory. But, as we know, it is not unusual for music in all periods to lag behind its sister arts. Music is a highly specialized language; indeed, many would count it the most complex of all. It is hardly surprising that such a complex language and art form should take a long time to reach its apogee.[30]

What impresses us most in the end is not so much the surface cleverness – the madrigalisms and *augenmusik* – as the more far-reaching devices. Galilei is often quoted for his attack on naive text illustration,[31] and in a sense he is right: it is only when surface illustration gives place to something more fundamental and far-reaching that real music emerges. This music may address the *cognoscenti*: but, like all good music, that does not prevent it from appealing on another level to those who are not 'in the know'.

There are various levels of appeal, and I cover some of them in the following chapters. The shape of this book is largely governed by the uncovering of these various levels. We may see the ordinary use of solmization as having an appeal mainly to the ordinary singer, whereas the more abstruse uses of hexachord syllables are addressed to the more deeply knowledgeable. We are, nevertheless, dealing with the period just prior to the disappearance of the hexachord as a force for the organization of musical structure. This is quite clearly evident in Dowland's introduction 'To the Reader' in *A Pilgrim's Solace*: in this passage he regrets that his *avant-garde* contemporaries do not understand the hexachord.[32] Dowland's implication is that 'the learneder sort of Musitians' (for him, these are more or less equivalent to conservative musicians) do have this knowledge. We shall see how vital a knowledge of the system is to an understanding of the music and (in some instances) to its performance. The gradual development of the new style of composition can readily be seen in those series of madrigals in the emulative tradition, each of which sets a text already used by a previous composer but seeks to improve upon it in expressiveness. Such a series of emulative works, as we shall see, pushed the art of composition to its limits, and analysing them acts as a barometer of progress by the *avant-garde*. This can involve chromaticism, new treatments of dissonance, new means of formal organization, new textures, and sometimes abstruse uses of the hexachord system: but progress could also be made towards diatonic tonality by composers who, being equally keen to write expressively, reached out towards the methods of the major/minor system without going to such extremes, and by remaining basically within the classical style.

Hexachords

The hexachord was the very ground of musical learning, and it was normal for treatises to start with an explanation of this system.[33] As if to illustrate the point, Shakespeare introduced a basic lesson in sight-singing, which Hortensio uses as a cover for courtship, into Act III, Scene I of *The Taming of the Shrew*. One learned to read music by using the *gamut*, a system which formed the basis of music as understood at that period. Devised by Guido d'Arezzo in the eleventh century, it was taught by imagining the notes to be spread across the fingers of an outstretched hand: another name for the system was therefore 'the Guidonian hand'. Only with the burgeoning of chromatic music did the system, which is basically diatonic, die out.[34] The gamut system consisted of three fundamental hexachords, available in various octaves, built on G (the durum or 'hard' hexachord), C (the naturale or 'natural' hexachord), and F[35] (the molle – i.e. 'soft' or 'sweet' hexachord). (See Example 1.) Hexachords are not keys or modes, but merely a means of identifying notes. They are identical in shape, having the sequence TONE–TONE–SEMITONE–TONE–TONE (a sequence which is the same when inverted). The notes in ascending order were known by the sounds derived by Guido from the opening syllable of each line of the medieval Office Hymn for St John the Baptist (*Ut queant laxis*), a hymn in which each line starts a note higher. These sounds, UT RE MI FA SOL and LA, were often known as the *voces musicales*.[36]

The semitone – which, as we have seen, was the most characteristic interval of the hexachord, and the one most often invoked for expressive purposes – occurs in the very centre of each hexachord, between MI and FA.[37] It is this interval (or rather, its position) that does most to determine which hexachord is in use: the importance of the semitone for this purpose is paramount.[38] The symmetry of the system, with each hexachord revolving around its most characteristic interval, must have appealed strongly to the Medieval and Renaissance mind. Such orderliness was not dissimilar to the orderliness of music itself and of 'the harmony of the spheres' which was thought to reflect the glory of God's creation. It is, then, easy to see how the system survived for so long: but it is not so easy for us to understand why a hexachord containing B♭ sounded 'soft' or 'sweet', whereas one with a B natural sounded 'hard' – we must simply register that this was so. The durum hexachord used B natural, the molle used B♭: the signs for the two pitches were different (♮ and ♭ respectively), and eventually durum came to mean 'major' and molle 'minor'.

Example 1

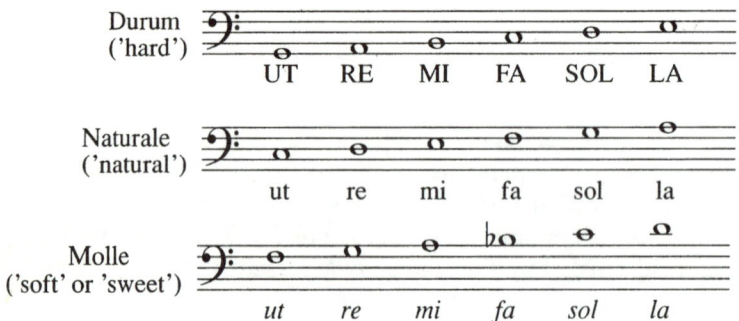

One of the difficulties of the gamut system was that, since no hexachord spans an octave, it was necessary to change ('mutate') from one to another when going beyond the confines of a single hexachord. Performers would, however, remain for as long as possible in one hexachord so as to avoid over-complication.[39] 'Sol-fa-ing' songs were devised in order to help train musicians in the art. The complexity of the system was one of the reasons for its eventual eclipse. The complete range of notes in the system is shown in Example 2.

Many notes can belong to more than one hexachord, and were known by the combination of their various possible hexachord syllables. The compound names shown in Example 2 were used for identifying pitch (though even this was not without ambiguity): such compound names also helped in the process of mutation between the hexachords.[40] Accidentals (apart from B♭ or E♭ – see Chapter 1) could be reckoned as merely inflections of the note and did not necessarily alter the sound-name, as is shown by Morley.[41] But B♭ or E♭ will always be 'fa' in this system, except on the rare occasions when extremely flat hexachords are in use (see below).[42] Moreover B natural (and, very often, notes signed with a sharp) will be considered as 'mi'. Indeed, it will be evident from Example 2 that B♭ and B natural are the only pitches above the lowest three that do not have compound pitch descriptions.

Example 2

Throughout this book DURUM solmization syllables will be given in CAPITALS ('UT'), naturale syllables in lower case ('ut'), and *molle* syllables in *italic* ('*ut*'). <u>Underlined</u> italic syllables ('<u>*ut*</u>') will indicate the hexachord on B♭ (i.e. *molle* transposed one degree flatwards). Solmization of the correct melodic shape that does not conform to one of the recognized hexachords is followed by a query ('ut?').

Changing from one hexachord to another was a natural part of the system. Any line spanning more than a sixth was in any case bound to require a change of hexachord. Being able to make such changes automatically probably explains why composers made them within a *soggetto cavato*[43] or, indeed, in any line of a composition. Josquin's *Missa La sol fa re mi*, for example, changes from naturale to durum (A–G–C–A–B: i.e la–sol–FA–RE–MI) and immediately back again (E–D–F–D–E: i.e. LA–SOL–FA–re–mi); the final E acts simultaneously as mi and LA of a new statement of the *soggetto cavato* without mutations (E–D–C–A–B).[44] Yet it is fair to say that mutations were not always applied: Josquin's *Missa Hercules Dux Ferrariae* uses the hexachord syllables re–ut–re–ut–re–fa–mi–re (the vowels of the name in the title) in both naturale and durum, but does not change from one to the other within a single statement. (There is one touch of molle: at the end of the second *Kyrie*, whose main subject derives a falling third from the re–fa leap of the *soggetto cavato*, there is a sequence which ends by basing the ostinato around the pitches G, F, G, B [flat, by *musica recta*], A, G. Each pitch of this ostinato is preceded by the note a third above: this is clearly derived by moving the solmization syllables to the molle hexachord.)

These procedures may have begun as a means of teaching sight-reading to beginners: as the basic way of learning music they became as much second nature to any musician of the time as the notes of the scale are to us today.[45] Theorists insist that the more experienced singers did not need to use the hexachords for sight-singing; despite this, there is a clear growth in the employment of the hexachord with, as it were, a knowing wink at the performers – once learned, the solmization syllables were never forgotten, and composers could use them as an additional means of communication. Josquin's *Missa La sol fa re mi* is one such; and we shall encounter many more in the following chapters.

Notes

1. See Wells 1984.
2. See Fenlon 1988, pp. 6 and 7, for instance.
3. An odd example is Arcadelt's First Book of Madrigals – an immensely popular publication. The reprint of 1603 provides a table explaining the hexachord system and its mutations, for presumably knowledge of the system had by then ceased to be general among performers. Yet the music generally does not make much use of solmization sounds, even if it makes a little use of the colour of the molle hexachord in the manner described in Chapter 1 below. See Lera 1989, p. 29.
4. For a discussion of 'aria' see Pirrotta 1982, pp. 247ff.
5. 'Modulation' in the modern sense: see Bent 1984, p. 18, fn. 26.
6. One finds more freedom in the early part of the sixteenth century than in the second half: the French chanson can be quite cavalier in its treatment of mode (for instance, Fevin's *Petite camusette* starts in the phrygian mode but ends on D: Mouton's *En venant de Lyon* ends in C, a key that has at no point been prepared: and Regnard's *Las, je me plains* starts in a kind of A major that eventually leads to an E–phrygian ending).
7. Haar 1986, p. 74, remarks that the word 'humanism' is overworked and misused. An excellent recent treatment is Fenlon 1989, pp. 2ff.
8. Arnold 1983.
9. Mace 1983, p. 120. The view that the madrigal developed from the frottola has been challenged: see Haar 1986, p. 59f, Fenlon 1988, pp. 8, 14, 15. Haar 1986, p. 66, makes a case for its development from the chanson.
10. Pirrotta 1982, p. 248. Pirrotta 1982, p. 22, points out that Humanists were suspicious of polyphony, associating it with scholasticism.
11. The monodic reform can, however, be dated well before 1600: see Pirrotta 1982, pp. 36 and 240. Pirrotta also points out that the idea did not originate in the Florentine Camerata: see ibid. pp. 63, 201, 244, 250.
12. Haar 1986, p. 146. See also Carter 1988a, p. 259.
13. Pirrotta 1982, p. 246f.
14. Berger 1987, passim.
15. See the discussion in Bent 1972, Bent 1984, and Zager 1987.
16. Morley 1597, p. 18.
17. In the chromatic or enharmonic genus there were two sizes of semitone: but such theoretical niceties had no real effect on practical composition, and are ignored here. See Haar 1986, p. 115, among others. See also Berger 1976, passim.
18. There are earlier periods in which such vertical tritones were shunned: see Zager 1987, p. 12, for example.
19. Schrade 1964 and Tomlinson 1987: see also Carter 1988.
20. Mace 1983, p. 151.
21. Novack 1983. Haar 1986, p. 135, refers to the concept of the rise of tonality as unhistorical. The earliest theoretical treatment of the modes in polyphony appeared as late as 1525 (see Owens 1990, p. 9).

22. Fanning 1988, p. 16.
23. Levy 1975, p. 236.
24. A splendid treatment of the theorists of the period is to be found in Berger 1976. Relevant quotations on which I have based the following passage may be found on pp. 40f, 73, 80, 87, and 93.
25. See Chapter 2.
26. *Musica reservata* has never been adequately defined: see Haar 1989, p. 245.
27. Palisca 1977, p. 115. Translation from Berger 1976.
28. Berger 1976, pp. 77–9.
29. See Haar 1986, pp. 138 and 147.
30. I owe the idea to a chance conversation with Professor Nicholas Temperley, to whom I offer grateful acknowledgement.
31. The whole passage is quoted in Strunk 1950, pp. 315ff.
32. See below.
33. See the remarks in the introduction to Rainbow 1982: see also Field 1996, pp. 5–9.
34. Though music teaching continued to invoke the hexachord for many years, and French composers still tend to describe music in terms of the hexachord on C. 'Tonic sol-fa', too, is based on the gamut system: indeed, 'ut' became 'doh' quite early on (see Haar 1990, p. 71).
35. The molle hexachord was not present in Guido's classification, being a late addition.
36. Some hexachord masses are entitled 'Super Voces Musicales'. Although the hexachord is invertible – that is, the same sequence of intervals occurs both upright and in inversion – I know of only one use of 'inversions' of the actual syllables apart from mi and fa: this is discussed below (see pp. 148–50). Instrumental and vocal music do, of course, often juxtapose rising and falling hexachords while *not* using the solmization syllables with ut at the top and la at the bottom. See the comments on the connection between hexachords and the Music of the Spheres in Godwin 1987.
37. On the affective quality of the semitone see Kerman 1981, pp. 97 and 121. Zarlino says that when the semitone is absent, the effect is bitter: see Palisca 1985, p. 363.
38. Allaire 1972, p. 24, says that fourths and fifths are the key elements: his discussion is based on music of an earlier period and a less chromatic nature than that with which the present book is concerned.
39. Zager 1987, p. 9.
40. A version with the hexachords descending as well as ascending is given in Morley 1597, p. 11.
41. Morley 1597, p. 17, and the example on p. 18.
42. See Allaire 1972, p. 35.
43. A musical phrase derived from a word by transferring its vowels to the corresponding hexachord sounds.
44. See Haar 1976, pp. 577–9. See also Blackburn 1987, p. 41.
45. This is certainly implied by Doni when he mentions that some singers paid so little attention to the text that they might as well have performed the pieces to solmization syllables and nonsense syllables: see Haar 1986, p. 107. In Ferrara in 1481 'a mass was sung entirely in solmization syllables, though apparently not in a liturgical service' (Reynolds 1989, p. 191).

1 Voces Musicales I

The Solmization Syllables

The gamut, as we have seen, was the very bedrock of musical knowledge. A composer could count on his performers, and on some of his listeners, knowing the solmization syllables as well as they knew their own names. It would scarcely have been possible for a Renaissance musician to sing B♭ without thinking 'fa', or B natural without thinking 'mi'. The solmization syllables can, as we shall see, act as a means of communicating with the performers: sometimes this was done in an obvious way, sometimes more covertly. The extent to which a performer was able to read the 'language' would depend on his experience, for the more seasoned singers clearly had the extra leisure in which to think about the implications of the notes as opposed to concentrating merely on sight-reading.[1] The composers, too, seem to have developed more abstruse ways of using the hexachord towards the end of the sixteenth century. As a means of expression it is sometimes more covert than overt: in either case, unless we have a knowledge of the gamut, we cannot hope to understand what the composer was attempting to communicate. Even if we have other methods of analysis not available to the *Cinquecento*, we are likely to overlook important features if we examine music of that period without this historical perspective.[2] Furthermore, analysis of vocal music that excludes any reference to the text cannot hope to tell the whole story: much can be learnt about text setting by studying the relationship between the words, the notes, and the gamut. If the composer is to express to us what he was attempting to express to his contemporaries, we shall have to take his own basis of musical thought into account.

Since notes were known by their solmization names[3] rather than by letters (though sometimes a letter-name for a note was prefixed – E la mi, or A la mi re, for example), a Renaissance singer would have in mind the solmization names of the notes he was reading.[4] Naturally, if a composer comes across

18

these sounds in the text he is setting, he may well write the note that corresponds to that sound. For this reason 'sola' is often set to the rise of a tone ('sol la') and 'lasso' to a falling tone ('la sol'), while 'mi fa' is often set to a semitone and 'ut sol' to a leap of a fifth upwards. It would have been farcical for Philips to have set the madrigal *Ut re mi fa sol la* (1596) with the solmization syllable names in any other order than that suggested by the hexachord;[5] it is clear, however, that not every composer reacted in this way when faced with just the occasional vowel sound that happened to match one of the solmization syllables, and it is likewise clear that those who did at times match sounds to corresponding pitches did not do so invariably. Yet there is overwhelming evidence that the practice of mirroring solmization sounds in the text with music suggested by them was widespread, even if it is equally clear that it was not universal.[6]

Straightforward uses of solmization of this type are well known, and examples like those in Josquin mentioned in the Introduction have been part of musical general knowledge for generations. In a similarly light-hearted way, Dufay is sometimes indicated in manuscripts by the letters 'du' followed by a B♭.[7] Pierre van den Hove (d. 1536) used the pseudonym 'Alamire', the hexachord description of the note A. As Martin Picker comments, this is '*la*, *mi* and *re* in the hexachords on C, F and G. . . . The name is appropriate to the many-sided Alamire; in addition to his musical activities, he was a diplomat and double agent . . .'[8] Although such treatments are not universal, it is clear that the influence of solmization is occasionally evident even when the words set are close to, but not exactly, hexachord syllables. As mentioned above, 'lasso' is normally set to the shape of a descending tone ('la sol') mostly in the correct pitches of one of the hexachords, occasionally not. This 'la sol' shape is used in Corteccia's setting of the word 'lassando' in *Se per onesti Preghi* (1543), and also in Luzzaschi's setting of 'lassa' in *Quando io miro* (1594). In *Crudel, perche mi fuggi* (1590) – a text often set as *Lasso, perche mi fuggi* – Monteverdi shows his knowledge of the alternative initial word by setting 'Crudel' to the 'lasso' shape. Even in such an extreme piece as Gesualdo's *Moro lasso* (1611, but written much earlier[9]) the descending step is used, though, like so much else in the piece, it is chromatically inflected.

Compound note-names – as shown in Example 2 – are only infrequently found in solmization of texts. In Palestrina's *Voi mi poneste in foco/Pero che da l'ardore* (1558) the word 'va-te' is set to the note D (so taking in the la and re sounds of la–sol–re): in Masnelli's *Non puo, dolce mia vita* (1582) 'dolce' is set to the note G (so taking in the sol and re sounds of sol–re–ut); and in Marenzio's *Se la mia vita/Pur mi* (1588) the first note (D) is set to sol–re in the hexachord sounds, for which the composer presumably regarded the first word 'Se' as an abbreviated equivalent. In the examples which follow it sometimes happens that the composer has set a diphthong or double vowel in such a way as to match solmization sounds in two different hexachords simultaneously: in such cases both the sounds are marked in the examples, bracketed together. On some occasions the result is that the double vowel sound is set to its corresponding compound hexachord description (as in the setting of the second syllable of 'assai' as la–mi or la–mi–re, E or A, in Example 8d).

Treatments of this kind are very clear to the singer, if not to the listener: it is, however, the less obvious treatments of solmization that are more interesting, even if more difficult to substantiate. Texts which do not have the exact solmization syllables may nevertheless include vowels with a close approximation to those in the gamut; and such syllables may still be matched in the music. A large proportion of Rore's *Ancor che col partire* (1547) is governed by the vowels in the text, and the whole opening phrase of Arcadelt's *S'infinita bellezza* (1544) is closely based around the vowels (as well as being in strict two-in-one canon, perhaps in an attempt to illustrate infinity[10]). In Marenzio's *Se la mia vita* (1588), to which reference has just been made, the opening two words are set as SOL–LA and sol–la, and the fact that 'mia' is then set as mi–la and MI suggests that this was a conscious use of solmization. Einstein's argument that such close following of the hexachord syllables leaves a composer no room for manoeuvre – or rather his suggestion that the inclusion of too many such syllables in a text restricts the composer[11] – is not borne out by such pieces.[12]

It is clear from Morley's treatise[13] that there is sometimes more than one way of describing the notes of a passage: by implication, therefore, there is often more than one series of pitches which accurately solmize a given set of syllables. Composers sometimes made deliberate use of these alternatives. For example, Orsolina Cavaletta's poem *Da le odorate spoglie/E quell'Arpa* ends by quoting the words 'Cara la vita mia' which occur in a madrigal by Wert. Luzzaschi, in his five-voice setting (1582), quotes precisely the closely solmized passage from Wert (see Example 3) in a manner which was clearly envisaged by the poet: but Gesualdo, setting the same text in 1594,[14] avoided an exact quotation from Wert's madrigal, using instead a closely solmized version of the text which is nevertheless quite different (see Example 4). The later setting of the words seeks to further the principles found in the earlier one; the idea of emulation evident here is characteristic of the period, and will be discussed at greater length below.

There are pieces which open with the same music sung twice, but with different words in the repeat,[15] and in which the composer has contrived to make such solmization syllables as occur fit for both performances of the music. The music must in such instances have been worked out with both portions of the text in mind, rather than casually repeated. Palestrina, for example, does this in *Vestiva i colli* (1566) and in *Voi mi poneste in foco/Pero che da l'ardore* (1558).[16]

Example 3   Luzzaschi: *Da la odorate* (from Wert)

By using a process known as *inganno* ('deception' – see below) a composer
can change from one hexachord to another within a phrase. Such a process –
not codified until the early years of the seventeenth century but practised, even
if not widely, before then[17] – can result in 'imitations' that differ in musical
shape while remaining close settings of the vowels of the text. The example
from Artusi (see Example 5a) shows just how basic a part of musical
knowledge the gamut was, for only if the hearer mentally associates the notes
of the upper and lower parts with their solmization names can the composer's
logic be appreciated.

Without a knowledge of the gamut there can be no discernible reason for
the one part to be associated with the other: the repeated-note opening (see
Example 5a) is a help in identifying the connection between the two strands,
but apart from that a relatively sophisticated understanding of the hexachords, and of mutations of them, is taken for granted. Solmization, then,
was not confined to vocal music in which text and hexachord sounds might
match: and if the solmization applied to instrumental lines, then it could apply
to all music. Example 5b, though, is a vocal piece: here, in an obvious
demonstration of *inganno*, Marenzio sets the first voice in naturale, but in the
alto he mutates from naturale to molle, a flatter area that persists for the third

Example 4   Gesualdo: *Dalle odorate*

Example 5a

Example 5b

and fourth entries. Furthermore, the setting of 'mi fa' (a semitone, as expected, in the soprano and first tenor) becomes a rising sixth in the alto and bass, where Marenzio shifts back from the flatter *molle* area (on *mi*) to the *naturale* (on fa).[18] The performer (and, indeed, the listener) is the more likely to recognize the use of *inganno* since the textual syllables are so exactly like those of the hexachord: the use of *inganno*, in this instance, renders the musical setting the more interesting, for the result is less predictable than an exact mirroring of the solmization syllables without a change of hexachord would have been.

The close mirroring of solmization syllables may result in a particular kind of modality, or a particular choice of chords. This would appear to be the case in Rore's *Ancor che col partire* (1547), where the phrygian mode has been chosen not only for its legendary associations[19] but also for the possibility of harmonizing cadences in such a way that the text is closely matched – in particular 'partire' and the last word, 'miei'. We shall encounter more examples of this later.

A slightly different but nevertheless interesting case is provided by Monte's *I'piansi, hor canto* (1570), which is written on D with a key signature of two flats. Here solmization syllables occasionally match for some of the notes at this pitch, but a vastly greater majority of correspondencies between hexachord syllables and vowels of the text is evident if one imagines the piece to have been conceived a tone higher in E phrygian.[20] Is Monte trying to have it both ways, or does this merely illustrate the danger of attempting to force a hexachord syllable background onto music which was not constructed – either consciously or subconsciously – on these principles? (We should, of course, remember that hexachord syllables might occasionally be 'correctly' set by accident.) It is quite possible for solmization to apply at more than one pitch: transposition upwards by a fourth (or by a seventh up, from G to F, for example) would not eliminate a close setting of hexachord syllables. Oddly, though, the solmization in *I'piansi* works at two distinct pitches for two different collections of solmization settings: it works at D phrygian, resulting in one very extreme note (Db, the only use of this note in any of Monte's madrigals); and it also works at a projected E phrygian 'original', which would include extremes of another kind – many B-major triads and an E-majorish sound. Sometimes one of these pitches is more appropriate than the other: for example, the use of Bbs and Ebs at 'dolce forza', 'molle' enough in the D phrygian, would much less vividly illustrate sweetness if the piece were pitched a tone higher.

The kind of writing so far described might be regarded as having a conscious wittiness aimed solely at the performers: for, since they will themselves be thinking in terms of solmization syllables, it is they who will most readily be aware of the wit. The fact that strong opposition to this manner of writing was expressed at the time[21] is in itself an indication of its frequent use; but nevertheless the technique continued to be widely used, particularly in the Italian Madrigal.

Whether or not this was done to produce a metaphysical wittiness addressed to the performers and *cognoscenti*, it is possible that there are other aspects to this matter. Firstly, and of lesser importance, a composer – especially one writing for amateurs – might combine the solmization sounds with their corresponding pitches in order to help sight-reading: the singer will then have one less element to think about, since he does not have to sing a different vowel from the one he imagines when 'solmizing'.[22] Furthermore, a use of close solmization of the text could help a singer to pitch accurately any unusual intervals that the expressive mannerist style might require him to sing: the solmization of the first syllable of 'fallo' as fa or *fa* (F or Bb) at the opening of Wert's *Amor, io fallo/Pero, s'oltra suo stile* (1561) is both an explanation of the expressive upward seventh leap (an interval forbidden in the *stile antico*) and a useful aid to the correct pitching of the interval. As if this were not convincing enough, Wert inverts the seventh immediately afterwards in his setting of 'fallire': here the second syllable is set to the note *mi* (A) for the same reasons, and the final syllable is also at times matched to its solmization sound (see Example 6).[23]

This argument is the more compelling when one realizes that many of the most popular madrigals of the sixteenth century – an exception is Arcadelt's First Book of Madrigals – are very closely set to the solmization syllables which are suggested (even if not always precisely) in the text.[24] Moreover, one suspects that certain composers felt that close solmization provided for a more resonant sound, perhaps rather like the effect achieved by later composers writing for open, as opposed to stopped, strings.[25] It is also possible that certain textual sounds automatically suggested certain shapes to a composer; so basic was the gamut to every musician's make-up that a text which provided a series of vowels that happened to match solmization syllables could scarcely fail to suggest a melodic line which mirrored those syllables. Example 7, for example, shows a series of settings of the word 'lagrime' (or 'lachrime') in works by Monte. Yet this cannot be taken as a general rule for settings of that word: Marenzio, for instance, writing his setting of *Dolorosi martir* some twenty years after Monte, in about 1580, does not use the shape. Nevertheless, at a time when composers were giving more and more thought to the close mirroring of the text in their musical settings, it was obviously much to the purpose to try to parallel the literary sounds with musical ones.[26]

Three objections may be raised to the analysis of vocal music by matching textual syllables to the hexachord sounds: each of these warning notes must be taken seriously. The first is the criticism that I have looked for the close setting of solmization syllables when they are not intended. It is clear that the system was in the process of being superseded, and that it was by no means

Example 6   Wert: *Amor, io fallo/Pero, s'oltra suo stile* (1561)

Example 7

Dolorosi martir (1558)

Poi che'l camin (1569)

Di piansi, hor canto (1570)

Amorosi pensieri (1583)

universally applied: we can, then, scarcely claim that all late-Renaissance music can be explained by it. On the other hand, it would be as well to remember that accidents of construction can occur, for a composer may subconsciously let his mind be led in a certain melodic direction by the solmization sounds that parallel the text he is setting. Perhaps it was some such process that caused William Byrd to say (in Fellowes's elegant translation[27])

> . . . as one meditates upon the sacred words . . . the right notes, in some inexplicable manner, suggest themselves quite spontaneously.

The second objection is that, since the vowel 'ah' occurs in two different hexachord notes, it is ambiguous to label any note setting that vowel, since one cannot be sure whether to apportion it to 'fa' or 'la'. This is a less serious charge, but one that emphasizes a fundamental difficulty about the solmization sounds: this difficulty raises questions of interpretation particularly when the syllables set are not exactly 'fa' or 'la', but only approximations to the 'ah' vowel sound. I have borne this in mind when dealing with the fourth and sixth degrees of the hexachord, and I have generally chosen only examples in which the correctness of the solmization is guaranteed by the presence of one of the other hexachord syllables in close proximity ('mi fa', 'sol la', for example).[28]

The third objection is that, if one takes transposition of the hexachord to extremes (rather like an infinitely 'moveable doh'), any syllable can be apportioned to any pitch. Perhaps for this reason many writers who mention the subject confine themselves to the most obvious and exact parallels with the solmization syllables. Yet, provided we bear in mind the ambiguities inherent in there being two 'ah' sounds in each hexachord (we shall later see that this could at times be a positive advantage) and that absolutely unrestricted transposition of hexachords can produce any solmization sound on any pitch, much can be gained from observing the correspondences. Transpositions of the mode are dealt with below; but there were clear limits to the extremes to which 'ut' could be shifted, and theorists considered it the mark of a dunce to mix up molle and durum[29] (though we have to remember that any major–minor alternations would imply setting the equivalent of 'molle' against its corresponding 'durum' at some basic pitch or other[30]). Normally, though, a mental imagining of hexachords of many chromatic hues co-existing would have been unthinkable to the late-Renaissance performer.

For these reasons, most of the examples chosen here involve passages which set more than one syllable (and those in similar or close hexachords); the greater the number of more-or-less adjacent syllables that coincide within the gamut, the more likely is it that the coincidence was intentional. I propose two exceptions in which a single syllable is used: the first is 'mi', used to refer to the major third of whatever key or mode is currently in use – a major third often unexpectedly introduced; and the second is 'fa', which often results in a rather 'flat' note or chord – again, often rather unexpectedly introduced. Both these are further dealt with below: it may be no more than coincidental that 'mi' and 'fa' themselves delineate the most expressive interval. In my discussion I have avoided stretching the system to include many remote hexachords: only the three basic ones and such transpositions as are clearly required by some feature of the text are normally used: any beyond these three in either direction will be clearly documented.

One further difficulty about my analyses must be raised here, for the sake of completeness; this involves the inversions of 'mi fa'. Whether or not the reader accepts my proposal that composers occasionally used inversions of these hexachord syllables, the main thrust of the argument of this chapter is not affected. In Example 3 'mi' and 'fa' were sometimes solmized in the reverse order: it is clear that, whatever the hexachord, the syllables 'mi' and 'fa' occurring side by side refer to the semitone, unless *inganno* is applied. 'Mi fa' or 'fa mi' were clearly treated as interchangeable – either was used rising or falling, but either referred to a semitone: in other words, the important thing about the syllables 'mi' and 'fa' is not the rise or fall, but the fact that a *semitone* is involved.

The knowledge that 'mi fa' and 'fa mi' were often used to indicate a semitone can be of some assistance in understanding performance practice. It is clear that the majority of solmization uses of the sixteenth century remained within the confines of the hexachords on G, C and F: yet, especially as music began to move more widely around the tonal spectrum, uses outside the basic three hexachords occurred. Composers, then, may use 'mi fa' (or 'fa mi') to

Example 8

a)

Rore: *Ancor che col partire*

b)

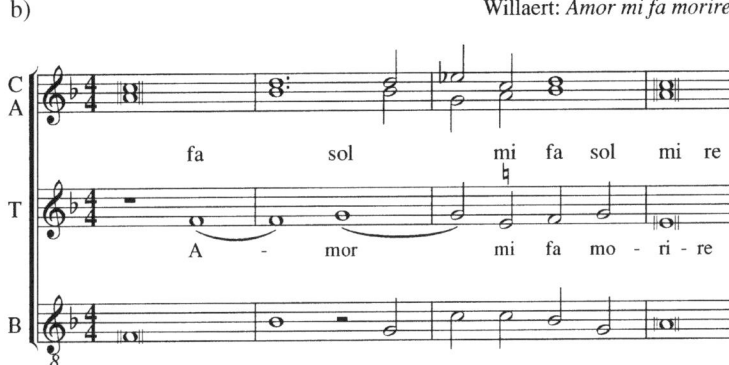

Willaert: *Amor mi fa morire*

c)

Caimo: *Anchor che col partire*

d)   Luzzaschi: *Se il lauro è sempre verde*

Example 8d *concluded*

pitches other than B–C, E–F and A–B♭. Indeed, of all the possible combinations of solmization syllables, 'mi fa' is the one most often transposed to other pitches, a fact which not only reflects its quality as the most easily identifiable and expressive interval of the system, but also its function as an indicator of the hexachord in use: 'mi fa' is like the pole star in navigation. Such syllables might therefore occasionally be of assistance in the application of *musica ficta*. (See Example 8a–c).[31] This cannot, however, be a universal law for the application of *musica ficta*: as the illustrations in Example 8d show, not every setting of the textual syllables 'mi fa' or 'fa mi' outside the three basic hexachords can be performed as a semitone.

Hexachord Colour

As we have seen, the molle hexachord was thought of as 'soft' or 'sweet', and so it was particularly appropriate for the illustration of sweetness or similar ideas. The feeling of sweetness seems to derive from the nature of B♭ – the only 'accidental' to appear in the strict hexachord system – for B♭ is quite often dwelt upon in illustrations of sweetness. Examples are legion and many will occur later in this book:[32] one rather unexpected use must suffice for the present. In *Quand'io pens'al martire* (1566) Merulo uses the molle hexachord (at 'Ma poi ch'io giung'al passo Ch'è port'in questo mar pien di tormento, Tant'èl piacer ch'io sento') to illustrate the sweetness of death and the poet's longing for it:[33] 'life' is pitched, by contrast, in a gloomy A minor. The two hexachords are juxtaposed at 'Cosi la morte mi ritorn'in vita', the tonal areas acting almost like leitmotives for 'death' and 'life'.

One arrives at B♭, in fact, by continual transpositions of the root of a hexachord up a fourth, so that each new hexachord begins on the pitch 'fa' of the previous hexachord. The tonality becomes flatter with each change of hexachord when moving in this direction. (Morley shows this use of the syllable 'fa' very clearly by setting it to each new B♭, E♭ or A♭ when such notes occur after music in which B natural, E natural and A natural respectively have been the norm.[34]) If one takes the process a stage farther and begins a hexachord on B♭, *fa* will become E♭.[35] Moreover, when music is written in transposed modes (with a flat key signature) – F ionian or G dorian, for instance – the use of a hexachord on B♭ has to be a theoretical possibility since it would merely be the transposition of the molle hexachord that would have been used had the piece been written in an untransposed mode.[36] Clearly, if all pieces with a signature of one or two flats were first conceived with the open signature and subsequently transposed, the naturale and durum hexachords would likewise move by one (or two) degrees flatwards. Sometimes this may have been the case: for example, some pieces survive in sources with two flats in one version and the 'open' signature in another – Dowland's *Lachrimae* is a case in point. Yet the majority of pieces with flats in the signature were clearly conceived as such from the start; and a study of the use of hexachords in these works shows that, despite the flatwards transposition of the mode, the durum hexachord is still the one on G (with B natural). It is clearly the use of B *natural* that gives the durum hexachord its hard quality – and that quality will not be preserved if transposition removes the B natural. The hexachords are a constant factor not affected by transpositions: many examples support this position, one of the most obvious being Rore's epoch-making *Mia benigna fortuna* (1557) – a piece discussed in detail below. The flatter the tonality, the 'sweeter' or 'softer' (and more dolorous, in some instances) the effect; the sharper the tonality, the 'harder' will the effect be.

All transposition of sixteenth-century polyphonic modes was by a fourth up (adding one flat to the key signature) or by a seventh up (adding two flats): this accurately reflects the fundamental notes of the three hexachords. We may therefore view E♭ as the 'fa' syllable raised to the fourth degree (G–C–F–B♭– E♭): it is, in a sense, sweeter than sweet – the *ultimate* 'fa'.[37] Moreover, as I have already pointed out, the mnemonic rhyme

> Una nota supra la
> Semper est canendum fa

indicates that a single melodic pitch above the sixth of any hexachord will be sung as a flat seventh (i.e. as 'fa' of the hexachord which follows next in the flatwards direction)[38]: it is clear that – particularly in works written with a signature of one flat – E♭ is almost bound to result eventually (see Example 9).[39] But, as we have seen, the durum hexachord does not by the same token transfer itself flatwards and become the hexachord on C, for if that were to be the case it would be rendered 'sweeter'. At a repetition of the word 'sweet' (or 'soft') a composer may well move in a flatward direction: just as in choral singing two chords that are required to be equally loud will not sound so unless the singers mentally imagine that the second chord is louder than the first, so two adjacent settings of 'dolce' would have less effect if both used B♭ than if the second 'capped' the first by moving on to E♭. This is illustrated at the words 'Pioggia di lagrimar' in Willaert's *Passa la nave/Pioggia di lagrimar* (1559), and it is the explanation for the use of the extremely flat chord (D♭) at 'dolcezza' in Rore's *Dalle belle contrade* (1566). The technique will be discussed in more detail later.

Because the solmization syllable for B♭ and E♭ was *fa*, the sixteenth-century mind clearly thought of B♭ and E♭ as being particularly suitable notes (and chords) for setting the vowel 'ah': one frequently finds F-ionian pieces that set this vowel to an E♭ chord (as in Marenzio's *Leggiadre Ninfe*, 1591), and even Weelkes, setting an English text – where such treatment is rare – wrote an unexpected B♭ chord in C ionian (C major in modern terms) for the first syllable of 'walking' in *Three Virgin Nymphs* (1597).[40] In addition F ionian

Example 9   Rore: *Per mezz' l bosch' inhospiti*

(F major in modern terms) became the accepted mode for the idyllic kind of Pastoral: since the publication of Sannazaro's *Arcadia* (written about 1480) in the early years of the sixteenth century, there had been a deluge of poetry, paintings and musical compositions which idealized the arcadian spirit. Many of the settings of pastoral poetry invoke the sweetness and softness of the molle hexachord, which was clearly considered the most appropriate vehicle for Arcady. Pastorals are found in other modes, of course (Marenzio's *Come fuggir per selva ombrosa* of 1591, for example, is in C ionian – the modern C major): but the vast majority are in F ionian (the modern F major).[41]

By contrast, the durum hexachord – with the 'hard' B natural – can be invoked to illustrate hardness or associated ideas. At this period there was no system for transposing sharpwards from the open signature to correspond to that of adding one or two flats for flatwards transposition:[42] any sharpness that is required is achieved by using accidentals. The opening of Gesualdo's famous *Moro lasso* is a good example of the use of a very sharp area to illustrate cruelty or hardness. A less well-known example is Frescobaldi's setting of Marino's *Se la doglia e'l martire* (1608),[43] in which the conventional 'sol la' shape is used for 'Se la . . .' but using hexachords on the sharp side of durum – on D and A. The harshness of such implicit hexachords illustrates the

Example 10

Frescobaldi: *Se la doglia*

harshness of 'martire' ('torture') at the poem's opening (see Example 10). The performers are unlikely to miss the point, though it is doubtful if non-performing listeners (should there be any) would be likely to understand. Just as the unexpected arrival of flats draws clear attention to any ideas of softness or sweetness in the text – or occasionally dolorous ideas – so the unexpected sharp can illustrate hardness, cruelty or pain: such a use can be seen at 'mio martire' ('my torment') in *Caro dolce ben mio* (1583) by Andrea Gabrieli. Naturally the use of these techniques raises serious questions about the performance of this type of music at any other than its notated pitch, though it is obvious that the composer is communicating through the written note and not through the ultimate sound (at whatever pitch).

Frescobaldi's *Se la doglia e'l martire* raises a further point – one that concerns *musica recta*. If certain flats are not notated but are nevertheless 'understood' because a flat hexachord is mentally applied by the performers, can it by the same token be true that sharps could also be 'understood' but not notated when the composer presupposes that the singers will have an abnormally sharp hexachord in mind? The opening of Example 10 clearly presupposes sharp hexachords: indeed, the passage looks as if it was originally conceived a tone lower with a key signature of one flat and subsequently transposed to a 'harder' key area. If this were so it would immediately become clear that the second soprano at the start not only freely inverts the material of the first soprano and alto, but that the inversion applies also to 'sol la' (set to 'Se la'), resulting in *la sol* (D–C). But since sharper hexachords than normal are in the singers' mind, would the second soprano and alto have sung C sharp in bar 4 of Example 10? If they had done so it would have provided a very appropriate falling semitone on the word 'farmi', but the harmonic content suggests that Frescobaldi really intended C natural (the use of B natural on 'farmi' in the tenor and first soprano argues against the idea that hexachord syllables in the text might be mirrored in the musical intervals). The fact that the use of hexachords on the flat side of molle is generally much more frequent than the use of hexachords on the sharp side of durum makes it appear unlikely that there was a recognized system for using *musica recta* in sharp hexachords; and *Se la doglia* is in any case rather late in the period for serious consideration of solmization.

It is not just a question of writing 'sharp' hexachords in isolation: the effect may well be the more striking if a composer moves to such a tonality from a flatter area. In *Dolorosi martir* (1558), for example, Monte moves out of G minor to a perfect cadence in D major to illustrate 'Duri' ('hard'): soon after this, for 'aspre' ('bitter'), he uses B naturals in place of B♭s to illustrate the bitterness by moving to the hard hexachord. To the modern mind such shifts of tonality may seem insignificant: to those brought up to the belief that each mode had its own character the chromatic shifts must have been the more striking; and to the hexachord-trained singer the mutations would have had the effect of mirroring the meaning of the text in a vivid fashion.

Just as some poems set in F ionian (modern F major) could be described as 'idyllic pastorals', so we might view a certain type of poem as an 'anti-pastoral'. Sannazaro's *Chi vuol udir* (from *Arcadia*), says

> Chi vuol'udir'i miei sospiri in rime
> Donne mie, carre e l'angoscioso pianto,
> E quanti passi tra la nott'e'l giorna,
> Spargend'indarno vo per tanti campi,
> Legga per queste querce e perli sassi,
> Che n'è già pien'omai ciascuna valle.

Denis Arnold gives the following translation:

> He who would hear of my sighs in verse,
> My dear ladies, and of my anguished plaint,
> And of how many steps both night and day
> I tread in vain in many meadows,
> Let him regard these oak trees and these rocks,
> For each valley is full of weeping.

Marenzio's setting of this poem (1585) is typical of 'anti-pastorals' in being cast very largely on the sharper side of the basic hexachords (though it is 'officially' in D dorian). There are many more examples, among the most instructive being Monte's *Per aspre horride* (1590), Marenzio's *Fiere silvestri* (1588), Caimo's *Piangete valli* (1564) and the *Cruda Amarilli* settings discussed in Chapter 4. Perhaps the ultimate anti-pastoral poem is Amanio's *Strane Ruppi*:

> Strane ruppi, aspre monti, alte tremanti,
> Ruine e sassi al ciel . . .
>
> (Strange cliffs, harsh mountains, trembling heights, ruins . . .)

This was set by Rore as early as 1542 in a very sharp-tending phrygian (though with a sprinkling of B♭s and avoiding B-major triads). Croce's *Valli profonde/Erme campagne* (1590) sets Tansillo's sonnet in D dorian, but using the 'hard' B natural most of the time. On the other hand, Rore's *Per mezz'l bosch' inhospiti* (1542) does not use sharp areas for another poem which is very much an 'anti-pastoral'. These 'anti-pastorals' find their parallel in such works of art as Giorgione's *The Tempest* and Leonardo da Vinci's *Virgin of the Rocks*. The world of Arcady illustrated a state of Utopia attainable in the present world – a vision at odds with that of Christian belief: but it was also an illustration of a world in which all was bliss and beauty, a world in which man was at one with Heaven, and in which the harmoniousness of earth reflected the harmony of the spheres. By contrast, the 'anti-pastoral' represents a situation in which man is out of tune with God. Shakespeare expressed this vividly in *My flocks feed not*, a section of *The Passionate Pilgrim* set by Weelkes (1597) with rather little attention to the underlying sense of the poem's 'all is amiss'.

But, just as not all uses of flat keys indicate an idyllic pastoral, so not all uses of sharp keys are concerned with hardness or 'anti-pastorals'. Weelkes's *O Jonathan* makes a very affecting use of an extremely sharp ending for the words 'passing the love of women'.[44] The extraordinary effect results, in this instance, from the alteration of the expected bass A–G–F–E phrygian cadence ending to A–G#–F#–E, with corresponding changes in the other voices: the use of the unexpected at this juncture 'caps' various passages in the piece where Weelkes has set up a pattern of expectancy only to break out of that pattern for an expressive purpose.[45]

By analogy with the treatment of 'fa' (though much less frequently), the textual sound 'mi' can be reflected by the arrival of an unexpectedly sharp chord – or one in which the major third is emphasized because it is unprepared.[46] In Frescobaldi's *Lasso io languisc'e moro* (1608), for example, a passage based around D minor and cadencing on B♭ is followed by a D-major chord which sets the word 'misero' ('wretch'). At the end of Monteverdi's *Ch'io t'ami* (1605) the middle vowel of 'morire' gives rise to an unexpected B-major chord which is not only very 'hard' but also matches 'mi' strikingly in the three voices that sustain the chord for a whole semibreve.

Hexachord Colour and 'Roving Tonality'

How far can we trace this expression of softness and hardness in the music of the Late Renaissance? Is it a recognized technique for text illustration? And can it result in what a later age has termed 'progressive tonality' – that is, ending in a different mode (or key) from that in use at the opening? We shall examine a number of pieces to see what answers can be found: but it is essential to make two caveats before doing so.

The first caveat is that not all musical illustrations of 'sweet' employ the molle hexachord: one other device was used, particularly in the late sixteenth century and the early seventeenth century. This device is the juxtaposition of major chords a third apart – as, for example, C major immediately followed by E major, or G major immediately followed by E major. A well-known example of this is Byrd's *O quam suavis est* (Gradualia, 1607). Joseph Kerman gives the picture admirably:

> *O quam suavis est* . . . moves much further afield harmonically than its companion and needs to, being more than twice as long. The harmonic range of this motet can be thought of as a projection of the unusual chromatic inflexion of the first

bars . . . . Byrd, who seems in general to have backed away from chromaticism for purposes of word illustration, here employs the technique in masterly fashion, the more so in view of the restraint which his temperament evidently set as a condition for the exercise. The caress of the first line is echoed only once, in a milder form, by means of the opening tenor motive imitated in the bass; a second motive for 'suavis est' allows the composer to dwell on the words and underline them with diatonic semitone motion instead of chromaticism. Later echoes are equally delicate. At the word 'dulcedinem' a veiled progression from a G major to an E major chord is followed by a single linear chromatic step in the tenor, and at 'suavissimo' there is no more than a single juxtaposition of G and E major. . . .[47]

The two methods of illustrating sweetness are not mutually exclusive. Philips, in *Tocca la vista mia* (1603), begins a basically F-ionian piece as in Example 11a. 'Soave' is emphasized by a move towards molle from an opening that has been virtually in C major: the lydian feeling that this creates also helps to illustrate Lydia (a lady who is similarly illustrated in several other madrigals of Philips's *Il secondo libro de madrigali*[48]). Within a short time, however, Philips illustrates 'soave' by using the other method, writing direct chromatic movement to a sharp triad (see Example 11b). We have also to take into account the fact that the two triads a third apart were not always adjacent, but separated by a further chord: the result is a much more old-fashioned modal sound, as in the extract shown in Example 11c.[49]

The second caveat is that composers did not use flats solely to indicate 'sweetness' or 'hardness': they sometimes used them to illustrate dolefulness or dolour: there could be no more vivid illustration of this than Josquin's *Absolon fili mi*, which is set on a final of B♭ (written with two flats) with the use of many A♭s and some D♭s and G♭s.

Our first example of 'roving tonality' comes very early in the history of the Renaissance madrigal. Willaert's five-voiced *Quanto piu m'arde/Non e ghiacciol* (c. 1538) may seem to the listener an oddly monotonous piece: that is partly because it is not primarily addressed to the listener, but partly because it relies to a certain extent on a recognition of the hexachords in use. The interest lies in the combination of molle and durum, a combination that was officially discouraged (though allowed eventually in chromatic music[50]). Listenius forbade movement between the soft and hard hexachords, and a move from dorian to phrygian was reckoned the mark of a dunce.[51] Morley castigates a piece of writing that begins in G and ends in F by his comment under the heading 'Going out of the key a great fault'.[52] But such tonal movement can have its uses, and Willaert combines molle and durum as a means of expressing in his music the contrast of sweetness and hardness which is the burden of the poem:

> Quanto più m'arde e più s'accend'il foco,
> Donna, per voi, più mi gradisce amore,
> Nè m'è doglia'l dolore
> Che dolce m'è'l morir, la pena un gioco.

Example 11

a)

Philips: *Tocca la vista*

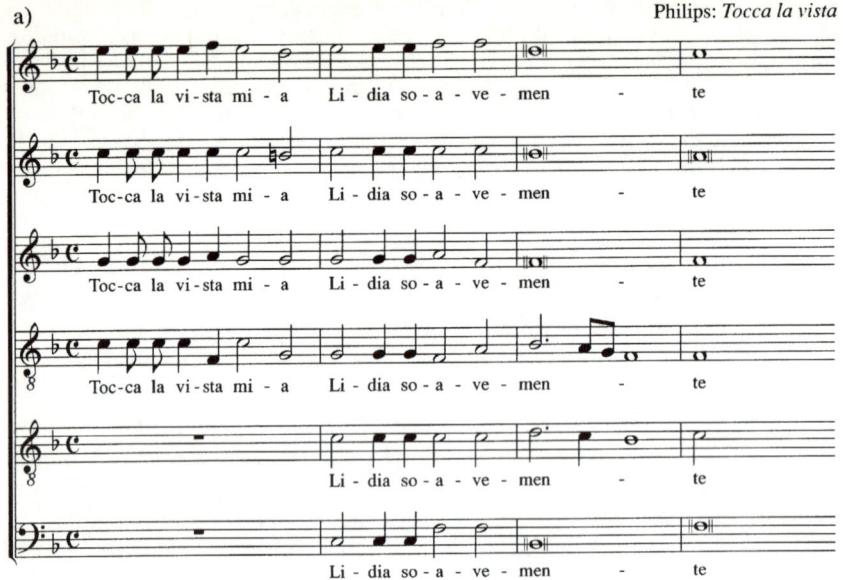

b)   Philips: *Tocca la vista*

c)   Marenzio: *Com'è dolce il gioire* (1595)

(The more the fire burns me and sets me alight,
Lady, for you, the more love pleases me,
Nor for me is the sadness pain
For sweet it is to me to die, the distress a game.)

The poem requires one to understand the sexual *double entendre* whereby, at this period, death can mean love-making. The second part reads:

Non è ghiaccio'l mio ghiaccio,
Nè la mia fiamma cuoce,
Nè'l dolor duol nè la morte m'ancide,
Tant'è soav'il laccio
E si dolce, mi nuoce,
Che non ange la vita, anzi gl'arride,
Onde nè pregh'amor che me ne sfide,
Ma che m'agghiaccie, infiamme, ancid'e stringa,
E nel mio cor dipinga
Vera fede, amor vero e dolce fuoco.

(It is not icy my ice,
Neither does my flame torment
Nor the pain sadden nor death kill me,
So gentle is the bond
And so sweet my hurt
That it distresses my life, but rather smiles upon it,
Wherefore neither do I beg Love to challenge me,
But to freeze, enflame, kill and clasp me,
And in my heart to depict
True faith, true love and sweet fire.)[53]

The Petrarchan tradition is full of opposites yoked together, as in this poem, and in his setting Willaert uses contrasting hexachord key-areas to emphasize these opposites: it is a technique which may very easily pass the modern listener by, since at this early stage of the development of the madrigal the contrasts are by no means extreme. In this piece the use of contrasting hexachords is most evident in the cross-relations between F natural and F♯, and between B♭ and B natural. The opening three bars illustrate the three basic hexachords; and the contrasts between these hexachords are used on the large scale throughout the madrigal, the appropriate tonal area more or less punctually arriving to illustrate sweetness or hardness in the text (see Example 12).[64]

Hoste da Reggio's *O beata colei* (1547) also sets a poem with typically Petrarchan juxtapositions – 'Io li fei parer dolce ogni martire . . .' ('For him I sweetened every suffering'), for instance. As is typical, all shades of feeling and all ideas are illustrated as closely as possible in the music. The words just quoted are therefore set to music which moves from durum with F♯ and C♯ into F (with a prolonged B♭ chord so as to draw special attention to the new pitch that indicates the change to the sweet hexachord): then, for 'ogni

Example 12

Willaert, c.1538

Quanto più m'arde

The more I am burned ...

Ne m'e doglia'l dolore

Nor for me is the sadness pain ...

Che dolce m'e'l morir

It is sweet to me to die ...

la pena un gioco.

the pain a jest.

SECONDA PARTE

Example 12 *concluded*

martire' ('every suffering'), the music moves back to durum and the use of sharps. This is not the only unsettled piece of tonality, for though the madrigal is technically in D dorian, it starts as if in F ionian, probably because of that mode's pastoral associations: the opening text, 'O beata colei' ('Happy is the woman . . .') presumably suggested that kind of atmosphere to the composer.[55]

There is a similar use of hard and soft hexachords in Lasso's *Cantai, hor piango/Tengan dunque* (1555). This is cast in the phrygian mode, but it veers backwards and forwards between the molle and durum hexachords in order to illustrate the text's juxaposition of sweetness and hardness. Such things as the shift towards flats for 'piango' ('weeping') and 'dolcezza' ('sweetness'), just after the opening, with the return to sharps at other points (and notably 'mio amaro la radice' – 'the root of my bitterness' – at the end) make this a companion-piece to Willaert's *Quanto piu m'ardre*.

Willaert set the same text, *Cantai, or piango* (1559), and so it must be dealt with at this point. As mentioned above, it was normal for Italian madrigal composers, when setting a text of which another setting had already been made, to try to improve upon the earlier one: this technique will be examined later. Willaert does, indeed, attempt to outdo Lasso's setting, and thus invites comparison: he chooses the same mode (phrygian), ends the *prima parte* on the same chord (A major) and uses B♭ for 'pianger', 'dolcezza' and 'languisca', just as Lasso had done. But Willaert writes a more expansive setting (longer by some twenty breves), uses more voices (six rather than five), and uses solmization syllables set to their corresponding vowel sounds much more widely than does Lasso. On the other hand, Willaert does not match Lasso's high bass notes at 'altezza' nor his solmization of 'luna', nor his molle hexachord at 'si dolce'; and Willaert does not use the molle hexachord for 'piango' ('weeping'), even though Lasso does. These matters, however, are only marginally relevant to the present purpose: more to the point is that Willaert does not follow Lasso in using a sudden chromatic shift to a sharp chord in illustration of 'durezza' ('hardness'). It follows that Willaert does not include such a decisive swing back and forth between molle and durum, even though he knew of the possibilities, having already used them in an earlier madrigal. In fact, at 'durezza' in bar 40[56] Willaert uses molle: this decision not to use the tonal colour suggested by the traditional descriptions of the hexachords might well serve as a check on the present discussion of their use. Clearly the system was at times used to illustrate hardness and softness (and similar ideas) in such a way as to modulate in a more or less modern sense: but equally clearly the system was not always invoked to illustrate such things.[57] Nevertheless, it is evident that in discussing the tonality of late-Renaissance music we need to take 'roving tonality' – that governed by the qualities of the hexachords – into account in addition to the modes with their long history of associations with different types of emotions.[58]

This can be illustrated by reference to a passage in Monteverdi's *l'Orfeo* (1607). John Whenham[59] sums this up admirably:

> The scene . . . in which Eurydice's death is announced to Orpheus and his shepherd companions, has long been regarded as one of the most powerful and moving in the opera. It is also one of the most interesting as regards Monteverdi's use of tonality, since its action is articulated on a large scale by the use of two contrasting modes – the Hypoionian, with cadence centres on C and G major, and the Hypoaeolian, with cadences on A minor, C major and E major/minor. The first of these, a 'cheerful mode' according to Zarlino, is used to suggest a state of blissful unawareness of the tragedy that has occurred off stage; the second, a mode apt for 'tears, sadness, solicitude, calamities, and every kind of misery', is employed for emotions associated with full knowledge of the tragedy.

The use of hexachord colour is another factor to set alongside this analysis. Messaggiera, with his tale of grief, interrupts the sylvan bliss of Pastore: the naturale and molle sounds of Pastore thus alternate with the harsher tones of durum (with a fair sprinkling of sharps). Orfeo's G minor–E♭ ('ohime che odo?') is dolorous, rather than pastoral, and the same is true of the G-minor opening of his 'Tu se'morta', which soon moves to the hard E major. This suggests that there was an ambivalence in the use of flats: F major may have suited the sylvan bliss, but G minor was much more inclined to illustrate grief.[60] Evident in this is a growing awareness of the particular qualities of major and minor keys – an awareness that looks forward strongly to later tonal music.

But music has not yet reached the point where we can say that a developed form of major/minor tonality has arrived. A knowledge of the significance of the various hexachords for depicting softness, sweetness, hardness, or cruelty, can act as a powerful aid to understanding music which has puzzled commentators who have tried to foist tonal characteristics onto works of this time. Monteverdi's *O Mirtillo* (1606), for example, has caused much difficulty among analysts;[61] its underlying tonal structure is one that, starting sweetly at the first announcing of the name Mirtillo (with an initial phrase in the molle hexachord), gradually shifts towards the durum and even harder areas as the cruelty of the situation unfolds. At 'chiami crudelissima' Monteverdi echoes this opening shift from molle to durum (and even sharper areas) by setting 'chiami' to *fa mi* (and 'fa mi'), but then moving to very sharp areas to depict the cruelty of 'crudelissima'. At 'infelici' ('unfaithful') the unexpected B–C♯–F♯ of the upper voice – a meltingly lovely touch for modern ears – illustrates the implied cruelty by using the hard hexachord (or rather, notes even sharper than durum): but, more than this, by writing unexpected sharps which would be solmized as 'mi', Monteverdi parallels the final two vowels of 'infelici' (B is already MI, of course). This hardness is maintained in the final cadence in order to emphasize the cruel nature of 'perfido Amore' ('faithless love'), and the choice of D major as the ultimate goal is logical in that the last syllable ('–re') can be set as D or A ('re' or 'RE') in the majority of voices – four out of the five, in fact. The piece clearly owes its tonal workings to the close tracking of the colour and moods of the words; attempts to force such music into a kind of proto-tonality that fails to recognize the part played by the hexachords fails to understand the structure fully.

The System Moves Towards Tonality

Yet this music is not modal either, and a clear but gradual shift towards the tonal system can be observed. Modulation such as I have described above was a factor in the move towards major/minor tonality that was eventually to oust the modes: but a further step towards the tonal system was the use of major and minor on the same tonic – a situation that enhanced the expressive power of the 'mi fa' interval, as we have seen. To the conservatives such a mixture of major and minor would imply a mixing of the characteristics of the modes, and was thus frowned upon – though the use of *modus commixtus* was sanctioned by theorists. Nevertheless, if a poem includes two clearly contrasted types of feeling it would seem logical to use two different modes to illustrate it, particularly if one is to take closeness of text illustration to its logical conclusion. On several occasions Monteverdi did this, and went a stage farther by changing the key signature.[62]

Ohimè se tanto amate, from Monteverdi's Fourth Book of Madrigals (1603), shows that the old concepts of solmization and hexachord treatments were being replaced by the newer conception of major and minor – but it also makes it clear that the change was by no means complete. Elements of both systems are evident in this madrigal, which also shows great subtlety of musical language in the service of text setting.[63] As one might expect, the text (by Guarini) is the driving-force behind the musical invention. It runs as follows:

> Ohimè, se tanto amate
> Di sentir dir *ohimè*
> Deh perchè fate
> Chi dice *ohimè* morire?
> S'io moro, un sol potrete,
> Languido e doloroso *ohimè* sentire;
>
> Ma se, cor mio, volete
> Che vita habbia da voi
> e voi da me, havrete
> Mill'e mille dolc'*ohimè*.

(Alas, if you take such pleasure
in the word alas,
then why would you slay
the one who says alas?
If I die, you will only hear
a single, moaning, miserable alas;

but if, my dear, you wish
to let me live
and wish to live for me, you shall have
a thousand times a tender alas.)[64]

The word *ohimè* ('alas') is the pivot around which this text revolves: along with 'ahi' it is a word that is found frequently in the texts set by the madrigalists, and in earlier years a composer might well have kept invoking the notes A or E (la–mi), or used the intervals F–E/B♭–A ('fa mi') or A–E/D–A ('la mi'), as the basis of his setting of that word, perhaps including slow and grinding suspensions to add a sense of grittiness to the sound. Monteverdi's approach, however, is quite different and fresh. There is no attempt to match the exclamation to its corresponding solmization syllables: instead the idea of 'aria' is invoked by choosing the second mode on G, a mode characteristic of laments, and by casting the sopranos[65] in parallel thirds – a device which is also characteristic of laments.[66] For much of the piece, indeed, the two sopranos move in parallel thirds, emphasizing this connection with laments. For once semitones do not form part of the expressive language (or, at least, melodic semitones do not): it is harmony rather than melodic invention that is of primary importance in this instance; and the third (in particular, as we shall see later, the nature of the third) is of vital significance.

But if solmization of *Ohimè* is avoided, dissonance plays its part most strikingly. 'Alas' is not an expression of anguish throughout the poem, for it changes its meaning subtly as the verse progresses: since the feeling of anguish is at its height at the start, dissonance is also at its height at the beginning of Monteverdi's setting. The underlying skeleton of this opening is shown in Example 13a: the composer, however, treats the upper four voices as two pairs, and divides the music of this skeleton between them in dialogue fashion: he also provides a gap between the two pairs, so producing not only a 'sigh' (sighs were conventionally illustrated by inserting rests into a phrase or into the setting of a word) but also making the entry of the upper voices more pungent (see Example 13b). The effect of the upper voices is in any case the more dissonant because they sing in an octave which is not prepared by the alto and tenor at the opening. John Whenham has commented that 'There is no doubt . . . about the intended meaning of *Ohimè, se tanto amate* and *Si ch'io vorrei morire*, both of which are brilliantly executed portrayals of sexual love'.[67] That being so, it might have been Monteverdi's intention to produce an underlying feeling, subsidiary to but alongside the main burden of his setting, that the beginning of *Ohimè, se tanto amate* represents the excited exclamations of a pair of lovers: this he does by creating antiphony between the *ohimè* of the lower voices and a parallel answering cry from the two sopranos.

The repeat of this opening pair of exclamations – or, rather, the answering phrase – is a third higher, so balancing the falling thirds of the melodic material: the deliberate marking of E with a sharp (meaning E natural, the natural sign having yet to be introduced into notation) counters any tendency to make the music 'molle'. The resulting E natural is 'hard' in several senses. Firstly, it belongs to the durum hexachord (indeed, it is also 'la–mi', which might well make the hearers and performers associate it with 'Ahi' through solmization). Secondly, it is a tritone from the bass B♭, and thus of quite unexpected nature: E♭ would have been more normal in these circumstances, and the change from an expected molle pitch (E♭) to durum (E natural) foreshadows the use of similar changes later. The resulting *mi contra fa* (E against B♭) is picked up later when an unconventional chordal progression at the words 'un sol potrete, Languido' (see Example 13c) juxtaposes a B♭ chord with a first inversion chord of E minor. Thirdly, since an unexpectedly sharp note was often used by composers of this period to set a 'mi' sound in the text, the E natural on *Ohimè* has yet another form of logic behind it. Clearly Monteverdi's tonality has been arrived at by mixing the second mode on G with the idea of durum hexachord colour (see Examples 13a and b).

By repeating the opening *ohimè* material (though with changes) at the ending of his setting of line 2 of the poem Monteverdi clearly connects the two: but the fact that there is no change of octave in the line 2 version makes that setting less anguished,[68] as befits its subtly changed meaning. The tenor part immediately repeats the *ohimè* line: it removes the 'sighs', though it adds an answering phrase (as had happened at the opening), but with the gap between model and answer extended to a fourth (rather than a third, as was used at the opening).

Line 4 of the poem is rather more concerned with 'die' than with the word *ohimè* that comes at its end: the melodic outline previously associated with *ohimè* is evident only in the first soprano. Anguish is, nevertheless, expressed in several ways (see Example 13d). The seventh in the bass – resulting from an octave transposition downwards of the expected goal of that part, an idea that reverses the octave shifts of the opening material – is one; it turns the bass G, which would be quite a regular passing-note if there was no octave displacement, into a dissonance from which this part leaps downwards. The odd note-values used by both the first soprano and the bass – a rhythm that could not be produced in the notation of this time without employing the recently invented tie – is expressive because it is unexpected: and the alto's use of A–G–A at the point where E–D–E would be more normal is a further such element. The leap off a dissonance in the bass prepares those in the two soprano parts

Example 13

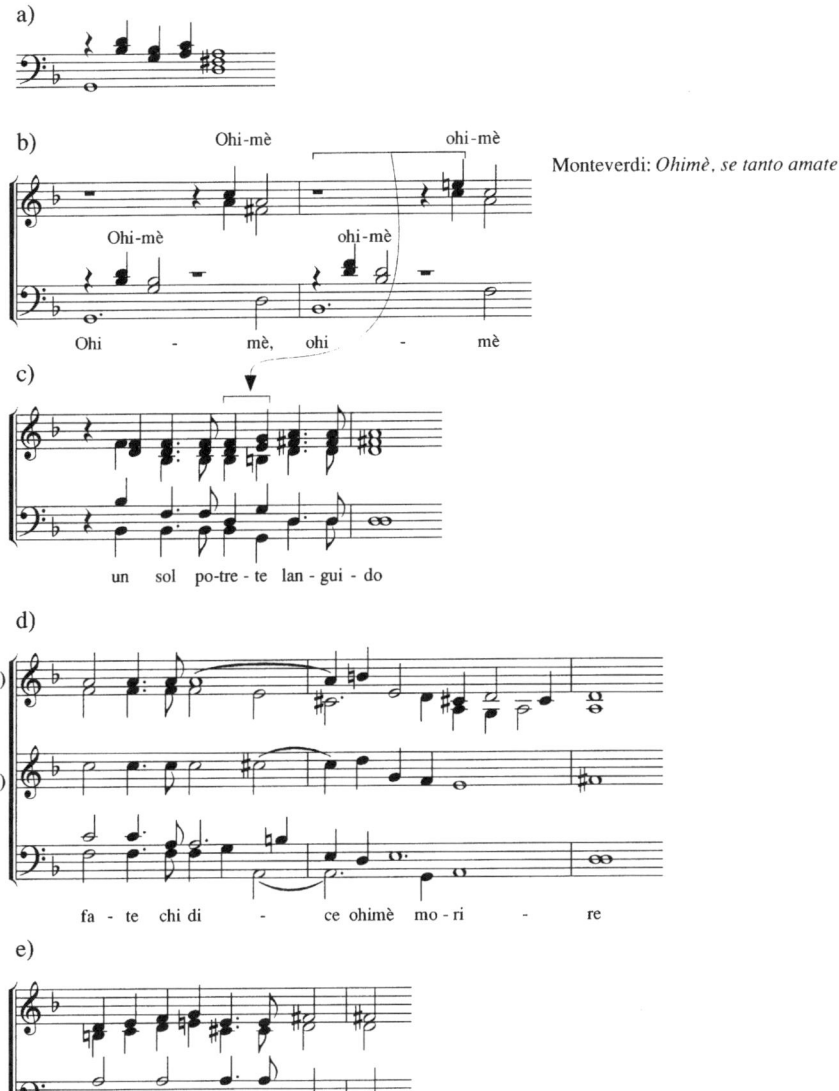

Monteverdi: *Ohimè, se tanto amate*

as well as the leap from a dissonant B natural in the tenor. Primarily, however, the D-major cadence, which tends to sound sweet to modern ears, is rather intended to express hardness by invoking the durum hexachord: indeed, it has been evident throughout the piece that the molle hexachord – in which the singers must basically have set their minds – is tempered by excursions into the harder, sharp areas: the chromaticism in the second soprano (middle stave of Example 13d) helps to prepare this, as do the unexpected B naturals (marked, of course, with a sharp rather than a natural) in the tenor and first soprano (see Example 13d). Moreover, the fact that both these B naturals are dissonances off which the voice leaps downwards – an idea not used in the classical polyphonic style – draws particular attention to the 'hard' B naturals in a manner that would not have obtained had they been treated simply as passing-notes.[69] (Indeed, one of these B naturals has added attention drawn to it because it follows such an unusual note-length – one that could not have been produced without the tie.) The function of dissonance both here and at the opening of the madrigal has been more than just a matter of illustrating anguish, for it also draws attention to the stages of the musical argument: moreover, the move from molle to durum is later encapsulated in the setting of 'havrete'.

The 'single, moaning, miserable alas' of the end of stanza 1 cannot be immediately repeated within any voice part without making nonsense of the poem, so Monteverdi resorts to repeating the whole phrase – which is set as a trio at first – in a fuller scoring and with some changes. The trio version is shown in Example 13e; as so often happens in music of the period, the repeat (using all five voices) moves flatwards to increase the dolorousness of the effect.[70] Despite this, features of the hard hexachord are included so as to illustrate the 'moaning, miserable' feeling; and the setting of *ohimè*, though not cast in the dissonant terms used at the opening, leaps downwards from a seventh, and uses the falling third shape: both ideas link this treatment of the exclamation with preceding treatments.

Ohimè is associated with death in stanza 1, but with life in the second stanza: in the latter, therefore, changes are made. The parallel thirds are largely maintained even though the 'lament' character is replaced by one of a happier kind (the trio-sonata feel that this gives is far removed from the 'lament' style which G dorian and parallel thirds produce: it is much more like the style of Monteverdi's *Chiome d'oro*, 1619). The 'thousands of *ohimès*' are illustrated by a sequence based on the opening shape, though with its sighs and antiphony removed, and announced in equal crotchets.[71] The 'thousands of *ohimès*' at the end of the poem clearly refer to love-making: by setting these *ohimès* to the melodic shape which is the underlying skeleton of the opening (see Example 13a) Monteverdi helps to make more convincing the idea that his opening could be interpreted as representing a pair of lovers. This melodic phrase cries out to be used in imitation (it is a shape perfectly adapted to stretto, and often used for this purpose in the Renaissance), though this is not at first part of Monteverdi's plan: instead the parallel thirds become parallel six-three chords,[72] and there is considerable juxtaposition of molle and durum in the F sharp–F natural, B♭–B natural, and E♭–E natural cross-relations (see Example 13f). The anguish which normally attends cries of *ohimè* is held in balance with the more idyllic feelings expressed in stanza 2, so the durum and molle hexachords are juxtaposed.

Example 13 *concluded*

f)

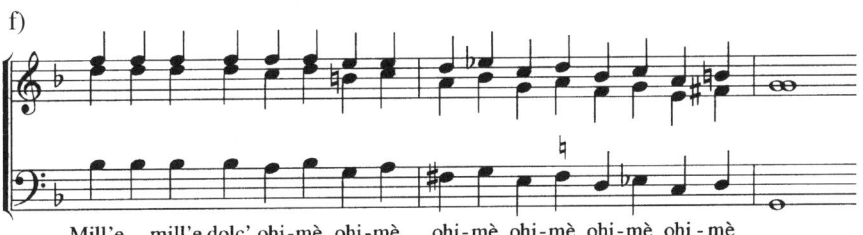

Mill'e   mill'e dolc' ohi-mè ohi-mè   ohi-mè ohi-mè ohi-mè ohi-mè

g)

dolci   ohimè,   ohimè.

At the repeat of this passage by the three lower voices, imitation of the *ohimè* shape is at last used: and there follows a further repeat for all five voices, over a dominant pedal. The unusual final cadence – where the normal and expected V–I cadence is replaced by major IIIb–I, with the expected melodic motion of II–I becoming major III–I (in a piece which is basically minor) – is shown in Example 13g; the unusual harmony and the shape used by the first soprano clearly derive from the cadence at the end of Example 13f (and ultimately from the opening exclamations of the madrigal), and the change from minor to major is, for once, not intended to conjure up associations of the durum hexachord, for the tonality here is a vivid illustration of 'tender'. The 'sighs' of the opening, however, are again heard, for the rests are reintroduced – an idea that helps to slow the music down at the end – and the repeat of the melodic shape of *ohimè* helps to provide a parallel to the continual echoing of that exclamation in the poem.

This gradual move away from modality and key areas governed by hexachords, and towards the use of major/minor tonality, was pursued further in Monteverdi's *Ch'io t'ami*. This madrigal, published in his Fifth Book of Madrigals in 1606, sets a long passage from Guarini's *Il Pastor Fido* in three *partes*. Monteverdi again sets this on the final G, but here he goes a stage farther by changing from a key signature of one flat to an open signature (no sharps or flats). The most obvious change of tonality is in the last six lines of the poem, where Guarini gives voice to the ultimate despair ('amor miseria . . . rigida Ninfa . . . al mio morire': 'wicked love . . . heartless Nymph . . . harsh . . . death'); but there is in addition a shorter change, also to G major, at line 8 – the end of the *prima parte*, which illustrates 'my lamenting'. To the modern ear the effect of hearing the final six lines in G major (F♯s are supplied by accidentals) is sweet, particularly since it follows the G minor which largely characterizes the preceding music. Yet the ending was clearly intended to be harsh rather than sweet;[73] Monteverdi's contemporaries would have considered this final passage as being a change from molle (B♭ in the key signature) to the harder durum – an ending clearly suggested by 'cruda voce' in the text.

This neat explanation, it must be said, is not borne out by some other features of the text setting. 'Dura' (in line 24 of the text), while using a B natural quite prominently, is naturale rather than durum; and 'crudele' (line 2) is strangely molle in feeling since it cadences on B♭. There are, nevertheless, many sharps at 'aspri' in line 26, so that the harshness is illustrated by harmonies on the sharp side of durum. On the other hand, 'soave' (lines 9 and 19), 'dolce' (line 15) and 'dolci' (line 17) – words which one would expect to use the sweet-sounding hexachord – while all belonging to passages with a flat key signature, are nevertheless not particularly 'molle' in sound.

'Cruda voce', at the end of the madrigal, does most certainly move the music into the harshest areas, well on the sharp side of durum; and several words in the text help Monteverdi to emphasize the point. The second syllable of 'l'armi' (in line 33 of the text), and 'mi' (in the same line) would be set to the major third of a hexachord if a composer was to match solmization syllables in his music. Monteverdi emphasizes this major-third quality by making the setting of these syllables rather sharp: first E and B sound together (naturale and durum), then G♯ and E sound together (E hexachord and naturale hexachord), and finally C♯ (A hexachord) is used.[74] In line 33 'l'armi' might also be thought of as 'fa mi', for it is set (in the first soprano) as the descending tritone D–G♯ as if illustrating *mi contra fa diabolus est in musica* by setting the syllables to hexachords a fourth apart (D is 'FA' in the hexachord on A, G♯ is 'MI' in the hexachord on E; see Example 14a). Here,

Example 14

a)

Monteverdi: *Ch'io t'ami*

55

then, is another version of the expansion of the 'mi fa' interval used in the interests of text expression. This example also shows that 'sola' – a word one might by now expect to be set to its corresponding solmization syllables – is given in the hexachord on D in the tenor (bar 54), with *inganno* in the bass (bar 55, hexachord on A to hexachord on E), and in the second soprano (bar 54) with a mutation from durum to hexachord on D.

All this indicates tonal motion in a sharpwards direction, illustrating 'cruda voce' ('harsh voice'): but the various soprano I versions of 'al mio morire' ('at my death') at the end – based on the drooping phrase Caccini had set to 'deh non languire' in his *Nuove Musiche* of 1602[75] – balance this trend with steady sequential movement back to G; the phrase first spans E down to A, then A down to D, and finally D down to the tonic G.

Monteverdi made another use of this minor/major technique, but on a larger scale, in his five-voice *Zefiro torna*, in the Sixth Book of Madrigals (1614). Petrarch's sonnet has a distinct change of mood after the initial octave, as is usual.[76] Monteverdi's setting is on G throughout, and again the key-signature changes from one flat (first eight lines) to open signature for the *sestet*. The poem, which changes from an idyllic, arcadian octave to a harsh *sestet* of an anti-pastoral nature, is thus given a setting that shifts from molle to durum. One might almost say that the pastoral and anti-pastoral types, which have already been noted above, are here juxtaposed, though the opening does not use the F ionian which so frequently characterizes settings of idyllic pastorals.[77] Nevertheless, the contrast is obvious, and must have been the more vivid to contemporaries in that mutation from molle to durum was frowned upon by contemporary theory. The 'modulation' is emphasized by a rhythmic change from triple to duple time, though the *seconda parte* includes a minute C-major recollection of the opening. The fact that there is not a single B♭ in the *seconda parte* would make the contemporary performer the more aware of the complete banishment of any molle feeling in that section: by contrast, it makes considerable use of the areas on the sharp side of durum, with frequent E-major and B-major chords.

Monteverdi set the whole of Agnelli's Sestina *Lagrime d'Amante* (1614) on the final D.[78] Of the six *partes*, all except IV have the open signature, whereas the fourth section uses a signature of one flat. It is not necessary – or particularly usual – to cadence on the same final for each section of a piece in many *partes*; but, equally, changes of key signature within a piece were still not usual at this period. In the fourth section – the one that uses a flat in the signature, and which begins 'Ma te raccoglie O Ninfa' ('Receive her, O Nymphs, in the lap of heaven') – the sweetness of the idea of reception into heaven makes the molle sound particularly appropriate.

The settings of 'Ahi lasso' and similar ideas throughout the *Lagrime d'Amante* are a touchstone of the tonal progress within the work. In Section I the words first appear with 'Ahi' set very often as 'la–mi' and with 'lasso' given the conventional stepwise falling shape (though the step is often a semitone in this instance): the overall shape of the phrases is similar to those found in Caccini's *Le nuove musiche* (1602) (see Example 14b). This setting,

Example 14 *concluded*   Monteverdi: *Lagrime d'Amante*

though sometimes implying a '*mi*' in the molle hexachord, is in fact on the sharp (durum) side: the sharpness of the opening of the whole madrigal is made more extreme if one takes into account the continuo part, which indicates opening chords of D major (not D minor, as the voice parts suggest). In section III there is a decisive shift towards flatter areas, though that section starts with a typical dorian phrase repeated a fifth higher to give an impression of moving in a sharpward direction – the repeat is virtually in the aeolian mode. The word 'lasci' is set to a descending tone; this is the correct shape for 'la sol', but the notes used are not always the conventional pitches belonging to the basic hexachords. The change towards the molle hexachord comes with the introduction of B♭s in this passage during which Glauco contemplates 'lasci quel seno / Che nido fu d'amor . . .' ('the breast which was the nest of love'). The closing phrase of the *parte*, in a clear aeolian, is repeated in the dorian mode with B♭s, so reversing the opening progression and making a satisfying frame for the section. The move to flats at the end prefigures the introduction of B♭ into the key signature for *Ma te raccoglie* (section IV): almost immediately a chord on E♭ emphasizes the shift to the sweeter areas.

At *O chiome d'or* (section V) the original key signature returns; and two phrases of text particularly attract our attention. The first is 'Ohime' (in bars 23–30), which Strainchamps[79] suggests is a reference to the famous opening phrase of the Lament of Arianna. 'Ohime' is repeated on what amounts to an inverted pedal E (alternating between the two sopranos); this note, 'la–mi' in the gamut system, would of course also be appropriate for 'Ahi me'. In the following phrase 'Ah muse' is continuously set as if the first word were 'Ahi', with 'la–mi' (or 'la' in either molle or naturale) the norm.

The *Sesta et ultima parte (Dunque amate reliquie)* makes a summary of these processes. 'Ahi Corinna' sounds on a single note, antiphonally called between the two sopranos over an ostinato-style G-minor passage much lower down in the other three voices: the style recalls that (in section V) at which 'Ohime' was set to antiphonal Es. 'Ahi Corinna', however, is set on monotone Ds for some time, until, at bar 38, the G-minor passage is transposed up a tone and repeated. B♭s are thus replaced by the harder B naturals, which – with the rise in pitch – give the music a yet more emotional and bitter quality: but, more than this, the repeated Es in the upper voices are set as 'la–mi' in order to emphasize 'Ahi'. It is as if the most powerful expression of that word has gradually emerged from the sweeter and more dolorous texture. This is immediately followed up by a setting of 'Ahi morte' which recalls the music for 'Ah muse' and 'Ahi lasso' in preceding sections (the la–#sol shapes will obviously make the performers associate this phrase with 'Ahi lasso': see Example 15).

In the madrigal which follows the *Sestina* in the Sixth Book of Madrigals, Monteverdi explores these ideas further. *Ohime il bel viso* is a setting of a Petrarch sonnet lamenting the death of Madonna Laura. The opening cries of *Ohime* – the word starts each of the first three lines – sound antiphonally on Ds in the two upper parts, as the three other voices sing in G minor very much lower in the texture; then, just as in *Lagrime d'Amante*, Monteverdi transposes the passage up a tone into A minor. B♭s therefore disappear in favour of the harder B natural, and the cries of *Ohime* now occur on 'la–mi' (E), a hexachord description that is a close parallel to 'Ahi'. This corresponds exactly to the 'Ahi Corinna' setting in the *Sestina* (VI, bar 32f). *Ohime* is the second word of line 5; lines 5 and 6 run

> Et ohime, il dolce riso ond'usci il dardo
> Di che morte altre ben già mai spero,

and Denis Stevens translates them as

> And alas, the sweet laughter whence came the dart
> From which I crave no other boon than death!

In Monteverdi's setting, the canto (first soprano) part has a series of semi-breves, rather like a *cantus firmus* in style, in a basic shape of three notes

Example 15   Monteverdi: *Lagrime d'Amante*

falling by step (a semitone followed by a tone). The words are repetitions of 'et ohime'. This quasi-*cantus firmus* follows the content of the text used by the three lower voices in that it shifts from the natural hexachord (F–E–D) to the molle (Bb–A–G) and on to the even sweeter hexachord on Bb (Eb–D–C). The process is then reversed so that Bb–A–G is followed by F–E–D: the return from the sweeter areas to natural (but not as far as durum) parallels 'no other boon but death'. The bold scale formation of this '*cantus firmus*' – which (not only because of its melodic shape, but also because it traverses several hexachords) may well have reminded Monteverdi's contemporaries of the ladder of being which, it was believed, linked all creation – is a neatly contrived tonal barometer paralleling the text (see Example 16). At times the sequential

Example 16

harmony of the lower voices duplicates the tonal motion, yet at other times it negates it: the constant ebb and flow between flats and contradictions of those flats (F♯ and C♯ are the only sharps used) is fascinating.

A well-known madrigal that, by contrast, does not use the traditional characteristics of the hexachords for its depiction of changing moods is Wilbye's *Draw on, sweet night* (1609). Here is a madrigal whose very construction is based on a juxtaposition of durum and molle; yet the sharp and flat areas are reversed in relation to what one might expect. English composers as a whole – Dowland is the exception – make much less use of these procedures: indeed, by the seventeenth century the hexachord system was in decline, and this piece is indicative of the change in fashion. Wilbye's use of tonality is modern in its use of minor (i.e. molle, D minor) for the sadder portions of the text and major (on the same tonic, and therefore durum) for the brighter portions, including all the mentions of 'sweet night', which are far from the molle hexachord.[80] Nevertheless, the tonal scheme of this madrigal – as in the others discussed above – is an expression on the large scale of that most evocative interval, 'mi fa': for here the expressive semitone, suggesting the alternation of durum (with its B natural) and molle (with its B♭) has resulted in large-scale alternation of major and minor sections.

Notes

1. See the comments in Zager 1987.
2. Perhaps it is time to suggest that analysis, as well as performance, should be 'authentic'. See Allaire 1972, p. 14; and Harper 1978. Buelow 1980 makes similar claims on behalf of Rhetoric as applied to music.
3. That is, the gamut sound.
4. Allaire 1972, p. 43f, suggests that the solmization process was used by beginners but not necessarily by more expert singers ('Once sufficient ability has been developed, reading becomes an automatic process'; see also p. 63). This does not invalidate the argument that there is a subconscious background of solmization names behind any piece of music from this period.
5. A more far-reaching use of solmization syllables is quoted in Einstein 1949, p. 229.
6. The most famous madrigal collection of all, Arcadelt's First Book of Madrigals for four voices (*c.* 1538 – no example of the first edition has survived) contains very few examples of the matching of solmization syllables in the text to their corresponding hexachord syllables.
7. Professor Brian Trowell makes out a case for 'faburden' being derived in the same way. See Trowell 1980, pp. 28ff. See also Lockwood 1985, p. 101; and Sandon 1984, pp. 56ff.
8. Picker 1989, p. 229.
9. See Watkins 1973, p. 167.
10. Augmentation and echo effects were sometimes used to illustrate similar ideas.
11. Einstein 1949, p. 230.

12. Perhaps the syllables may themselves suggest melodic lines: and perhaps this could be one of the forces which led Byrd to make the comment quoted below (see also note 27).
13. Morley 1597, p. 16.
14. Gesualdo, Second Book of Madrigals, Nos 16 and 17. Newcomb 1980, pp. 127f, confessed to being unable to understand why Gesualdo had not simply copied Wert's setting. The process of keeping the solmization while varying the actual hexachord is called 'Inganno' (see below; and Harper 1980).
15. Repetition of music to fresh words plays some part in the early madrigal: the most famous of all, Arcadelt's *Il bianco e dolce cigno*, is built around a quite complex scheme involving the repetition (with new words) of more than one section of music.
16. It is a pity that Powers 1974 fails to take into account Palestrina's use of solmization syllables.
17. See Harper 1980.
18. The rising 6th 'mi–FA' was a characteristic of the third mode: see Glarean 1547, Vol. 1, p. 71.
19. Zarlino 1558 gives the following descriptions for works in the phrygian (3) and hypo-phrygian (4) modes: '3 . . . tearful and full of laments. 4 . . . lamentful . . . contain sadness or suppliant lamentation, such as matters of love, and to words which express languor, quiet, tranquillity, adulation, deception, and slander. Because of its effect, some have called it a flattering mode.'
20. D phrygian is, indeed, a most unusual mode, and results in a move to D♭ very early in the piece. Mann 1983, p. 186, points out that it is Monte's only use of this mode: the extreme dolorousness obtained by transposing the phrygian mode to such a flat degree must be Monte's reason for using it.
21. Vicentino said: 'Some composers frequently think it a fine way of composing if in their compositions they dress up the text in the [corresponding] tone syllables. But this procedure has only the small advantage that by such a combination the pronunciation of the text is rendered a little easier for the singer; but a good singer will attach little value to such a composition, so that one sees it is of little importance'. See Einstein 1949, pp. 229f.
22. Vicentino recommended starting a composition in such a way that the singers will find it easy to sing in tune. See Maniates 1979, p. 172. It remains true that there are difficult pieces which also match solmization sounds: such pieces may, of course, be rendered the more approachable because of this.
23. Oddly enough, the word 'solea' later in the madrigal is not in any way mirrored in the hexachord sounds.
24. Readers wishing to verify this can do no better than check through Harman 1976: yet, as mentioned above, Arcadelt's famous First Book of Madrigals (*c.* 1538) does not use the device.
25. We shall come across a supreme example of this (in the music of Palestrina) later in the present discussion.
26. See the comments in Mace 1983, p. 121, and in Haar 1986, p. 134. It is interesting that Dowland copied the musical shape quoted in Example 7 in his setting of 'Sorrow stay' in the song *Stay, sorrow stay*: this is the piece that follows *Flow my tears* – another work that makes much use of such phrases – in The Second Book of Songs (1600).
27. Preface to *Gradualia* (Fellowes 1936, p. 80): see note 12 of this Chapter.
28. The end of Wert's *Valle, che de'lamenti miei/Ben riconosco in voi* (1588) illustrates this point perfectly. The last line of Petrarch's sonnet, 'Lasciando in

terra la sua bella spoglia', is permeated with ah sounds, and Wert sets most of them either to 'fa' or 'la': there are so many in this final passage that the device must have been intentional, and the continual use of D or A for the start of 'Lasciando' (to look no further) may well have been intended as an illustrative device. That is, the continual returns to the hexachord notes perhaps represent the 'confining to earth' of the beloved's mortal garb which the final line of the sonnet mentions.

29. See below.
30. Some examples of this are considered below.
31. See also Examples 43, 62 and 64.
32. Since so many examples in this discussion are drawn from Italian madrigals I might cite as other examples of the molle hexachord used to illustrate 'sweet' Lasso's chanson *La nuit froide et sombre* (1576), where B♭ contrasts with the sharps used to illustrate darkness; and Monte's chanson *Bonjour mon coeur* (1575), which takes one degree farther Lasso's setting (1564) of 'doux' in his version of the same text. See also Godwin 1987, p. 137.
33. It may be that the common sexual *double entendre* is implied here: indeed, if 'death' can mean physical union with the beloved, it seems logical that 'life' (used in a similar context) might stand for the absence of such union. The use of the gloomy A minor, along with the phrygian colour of these passages, takes on a new light when viewed in this way.
34. Morley 1597, p. 18.
35. See Morley 1597, p. 16. Indeed, in the example on p. 18 Morley implies a further transposition, with A♭ appearing as 'fa'. He tends not to use the solmization syllables 'ut' and 're': these syllables dropped out of use in seventeenth-century England (see Hughes 1980: also Rainbow 1982, where the system is called 'four-note sol-fa'). In his twelve-voice *Duo Seraphim* Francisco Guerrero specifically marks E with a sharp, since the syllable to be sung is the 'ah' of 'gloria': the ah sound would suggest a flattening of the E so as to produce the pitch *fa* (especially since that note is approached from below), and the sharp is a warning against this tendency. This indicates the importance of considering solmization when applying *musica ficta* generally in this period: it seems that Guerrero thought that singers would add *ficta* so as to fit the hexachord syllables unless he warned them against doing so in this particular instance. Nevertheless, as Example 7b shows, solmization is not a wholly reliable guide. Allaire 1972, pp. 27f, discusses both flatwards and sharpwards transpositions of the hexachord.
36. See Trowell 1980.
37. The flat hexachords can, of course, be written by using accidentals as well as by employing flats in the key signature. The introduction of new hexachords, including that on B♭, is discussed in Hughes 1980. In a similar fashion, the hexachord system was occasionally expanded in the opposite direction, beyond durum, so producing a hexachord based on D (see below).
38. Yet see the remarks in Berger 1987, p. 78.
39. As Newcomb 1980, p. 7, points out, fa cannot always be the note above la. Hughes 1980, maintains that the jingle *Una nota* . . . is not explicitly stated before Praetorius (1614–15).
40. Many – but by no means all – pastoral pieces are based around the molle hexachord: or, rather, they are in F ionian. Perhaps we may trace the use of this mode on to the many uses of F major for pastoral music in later centuries. The continual leaning towards 'fa' – i.e. the subdominant – that results in the use of B♭ undoubtedly makes for music of a relaxed nature. (It may be no more than a

coincidence that 'fa' is a very relaxed vowel to sing; 'mi' – the major third and the result, at times, of 'sharp' music – is, by contrast, brighter and harder. [Allaire 1972, p. 45, quotes a treatise of Guilliaud, 1554, which maintains that fa and ut are soft sounds, sol and re are medium, and la and mi are hard sounds. It is difficult, though, to understand why la should be hard when fa is soft.] Perhaps these facts may, even if subconsciously, have contributed to the feeling of 'rightness' about the use of the hexachord.) The relaxed feeling which this key area gives may account for its use so often in later music for pastoral scenes: this would certainly help to explain the strong subdominant tendency of such pieces as the final movement of Corelli's *Christmas Concerto* and Beethoven's *Pastoral Symphony*. The hexachord background may explain the cryptic remark 'Melos suave' which occurs in the Mulliner Book at Blitheman's second setting of *Eterne rerum* (*MB* Vol. I, No. 51). Of Blitheman's four settings of this chant, this is the only one that does not begin with a chord of F. Perhaps the fear was that the opening (which begins with a D-minor chord) would be taken for pure dorian (rather than 'D minor' or D aeolian) and that B naturals rather than B♭ would result, were it not for the warning to observe the 'sweet' hexachord.

41. See Tomlinson 1987, pp. 49 and 50. Chater 1981, p. 96, says, 'Also significant is the predominance of modes 11 and 12, symbolizing the humble and rustic'. There are, of course, F-ionian pieces that are not idyllic pastorals.

42. See Berger 1987, p. 60. Sharp key signatures are so rare before the seventeenth century as to be not worth taking into account: Allaire 1972 notes some examples – see pp. 33, 110, 115ff. He also deals with the transposition of hexachords in a sharpward direction without a change of signature; see pp. 19, 27f. Theoretical evidence about the use of an unexpected sharpness for illustrating harshness is quoted in Haar 1990, p. 73: Cimello gives an example of the use of the tritone in a suspension figure, normally forbidden but allowed 'to show the harshness and cruelty of some word'.

43. Frescobaldi may have been influenced by the opening of Marenzio's *Dolorosi martir* (1580).

44. The unexpectedly sharp (for an E-phrygian piece) penultimate chord of Marenzio's *Dolorosi martir* (1581) may have been the inspiration here.

45. See Pike 1993, pp. 69f.

46. See the fifteenth-century 'Anonymous XI', quoted in Allaire 1972, p. 35.

47. Kerman 1981, p. 292. The technique occurs in as early a madrigal as Lasso's *Alma Nemes* (1555) (and in the sacred contrafactum, *Alme Deus*), where sharps are used at the end for 'dulce novumque'. Cf also Monteverdi, *Luci serene*, and Marenzio, *O dolcezze amarissime*, among many others. See Tomlinson 1987, pp. 48, 68, 136. Another well-known example is at the word 'dolce' in Monteverdi's *l'Orfeo*, Act IV ('Ahi, vista troppo dolce'): the vocal line here fills in a falling diminished fifth: it may be relevant, then, to point out that Monte several times uses a direct downward leap of a diminished fourth to illustrate 'E nel soave' in *Fui presso fui ferito* (1595). Weelkes uses a chord of B major (in a G-mixolydian piece) at 'sweet lass' in *My flocks feed not* (1597), having previously used an unexpected B major on 'afraid'.

48. Notably *Chiesi un guardo* and *Correa vezzosamente*. We might note that Zarlino 1558, Part IV, does not use the old names for the modes, but prefers numbers. Nevertheless, the use of the 'aria' of the lydian mode has the advantage that it conjures up such descriptions as Zarlino's '. . . modesty, happiness, and relief from annoying cares'. This certainly seems to be the thinking behind Monte's use

of lydian colour at the start of *Vergine pura* (1583), and Willaert's at the start of *Qual dolcezza giamai/Alla dolce armonia* (*c.* 1538).

49.   See, too, the somewhat different examples at 'Men dolci si ma non . . .' in the *seconda parte* of Wert's *Giunto alla tomba/Non di morte sei tu* (1581).

50.   Allaire 1972, p. 47n.

51.   Maniates 1979, p. 194: Allaire 1972, pp. 23, 31, 47, 49f, 52f.

52.   Morley 1597, p. 248.

53.   This English version, by Alec Harman, is intended to be a word-for-word translation rather than a poetic rendition.

54.   From the same year (1538, though the date is not quite certain) comes Arcadelt's *Qualor m'assal' Amore/Ma quell'in un momento*, which has an opening alto part using the notes F–G–A–B natural–G–A; the B is specifically marked with a sharp (meaning B natural since the natural sign was not used at the time) so as to avoid the use of '*fa*' at that point. But B♭s are often required elsewhere in the piece, and they conflict with the B naturals: this dichotomy is a neat illustration of the love–death dichotomy of the poem ('wherever love assails me, I feel death approaching . . .'). Monte's *La dolce Vista* (1569) begins with a chord of F moving to B♭ for 'dolce', but soon moves to a perfect cadence on E (with G♯) to illustrate 'morte'.

55.   As mentioned above, many texts of an idyllic, pastoral nature are set in F ionian.

56.   Of the edition in Harman 1983.

57.   Taglia's *Come'esser puo che si contrari effeti* (1555) sets a text that sums up the juxtaposition of opposites that is such a feature of Petrarchan poetry. The prevailing aeolian mode is banished in favour of a very remote flat key area which illustrates 'Ice can be fire and sweetness', only to return to aeolian for '. . . torment'.

58.   For example, Nasco's *Madonna, quand'io penso* (1561) illustrates the pain of love by playing off the 'hard' B natural against the 'soft' B♭: indeed, soon after the opening (which is dorian, though the piece ends in the aeolian mode) a B sharp (meaning B natural) has to be marked – despite the lack of any flat in either the preceding music or the key signature – to warn the performer against singing a ♭ in a D–A–B–A phrase that would normally invoke the *una nota supra la* rule. The chromatic mixture of flat-side and sharp-side chords in Gesualdo's *Ecco, morirò dunque/Ahi, già mi discoloro* (1596) is not merely wilful, but the result of mixing molle and durum in order to illustrate the idea of death for love. The use of a B-major penultimate chord in Marenzio's *Dolorosi martir* (1580) illustrates the last word, 'amara' ('bitter'): with the final E-major chord, and taking the sharp-side opening into account, this could be described as E major; yet tonal E major, with the associations it eventually attracts, is not what Marenzio is invoking here; rather it is the 'aria' of the phrygian mode ('tearful and full of laments') alongside the hard sharps.

59.   Whenham 1986, p. 56. The change of tonality in *l'Orfeo* is not so very remarkable when one considers the move from A major to C minor at '. . . dolente? Ahi crud'Amor' in Rore's *Dalle belle contrade* (1566).

60.   The G minor–E major idea was one that Monteverdi picked up from Peri's *L'Euridice* (1601).

61.   See the discussion in Chew 1989. It is worth noting that the passage at 'chiami crudelissima' is based on the conventional expressive device of parallel six-three chords over a further expressive pattern, the descending tetrachord; the devices

are, however, made the more pungent by the application of unexpected suspensions.

62. See *Dixit Dominus* in the *Vespers* of 1610, where the prevailing A minor shifts into G minor for the first part of the Doxology: after 'sancto' A minor returns, but the polyphony ends with a chord of E major. The *cantus firmus* is used at three different pitches.

63. Salzer 1983 analyses this piece without realizing either the importance of the hexachord background or the importance of dissonances (the latter is a common failing in analyses of the Schenkerian type): but Salzer's discussion (p. 140) of the verse-form is valuable, as is his comment about 'Deh perchè fate', 'The musical setting ... can do here what cannot be done in a reading or recitation of the poem: an exciting and challenging statement can be made to enter prematurely, as if one person's statement were interrupted by another's'.

64. Translation from the notes accompanying the record of Monteverdi's *Quarto libro dei madrigali*, L'Oiseau Lyre, Decca, London, 1986.

65. The upper parts are both of soprano range, though their clefs differ.

66. See Haar 1986, p. 142.

67. Whenham 1986.

68. It also removes the underlying feeling that the music might be imitating a pair of lovers.

69. There are also leaps downward off two dissonant D's.

70. Salzer 1983, p. 143, says that at the repeat the music is 'shifted upwards[!]. The latter compositional procedure, as well as the change from a three- to a five-voice setting, creates the heightened emphasis that is characteristic of a warning reiterated in a raised voice'. I submit that Monteverdi's purpose is different – it is that of moving flatwards to create a more 'dolorous' sound.

71. The passage bears a strong resemblance to the setting of 'Onde con dolci ed amorosi' in Monteverdi's setting of Tasso's *Mentr'io mirava fiso* (1590), where the cross-relations also depict 'the sweet pangs of love'. There is another connection between *Ohimè, se tanto* and a different madrigal in that the 'e dolorosa' phrase occurs again in *Cruda Amarilli* (discussed below): both settings use a leap of a seventh.

72. One of the associations of six–three chords at this period was with sweetness: see Beebe 1983, p. 91.

73. The same is true of the A-major end of Gagliano's *O sonno/Ov'è'il silenzio* (1602), which illustrates 'hard and cruel nights' by using a sharp passage. In Wert's *Giunto alla tomba/Non di morte sei tu* (1581) the words 'Di color di moto privo' sound sweet to modern ears, for they are set in 'recitative' on a chord of A major; but the effect would not have been sweet to Wert's contemporaries.

74. Monteverdi might also have done this at the start of the madrigal, for the first line is full of 'mi' sounds: but at that point he ignores the solmization. The opening in fact provides one of the places where 't'ami' cannot be interpreted as 'fa mi', and solmization cannot be an indicator of *musica ficta*. Wert, in *Egressus Iesus* (1581), gives an unexpected major chord at 'Miserere mei'; this partially illustrate the entry of a new voice into the narrative, and partially shadows the 'Mi –' of the text with MI.

75. The descending sixth, whether major or minor, formed no part of the *stile antico*; yet Caccini, even if he popularized the motive, was not the first to use it. See, for instance, Wert's *Giunto alla tomba/Non di morte sei tu* (1581) at 'languido ohime' and 'il pianto' in the *prima parte*. Other examples that predate Caccini's publication are Marenzio's *Cruda Amarilli* (1591) and *Crudele acerba* (1599),

Monteverdi's *O come è gran martire* and *Vattene pur crudel* (both 1592), and Wert's *Amor, io fallo* (1561).

76.   Monte's setting of 1554 divides into two *partes* at this point, though without changing tonality.

77.   Monte had used a similar ploy, though in reverse and without changing the key signature, in *Per aspre horride* (1590). This is in A phrygian: the opening description of the 'horrid paths, woods and wild rocks' is cast in sharp areas (with no lack of E-major triads) – an 'anti pastoral'; but at the poet's response in the second half of the madrigal (it is not divided into two *partes*) there is a return to a more pure A phrygian (with only a single crotchet B natural), the flatter area paralleling 'And then, Sorrowful . . .' Monte changes from a key signature of one flat to the open key signature from section 11 to the end of *O voi c'havete* (1578), which is in 18 *partes*.

78.   The Sestina is an elaborate verse-form of six six-line stanzas, followed by an 'envoy' of three lines: the line endings of stanza one are repeated in a different order in the subsequent five stanzas.

79.   Strainchamps 1985, p. 172f.

80.   Wilbye's *Adieu sweet Amaryllis* (1598) provides another example. Several works by English composers of this period show a marked interest in the possibilities of contrast between major and minor on the same tonic: Bull's *Starre Anthem*, Weelkes' *O Lord arise* and Ramsey's *Sleep, fleshly birth* are among these – but lack of space precludes a discussion here.

2 Voces Musicales II

More Abstruse Uses of the System

The uses of solmization and of the expressive colour of the hexachords so far described are straightforward. The veering towards molle or durum in order to illustrate features of the text would have been very clear to the performers, and most singers would probably have been surprised to find a prominent 'sola', 'lasso', 'mi fa' or 'ut sol' in the text not set to its corresponding hexachord sounds. Such settings are purely mechanical; but there are occasions when this kind of sound language can be made to create real music. As we have seen, the progressive elements in the music of the period mostly resulted from the attempt to express the meaning of the text with ever greater vividness and fidelity. The examples of solmization discussed in this chapter – largely but not entirely in chronological order – are part of this trend: the solmization is used as a way of emphasizing the meaning – sometimes explicit, sometimes implicit – of the words.

Willaert's *Amor mi fa morire* (1536) sets a poem (by B. Dragonetto) in which the opening line ('Love, you cause me to die') is the basis of the whole poem, the idea from which everything else logically derives. The musical setting parallels this textual idea by using an opening phrase which mirrors the solmization exactly (see Example 8b): the tenor part, fa–sol–mi–fa–sol–mi–re, gives a short musical tag which recurs from time to time throughout the piece, usually to different words which do not themselves share the hexachord sounds suggested by those notes. By using this tag to recall the hexachord sounds of the opening line of the poem, Willaert reminds the singers, at intervals, of the text's opening – and fundamental – idea.[1]

Several pieces from the final years of the 1550s display a virtuoso treatment of solmization syllables in the service of text illustration. First came Rore's 1557 setting of Petrarch's lament on the death of Madonna Laura, *Mia benigna fortuna/Crudele acerba* (1557), a famous text which inspired several

67

highly expressive avant-garde settings. This madrigal will be discussed at length later: for the moment it is sufficient to note that one of the attractions for musicians was the line maintaining that the poet's grief 'vince ogni stile' ('defeats every style'). Composers were glad to accept the challenge. Rore chose to illustrate the idea by *bending* the hexachord: this is partially the result of his choice of conflicting key-signatures (some voices have one flat, some have two)[2]. 'Stile' is set to 'mi re', but 'mi' is on occasions flat, producing a shape more characteristic of 'fa mi': but there is an additional point. As we have seen, the 'mi' vowel sound will at times lead to the use of an unexpected major third; the use of an unexpected Eb in the soprano just before the end at the first syllable of 'stile' thus runs directly counter to the conventional process used by those who invoke hexachords. In a sense, then, this defeats the hexachord itself: for, as Petrarch says, 'I miei gravi sospir non vanno in rime' ('My heavy sighs find no outlet in song': see Example 17).[3]

It may be that Monte knew of Rore's setting, for in his own *Dolorosi martir*, published a year later (1558) he applied a similar solmization process. The resonances of solmization are set up by an opening passage very closely built on the syllables of the text. Because of this, when he sets Tansillo's words, 'Misero piango e'l mio perduto bene. Triste voci . . .' ('I sadly bewail my lost joy. Sad voices . . .') he can use a 'saddened' version of the hexachord in which the *voces musicales* become 'sad voices', and the resonances already set up will help the performers and hearers to take the point. In this passage 'misero' becomes 'bmi re' instead of 'mi re', in a manner that takes its inspiration from Rore's example (see Example 18). Besides E natural/Eb cross-relations, Monte imitates Rore's characteristic final cadence, demonstrating clearly that he was parodying the earlier *Mia benigna fortuna/Crudele acerba*.[4]

Lasso expanded the idea in his sacred madrigal *Quanto il mio duol* (1560). Here the hexachord witticism is encapsulated in a piece which is largely built on the descending tetrachord, a musical phrase often used as an expression of grief during the period.[5] Several treatments of hexachord syllables suggest that solmization is 'in the air'. For example, soon after the opening Lasso sets 'sia'[6] unexpectedly high by comparison with the music that precedes it, and with the solmization syllables reversed. (The D–C# is harmonized by a cadential Bb–A in the bass, also set to 'sia'.) Later, the 'repeated invocations' ('Tanto ti chiamo') in the treble voice (though not invariably in the lower parts) set 'ti chia–' to 'mi fa'. Having set up these resonances, Lasso builds on them. In the following passage, the text 'con dolorosa voce' ('with a sorrowful voice') clearly calls for a treatment in which the *voces musicales* must, as in Rore and Monte, themselves become sorrowful. The bass therefore begins with an unconventional, 'sad', version of the hexachord, starting on Bb and descending by step to D. This is followed by naturale and durum hexachords, sadly harmonized, and often repeated so as to draw unmistakable attention to them.

Example 17   Rore: *Mia benigna/Crudele acerba*

The 'sad' harmonization consists of descending parallel first-inversion chords over a pedal, resulting in minim passing-notes; this technique was often used to express grief in late-Renaissance music.[7] There follows a 'sad' (and at the end unexpectedly twisted) durum hexachord in the soprano, with B♭s instead of B naturals, in long-note style and looking for all the world like a typical hexachord piece (bars 60–65, at the text 'la morte bramo' – 'I long for death'). The B♭, as well as twisting the expected hexachord (nothing but durum has been used for some time), also gives the syllable 'bra–' a matching 'fa' setting.

Example 18   Monte: *Dolorosi martir'*

The idea of the 'sad' hexachord seems to be recalled at the very end, for the final soprano phrase has a similar line. It is possible that the use of the molle hexachord here refers to the slight sweetening of tone ('. . . ch'ove ch'io vada sentirò minore' – '. . . for wherever I go I shall feel less pain') in the poem at this point.

These three impressive pieces had considerable influence on later composers. Indeed, it was acknowledged that Rore's music provided the starting-point for the *seconda prattica*.[8] The influence of the grinding nature of the tonality in his *Mia benigna fortuna/Crudele acerba* – provided by the E♭/E natural dichotomy, by the phrygian cadences which result, and by the 'flattening-out' of the hexachord – continues to the end of the century.[9]

Monte again uses solmization for structural reasons in his *Ahi, chi mi rompe il sonno* (1570). At the end of both *partes* solmization is in evidence, though at the close of the *prima parte* it is not built around the conventional hexachords. It is possible that the tonality of the piece was chosen so as to fit the solmization of the end of the text, though (as mentioned above) it is equally true that more than one 'correct' setting of the solmization sounds is possible. As so often at the end of madrigals, the last section (the final couplet of the text, usually) is repeated: in this piece, Monte alters the repeat so that, on singing the passage a second time, the music more closely fits with the solmization pitch-names suggested by the text. Thus, whether or not the singer (and, indeed, the listener) feels a sense of dissonance when the syllables are *not* all 'correctly' solmized, there is an unmistakable feeling of rightness – of 'resolution' or 'homecoming' – when they are. This feeling is obviously very fitting at the end of the piece.

As the century draws on, the uses of solmization tend to take on the nature of metaphysical wit, inevitably reminding one of the virtuosity of Donne's poetry. Luzzaschi provides an example of this kind of writing in his *Se il lauro e sempre verde/Dhe, se pur secco* (1582). We may be the more inclined to believe that Luzzaschi was consciously employing solmization if we remember that his piece was written for private performance within the *musica secreto* of the court at Ferrara – when few people were present, and those people connoisseurs – and that the dedicatee (whose name is included in punning form in the title) was that leading member of the *Concerto delle Donne*, Laura Peverara. The piece has an immense concentration of solmization in the middle[10] (see Example 8d), but almost none outside this passage (and even that little may well occur merely by accident). By his sudden change to a reliance on solmization Luzzaschi apparently emphasizes a point made in the text: the poet says that all is 'dried up' ('se pur secco fosse'), and the composer responds to this by suggesting that inspiration, too, has 'dried up', leaving him to fall back on hexachord solmization. The 'greenness' ('che mai verde fiorisce') which follows this passage in the poem is illustrated musically by a return to free (non-solmized) music with a considerable burgeoning of melismas. If I am right, this amounts to a criticism of solmization-based composition, for Luzzaschi seems to imply that 'free' composition shows inspiration, but that those for whom inspiration has dried up rely on solmization. (We shall, however, shortly see that Luzzaschi is by no means averse to using close solmization in his other madrigals.) In bar 54 the text results in a *vertical*, rather than horizontal, setting of the solmization syllables: that is, the syllables which suggest 'mi' and 'fa' are sounded together, though the voice with 'mi' sings F and the one with 'fa' sings E – an inversion of the solmization syllables such as we have already encountered. The inversion, the crossing of the voices, and the strong dissonance,[11] all help Luzzaschi to give pungent emphasis to 'languisce' ('withered').

Marenzio, who quite often used solmization, does so in a particularly interesting way in *Affliger chi per voi/Nulla da voi* (1588). The piece contains a considerable amount of solmization, though for our purposes the most interesting portion is the end of the *prima parte*, which sets the text 'Manchi per dura via d'aspre montagne' ('faint on the hard journey through rough mountains'). A hard journey through rough mountains could scarcely be described as an idyllic pastoral; and there is considerable bitterness in the text as a whole. Marenzio, writing a piece in D dorian, chooses to manage without using a single flat of any kind (though there are plenty of sharps, and there is some chromaticism which one might well have expected to produce the occasional flat): there is no softness, then, to be encountered anywhere in this piece. It has the character of an anti-pastoral, perhaps: the modern ear may hear the tonality as D major, but to Marenzio's contemporaries it would have seemed a very bitter, hard-sounding madrigal. By first solmizing 'Manchi per dura via d'asp[re montagne]' as FA–MI–RE–UT–fa–mi–fa a descending stepwise line, with the beginning of an ascending line, results. Obviously, the topography of the landscape is being illustrated: but the descent may also be intended to illustrate 'faint'. This descent fits in parallel tenths over a descending naturale hexachord (in the bass). Why, though, should Marenzio use clear statements of hexachords and six-note scales in parallel with them (but with a different combination of tones and semitones) at 'hard journey through rough mountains'? I suggest that he intends to remind the performers of the hard journey which every musician had to undergo – for the gamut system (or any other kind of *Gradus ad Parnassum*) is just such a hard climb as the text mentions[12].

If performers subconsciously thought of the solmization names as they sang, then obviously those sounds must have been in the back of their minds. By choosing notes carefully, therefore, a composer could construct a pattern of sounds which might suggest a word or a short sentence: we have, in fact, already seen how, in Willaert's *Amor mi fa morire*, the repetition of the opening solmization of the text is repeated later in the piece so as to recall, like a *leitmotif*, the main burden of the poem. Einstein maintains that the secondary meaning can at times be obscene.[13] In *Quando io miro* of 1594, Luzzaschi uses this type of hidden language. He sets the mind thinking in solmization by his careful and very beautiful setting of 'Ahi lassa':[14] 'lassa' has the shape normally reserved for 'lasso', and 'mi fa' is also present, with 'Ahi' sometimes set to the note la–mi or la–re–mi (see Example 19). Having set up the resonances of solmization in this way, Luzzaschi capitalizes on them. The next phrase, 'Favor d'amica stella', which actually has no religious connotation, must all the same have brought to mind the phrase 'Ave maris stella' – the more so when one considers that that particular Marian antiphon must have been extremely well known to Catholics because of its regular liturgical performance for three months of every year. Luzzaschi seems to have recalled

Example 19   Luzzaschi: *Quando io miro*

the antiphon, for, after setting the first syllable of the line 'Favor d'amica stella' to the obvious 'fa' syllable, he then follows this up by using 'mi' and 'fa' in that order (at least, in the soprano, second entry of the alto, and second tenor): 'fa mi fa' must, in connection with 'amica stella', have suggested *Maria* to most performers (see Example 20). One would expect this 'fa mi fa' shape to be used for the word 'amica': Luzzaschi in fact only sets that word to solmization syllables which involve mutation between somewhat distant hexachords (the suggested solmization is thus highly problematical), or which involve the inversion of 'mi fa' (though many composers did this). Since the actual uses of 'fa mi fa' are 'out of phase' with the expected uses, the thinking musician might well have tried to discover the reason. It would not take such a person long to discover the connection between 'amica stella' and 'Maria'.

Marian Symbolism

The use of Marian Symbolism, though, is more appropriate to church music than to the madrigal; and such symbolism was indeed found at times in the liturgical music of the period.

Example 20   Luzzaschi: *Quando io miro*

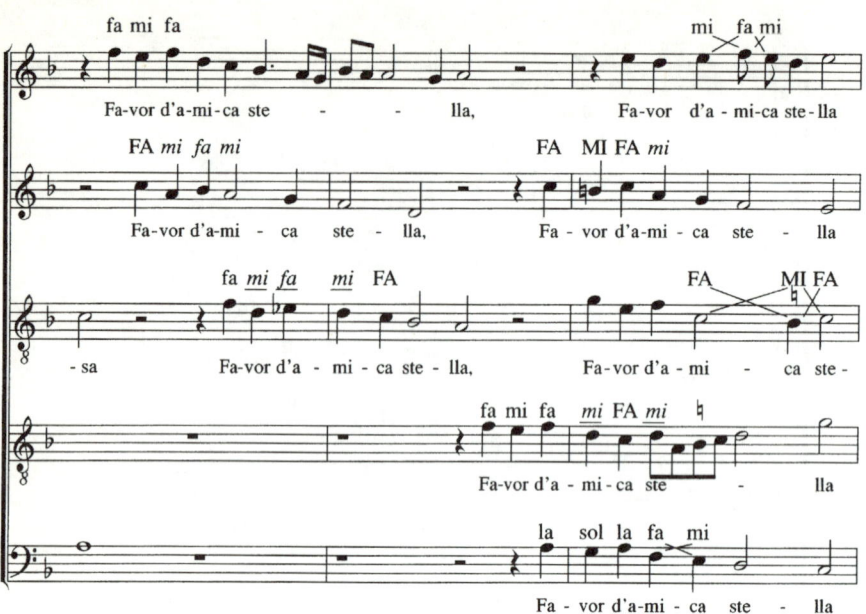

Peter Philips's volume of five-voice *Cantiones sacrae* (Antwerp, 1612) represents his earliest published church music. The writing is relatively conservative, and although a basso continuo part was added to the volume in 1617 the novelty of this feature does not succeed in making the music feel any more modern. The basically old-fashioned polyphonic nature of the collection – and its Roman Catholic contents – would have suited Philips's employers admirably. From 1597 the composer had been organist to the Brussels court of the Archdukes Albert and Isabella (as they wished to be called); this was virtually a Spanish court on Netherlands soil. The Archdukes considered themselves the spearhead of the Counter-Reformation in the north, and the life of the community was expected to be dedicated to their aim of reconverting to the Roman obedience those lands lost to the Protestants.[15] Ultimately Albert and Isabella were subject to, and dependent upon, Spain, so it is not surprising that elements of conservative, mystical theology should be evident in Philips's music. Spain, always conservative in theological matters, still preserved medieval thinking to a considerable extent.

Gaude Maria virgo and its second part *Virgo prudentissima* is one of the most old-fashioned motets in Philips's 1612 collection. I have concluded that it must have been written between 1582 and 1585[16] when Philips was in his early 20s, thus predating his time at the Brussels court. There is much in the piece, however, that would commend its composer to a man of Albert's outlook. The text is

Gaude Maria virgo cunctas haereses sola interemisti in universo mundo.
Alleluia. Virgo prudentissima quo progrederis quasi aurora, valde rutilans.
Filia Syon tota formosa et suavis es, pulchra ut luna, electa ut sol.
Alleluia.

(Rejoice, O Virgin Mary, alone thou hast destroyed heresies in all the world. Alleluia. Most prudent virgin, who comes forth like the ever rosy dawn, daughter of Zion all comely and sweet, beauteous as the moon, mighty as the sun, Alleluia).

A text aimed against heresy (in this context against the Protestants) would be of the utmost relevance to a composer in Philips's position. He had originally left England because of his adherence to the Catholic faith; and the text is equally relevant to Albert and Isabella's purpose in 1612. Moreover, by basing the opening of his motet on a setting of *Gaude Maria virgo* published by Victoria (Rome, 1572) Philips may well have been intending to state his own allegiance to the Roman church and in particular to its Spanish branch, which was so actively involved with the Counter-Reformation. Philips was in Rome from 1582 to 1585; Victoria was also there during these years and both were at Jesuit colleges. It seems likely, therefore, that Philips came across Victoria's *Gaude Maria virgo* (which has no *secunda pars*) during his stay in Rome. For the present purpose it will be enough to consider just a few elements of both settings.[17]

At the words 'sola interemisti' Victoria sets not only the first two syllables (which have an exact counterpart in the hexachord system) but goes on to set the first syllable of 'interemisti' to 'mi' (see Example 21a). As we have seen, 'sola' was commonly set as a rising tone; indeed, Sheppard (*c*.1512–*c*.1550) made use of this device in his much earlier setting of the same text.[18] Victoria additionally uses *inganno*, producing the line shown in Example 21b by moving from the *naturale* hexachord to the *durum* and back.

When Philips later set the same text he extended the device – as so many madrigalists in the emulative tradition did – so that two more syllables were solmized (see Example 21c); and like Victoria, he also used *inganno* (see Example 21d). Is this any more than a learned device, aimed – perhaps with a knowing wink – at the *cognoscenti*? The answer is, I suggest, found in Philips's setting of the second part of the motet, *Virgo prudentissima*. The obvious use of solmization in the first section nicely prepares the listener so that he or she will recognize the relevance of later events, even if that recognition is only subconscious. Solmization is clearest at the words 'electa ut sol', where not only are the last two syllables set in a very obvious fashion, but two other syllables are also possibly solmized (though with a change of hexachord). This phrase, much repeated, is shown in Example 22a. Furthermore, by applying *inganno* to it, on five occasions Philips produces an upward leap of an octave between 'ut' and 'sol' (UT–sol, an octave G, or ut–

Example 21

a)   Victoria

b)   Victoria

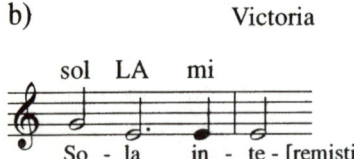

c)   Philips

d)   Philips

sol, an octave C), providing a valid extension of the phrase shown in Example 22a that additionally illustrates the text by placing 'sol' ('sun') markedly higher that the surrounding music.[19]

Similar devices occur, rather less obviously, in the rest of the motet, and Philips illustrates 'et suavis est' by moving to the *molle* hexachord, so illustrating musically the 'sweetness' mentioned in the text. In view of the amount of close mirroring of syllables, one cannot help wondering why, in the second part, Philips nearly always sets the word 'luna' ('moon') as a stepwise descent (see Example 22b). When this step is a whole tone (as it is when placed in the lowest sounding voices of the the passage) it is an exact inversion of 'sola' as that word had been set in the first section of the motet; but when

Example 22

a)   Philips

b)   Philips

the step is a descending semitone it is a rather free inversion of the 'sola' shape. Although the Latin for 'sun' is 'sol' and not 'sola', an Englishman might very well, by faulty etymology – or, more likely, with punning wit such as we associate with the metaphysical poets – consider 'sola' and 'luna' as being complementary, since 'solar' and 'lunar' are English words.[20] As Example 23a shows, the phrase had already occurred early in the first part, at the words 'Maria virgo', and a similar phrase is used to set 'Virgo prudentissima' in the second part ('In universo mundo' in the first part is also somewhat similar).

This correspondence may well be accidental, but nevertheless it neatly ties together the mention of the Virgin Mary and the description of her as 'beauteous as the moon'. The demonstration of 'luna' as a complementary idea to 'sola' would also have some relevance here, since there is a theological background to it. The sun itself stands for Christ. As Edward Hulme put it: 'The beneficent sun, the source of light and heat, has naturally been accepted as a symbol of the "sun" of Righteousness, the dayspring from on high, to give light to them that sit in darkness'.[21] Just as Diana, the classical patroness of

Example 23

virginity associated with the moon, is the counterpart of the ancient sun god Apollo, so the Blessed Virgin Mary is the counterpart of Christ. The medieval mind loved these opposites and viewed such balances as the complementary forces that kept the planets in their orbits and governed the purposeful organization of the universe. Indeed, a man in a really 'metaphysical' frame of mind might easily make the reverse of 'sol la' into 'female sun' (la = she, sol = sun); this, to those brought up in the late sixteenth century, would be more likely to be taken as an illustration of the eternal truths than as a weak etymological joke. Konrad Mut (1472–1526) put it quite succinctly: 'There is only one god and one goddess, but there are many forms and many names – Jupiter, Sol, Apollo, Moses, Christ, Luna, Ceres, Prosperina, Tellus, Mary . . . In religious matters we must employ fables and enigmas as a veil'.[22]

In art Mary is often represented with a crescent moon at her feet; a well-known example from the period under discussion is El Greco's *The Coronation of the Virgin* in the Prado at Madrid. Philips makes the correspondence clear by using a backwards form of the 'sola' music to set the word 'luna' (in spite of the fact that 'sola' in Latin does not mean 'sun'). One could perhaps maintain that Philips has replaced the strict nature of Victoria's underlying 'rule' (the Spaniard's motet is in canon at the unison, a feature Philips did not copy) with a different underlying structure of some strictness. This structure involved close solmization as well as symbolism enshrining the very Catholic notion of placing the Virgin Mary on an extremely high level. Perhaps both men, in their own way, were trying to parallel in music the idea of conforming to the strict rule of Rome; for to both men the breaking of the Catholic rule would have seemed heresy.

This interpretation might be thought impossibly far-fetched, particularly since 'luna' does not appear many times in the motet (compared with 'sola'), and is not invariably solmized as 'la sol'. Nevertheless, Philips himself virtually proves the accuracy of the interpretation by reworking and developing the symbolism in a much later motet. We find it in his setting for two voices and *bassus generalis* of *Virgo prudentissima* (this time without a *Gaude Maria virgo* to precede it and so without any reference to heresy), which was included in the last publication given over solely to his own music, *Paradisus sacris cantionibus consitus* (Antwerp, 1628). This motet is a much more up-to-date and mature work than the five-voice piece discussed above, and it must have been written during Philips's time at the Brussels court. Like the earlier version, the 1628 work sets 'electa ut sol' with a rising fifth between the last two syllables. By contrast, 'luna' is usually set to a falling fifth (see Example 23b) in a phrase repeated many times in both voices as if to give the ear ample opportunity for recognizing that 'luna' is an exact inversion of 'ut sol'. In this piece there is no need to suggest the use of puns or faulty etymology behind the composer's thinking; nevertheless at times Philips also set 'luna' to a descending tone, as he had done in the earlier setting (i.e. as the reverse of 'sola' rather than as the reverse of 'ut sol' – perhaps he was thinking of his five-voice setting). The inversion of the rising fifth 'ut sol' to form the falling fifth 'luna', however, seems to suggest that Philips consciously thought of the sun and moon as complementary, and by implication that he was illustrating the corresponding positions of Christ and Mary.

Such hidden meanings in music need not surprise us, for this kind of thing is fairly common in other art forms of the time. The complex symbolism of the contemporaneous Antwerp altarpiece by Rubens[23] is, for example, widely acknowledged; and there seems no commonsense reason why symbolism accepted in one art should not be practised in another. When one recalls that Rubens and Philips were connected with the same ultra-Catholic court the possibility that some of the latter's music may also have a hidden meaning does not seem far-fetched.

Could such symbolism have been understood in the early years of the seventeenth century? *Difficoltà* – difficulty in writing a work or in understanding it – was much prized at the time;[24] and religious composers were not necessarily only addressing humans, for worship was firmly God-centred. But it remains true that singers versed in the hexachord system could scarcely fail to be aware of the solmization; and it would seem difficult to miss the inversions in the setting for two voices (I have not quoted them at length, but they are clearly audible and very numerous). By hindsight we can see that such principles of symbolic writing apply, in a less mature and less thoroughly worked-out way, to the earlier five-voice setting, though whether this could have so easily communicated itself to the hearers or performers must remain more open to doubt.

Palestrina's *Stabat Mater*

With this whole armoury of the possibilities of solmization in mind, it is now time to look in greater detail at a section of music. So far we have dealt mostly with secular music, for that is the main home of this kind of writing. Solmization is also found in the church music of the period – that of Wert, for instance:[25] but since the liturgy is scarcely the place for brilliant wit, such devices are much more rare in sacred polyphony.[26] I nevertheless propose to take one of the most solemn pieces of writing from the end of the century – written at a time when solmization was, in any case, past its height – as an example of the gamut system used in church.

Palestrina composed his eight-voice setting of the Sequence *Stabat Mater* at the end of his life:[27] it was written for, and was for a while sung exclusively by, the Papal Choir. It has for long been regarded as a work in which the composer distilled the experience of a lifetime, and in which he tailored his music precisely to the requirements of the text. In its avoidance of imitation and its concentration on audibility of the words – there are few melismas – Palestrina was fulfilling the requirements of the Council of Trent.[28] The concentration on chord spacings, chord progressions and a careful following of the metrical rhythm of the Sequence has been universally admired. But in fact, Palestrina gets even nearer to a close interpretation of the text of the Sequence than these matters alone suggest, and closer than most commentators have realized. The opening chordal progression, which has excited much favourable notice, offers considerable evidence to support this view.[29] In order to study the opening, however, it is necessary first to examine one of Palestrina's madrigals, the four-voice *La ver l'Aurora*. This madrigal, a setting of Petrarch, dates from some thirty years earlier in Palestrina's life than the *Stabat Mater*, being first published in 1568. The opening is shown in Example 24.

The text of the first phrase begins and ends with the vowel ah: Palestrina could either use 'la' or 'fa' if he wished to set this to the corresponding sounds in the gamut. Clearly he did so wish, for the topmost voice is set to the note A ('la') at both the beginning and end of the phrase. Although it is 'fa' rather

Example 24   Palestrina: *La ver l'Aurora*

('Towards dawn, when the breeze so gently ...')

than 'la' that is concerned, the tenor part likewise uses the same hexachord sound at both ends, though with a mutation from durum to naturale. The sharp added to the first C in the tenor does not necessarily change that note from FA. Morley, as we have seen,[30] gives F♯–G as 'fa sol': it is, however, true that a semitone progression like this could also have been imagined as 'mi fa' (though one would have to consider the possibility of a hexachord built on D to make this viable – and this was quite possible). There is therefore, because of the sharp, a small element of ambiguity in calling the tenor FA.[31]

The other two voices, alto and bass, start on 'LA' (or 'la') and end on 'FA' (and 'la'): this is because Palestrina has moved from a chord of A at the start to a chord of F at the end of the phrase. Despite this, the ah vowels of the text are still paralleled in the hexachord. (Here, clearly, is a passage where the fact that there are two ah sounds in each hexachord is used to advantage). But why does Palestrina move to a chord of F? The word 'dolce' provides the clue. After writing an opening chord in which each voice expresses the ah vowel of the first word in a precise way according to the hexachord, Palestrina introduces B♭ so as to cause a mental shift towards the sweet hexachord. Indeed, as if to emphasize this, the six-note descending scale in the bass (bars 3–5, imitated in the treble in bars 5–7) is turned into an exact molle hexachord in the bass at the end of the phrase quoted in Example 24. The final F-major chord of the Example reflects the introduction of this molle hexachord, and the voices are set with two 'fa's, one 'FA', and one 'la'. The sound of the text is still paralleled, despite the change of hexachord: indeed, because of the change to molle the music must, to Palestrina's contemporaries, have seemed sweeter. This nicely illustrates the idea of sweetness in the text.

In fact, an F-major triad had already occurred at the beginning of bar 3. There is something approaching musical rhyme in this, and its purpose is to draw attention to a literary rhyme (or rather, an assonance with – perhaps – a pun intended) between l'Aurora and L'aura.[32] The significance of this musical rhyme is the more evident because the piece begins some distance away from F, on a chord of A major: the point would have been lost if Palestrina had begun the piece on a chord of F, and then immediately cadenced twice more on that note. Obviously, the F chord in bar 3 sets the rhyming ah sound just as accurately as the final F chord of Example 24. Indeed, every ah vowel in that extract is carefully matched to a solmization syllable: this includes the tenor run in bar 3 which starts on fa in the naturale hexachord and ends on FA in the durum.

The last two syllables of the word 'l'Aurora' are close in sound to 'sola', which, as we have already seen, is often set to a rising tone on the notes D–E, G–A, or C–D. Palestrina therefore uses G–A ('sol la') in the alto at the word 'l'Aurora'. Indeed, if C be construed as '*sol*' in the sweet hexachord, the outer voices in bars 2 and 3 of Example 24 also have gamut sounds which match the text ('*sol* FA' in the soprano, and '*sol* fa' in the bass). This, however, may be taking things too far, since a direct mental mutation between the molle and durum hexachords is farther than most singers would normally go in their singing of a repeated note:[33] as we have seen, theorists discouraged it except in chromatic music.

In passing, we may note that 'si' is set to the hexachord syllable 'mi' on two occasions, but by no means on all its appearances in the text. 'Ver' in bar 2 could perhaps be construed as 're' (or '*re*') in three of the four voices; and 'che' is set as 'RE' on three occasions out of a possible seven. Indeed, in the tenor part, the leap up from C to A natural is exactly solmized as 'FA RE': there is possibly a practical reason for this. The upward leap of a major sixth was not used in the strict *stile antico*, apparently because it was found difficult to sing in tune. Though the leap here is a dead one (that is, the notes are separated by a rest) correct solmization will help the singer to tune the interval accurately. The fact that the text and solmization syllables match each other means that there is one less element for the performer to consider while singing: the leap is therefore that much more likely to be correctly tuned.

When, towards the end of his life, Palestrina wrote his eight-voice *Stabat Mater*, he was faced with a text whose opening had some similarities – despite an outwardly quite different atmosphere – to the opening of *La ver l'Aurora*. For this reason the austere note-against-note writing in eight voices makes a striking contrast to the start of the madrigal; yet there are similarities that make one believe that Palestrina was building on his earlier piece when he came to write the *Stabat Mater*. For one thing, the first line of Jacopone da Todi's Sequence (the portion set for Chorus I in Example 25) contains many ah vowels, including one at the beginning and one at the end. In this it resembles the opening of the Italian poem set in *La ver l'Aurora*. Yet again, therefore, Palestrina chose to begin and end the top voice of his first phrase on A ('la'): but in *Stabat Mater* the bass part not only starts on that note – it also returns to it. Moreover, Palestrina chose to start and end the alto part on the solmization 'LA', and the tenor begins and ends on 'FA' (though it is sharpened, as in the madrigal discussed above). The sound of the text is thus carefully followed by the solmization: but Palestrina takes the idea further, for the first syllable of 'mater' is set in all voices either to 'fa' (or 'FA') or to 'la' (see Example 25). Furthermore, the sweet F-major chord on 'mater' ('mother') is very fitting for the Mother of God. (It will be recalled that *La ver l'Aurora* also moved to F in order to illustrate 'dolce'.) In *Stabat Mater* the move to F may be coincidental, for though some mentions of Mary in this piece are set to the molle hexachord, others are not: moreover, the molle hexachord is also employed later in the Sequence for quite opposite ideas such as 'tormenting'. One explanation for this may be that it recalls the dolorousness of the mother who watched her son undergo great suffering: for the singers must have been forced to make continual mutations to the molle hexachord, and this in turn must have made them call to mind the extraordinary opening of the piece. One cannot help but think that the sweet hexachord (which, indeed, persists for several chords) after the A major at the start, is peculiarly suitable for 'mater': the placing of the solmized ah sounds in the opening phrase not only helps the singer to accentuate the text correctly, but (having the widest spacing on the F-major chord) automatically gives the greatest emphasis to the molle chord on the important word 'mater'.[34] Here again the two ah sounds of the hexachord are used to advantage. The G-minor chord that occurs during the word 'dolorosa' is one that, as we have already seen, is associated with the

Example 25

Palestrina: *Stabat Mater*

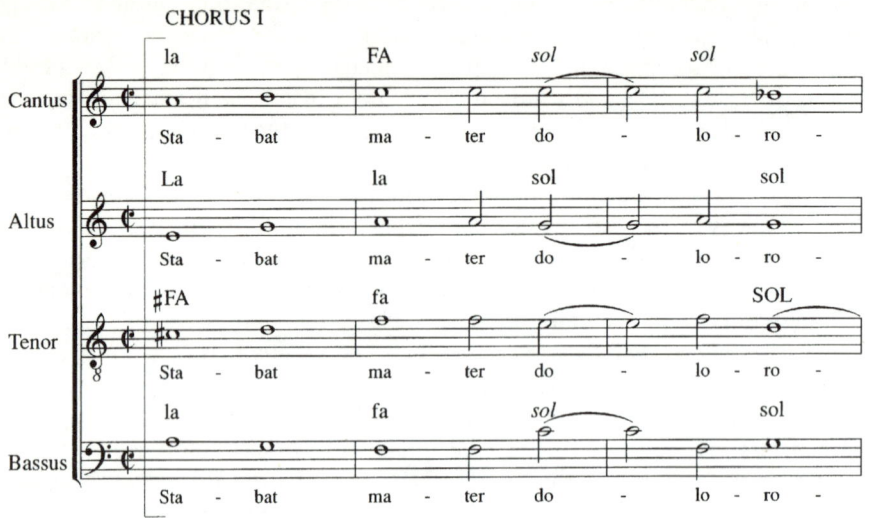

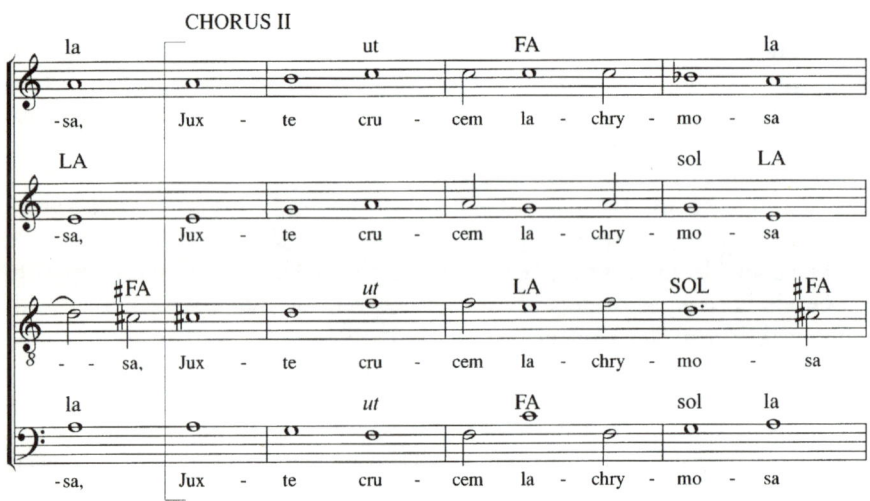

('The mother, sorrowing, stood weeping beside the cross ...')

dolorous in madrigals of this period. The changes of harmony within this first phrase help to indicate the underlying trochaic rhythm of the poem.

But it is not only harmony that must concern us, for the topmost part of the opening phrase has its own expressiveness. This derives from the juxtaposition of durum and molle – for B natural can only belong to durum, and B♭ can only be molle: not only does this constitute a further use of *mi contra fa* for expressive ends, but the cadence at the end of that phrase is given an A-phrygian feel because of the preceding B♭. There is considerable sense in this, for the phrygian was traditionally the mode for laments, and – as we have seen – its flatwards transposition onto A rendered it the more dolorous, and the more unusual.

We cannot, however, study the first phrase in isolation: Palestrina draws attention to the strophe–antistrophe scheme characteristic of Sequences by repeating the opening phrase of music precisely – in Chorus II – to the second line of the poem. The rhyme in the text is therefore paralleled by one in the music; and it may be that the more attention is focused on that rhyme since the bass part carefully solmizes the words that form it: that is, '–rosa' and '–mosa' are both set to G–A ('sol la'). A somewhat similar device for paralleling assonance had been used in *La ver l'Aurora* – a chord of F major, in fact;[35] and perhaps it is not without significance that the hexachord syllables sol and la were used there, too (see Example 24, bars 2–3).

In the second line of the text (that is, the portion sung by Chorus II) the solmization is not so close as it had been in line 1. One might imagine that this would of necessity be the case; yet, as we have seen, Palestrina did elsewhere sometimes make the solmization match on both occasions in a passage whose music is repeated but whose words are different. In the present Sequence, 'crucem' might be thought to use 'ut' and '*ut*' for three of the four voices; and the first syllable of 'lachrymosa' is set to 'FA' or 'LA' in three of the four voices. But perhaps still more relevant is the switch over to the molle hexachord at 'lachrymosa' ('weeping'), since music written with flats was considered doleful. The veering of the harmony from sharp to flat gives a mixture of hardness (durum) and softness (molle), perhaps in an effort to parallel the hardness of crucifixion on the one hand and the softness (sweetness) of Mary and the dolorousness of her mourning on the other. Although the techniques are recognizably the same as those used in Willaert's *Quanto più m'arde* discussed above, Palestrina writes in such a refined way that each chord is made to 'tell': as a result of this one can almost account for each individual sound. The language of expressive music has travelled far from that of *Quanto più m'arde*, in which the technique was a relatively blunt instrument.[36]

It would be idle to pretend that Palestrina's careful use of hexachords at the opening of these two pieces reflects the general manner of writing throughout. In both pieces much of the text is not solmized. Yet an examination of Palestrina's setting, in *Stabat Mater*, of 'Virgo virginum praeclara, mihi jam non sis amara, fac me tecum plangere. Fac ut portem Christi mortem . . .' and also of the closing words 'paradisi gloria' (in both of which sections there is very widespread use of solmization) shows that the idea certainly recurs from time to time. Example 26 shows the former of these two passages. Here the climax of the first two phrases (on the second syllable of 'praeclara' and of 'amara' is emphasized by making the solmization sounds of the notes correspond with those of the text: in spite of this, Palestrina has actually harmonized the second phrase differently from the first. The full choir then enters for a final section (only two sopranos, one alto and one tenor have sung in the previous section), and the resulting fullness is intensified by closely following the textual sounds with solmization (see Example 26).

This final section ends with the words 'Paradisi gloria' – one of the very few passages of imitation, and of text repetition, in the piece. As Example 27

Example 26   Palestrina: *Stabat Mater*

Example 26 *concluded*

shows, some elements of the imitative point are derived from solmization; and the glory of Paradise is marvellously emphasized by closely solmizing all eight voices ('la' in either naturale or molle hexachords, with the '#fa' in the naturale hexachord). The effect of this, for the performer, must have been to give added resonance – and a great sense of resolution – on the final ah sound similar to that already mentioned in connection with Monte's *Ahi, chi mi rompe il sonno* (see Example 27).

It is by no means far-fetched to maintain that the opening of *Stabat Mater* is a reworking of the opening of *La ver l'Aurora*, the 'originality' – for so it is often considered – of the use of root position triads of A major, G major and F major one after the other being derived from a progression in the 1568 madrigal. In that madrigal the progression was interrupted by a chord of C

Example 27

Palestrina: *Stabat Mater*

88

major; but the overall A–G–F progression was the result of following the dictates of the text with absolute precision. In *Stabat Mater* it was a stroke of genius to omit the C-major chord which would have resulted if Palestrina had made an exact parody of the madrigal: the chord progression as it stands has an austerity and an unexpectedness that must have sent shock waves through its original performers and hearers – as, indeed, it still has the power to do today.

The *Stabat Mater* was written at a time of controversy between those who supported classical polyphony and those who wanted to return to the delivery of the text in a rhetorical manner such as they supposed the ancient Greeks to have used. Palestrina has always been considered the high priest of the classical polyphony; but there is no doubt that in certain portions of his eight-voice *Stabat Mater*, where there is an attempt to mirror in musical notes the exact sound of the text as well as its precise rhythm, Palestrina has a claim to belong – momentarily – to the 'new music' camp as well.[37] 'The words are mistress of the harmony' (*Ut oratio sit Domina harmoniae*)[38] was the battle-cry of the Monteverdi camp in their controversy with Artusi, and its use as a slogan can be traced to an interest in the power of ancient music as attested by authors of Classical Antiquity, and especially to an interest in Plato. Claude Palisca[39] shows that both Bishop Jacopo Sadoleto (later a member of the Council of Trent), in his *De liberis recte instituendis* of 1533, and the Monteverdi camp (in the early years of the seventeenth century) quoted the same passage of Plato in support of the contention that the text must be audible and intelligible. Without a doubt the words are in a very real way the mistress of the harmony throughout *Stabat Mater*: indeed, in the closely solmized passages they are so in a more far-reaching manner than in some examples of the 'new music'. Yet Palestrina would scarcely have chosen such a solemn text in order to hoist a banner for his own faction; it is more to the point that a lifetime's experience as a madrigalist and church composer has been harnessed in order to make the most direct approach, through the music of the *Stabat Mater*, to the hearers – and, indeed, to the performers. The composer has not, of course, gone as far as the Monodists or the writers of Protestant psalm tunes in making the text pre-eminent; yet the words are so carefully matched to the music that they can scarcely fail to be audible and intelligible. Palestrina could not have gone any further than this within the realms of the polyphonic style.

The Circle of Fifths

In the discussion of Example 26 above we saw how the ah vowels in 'praeclara' and 'amara' were differently harmonized, though both were carefully set to solmization syllables. This was done by setting the syllable first

to a chord of F (that is, 'fa' in the naturale hexachord) and then to a chord of
B♭ (that is *'fa'* in the molle hexachord, the hexachord based on the note
previously understood as 'fa'). In other words, 'fa' has been raised to a higher
power, and the harmonic result has been to produce an embryonic circle of
fifths, a device implicit in the very nature of the hexachord system, and which
results in frequent occurrences of that harmonic scheme.[40] A composer can
use the circle of fifths to emphasize some feature: this will be discussed in
more detail below. Whether or not Gesualdo knew of Palestrina's use of the
device, he himself used it in his Second Book of Madrigals (1594): it occurs in
the *seconda parte* of the madrigal *Se per lieve ferita* in order to illustrate the
text

>Ahi, che a maggior dolore
>Convien pietà maggiore!
>
>(Ah, because of greater grief,
>One shows the greater pity).

Here the word which results in the circle of fifths is 'Ahi', set (as it frequently
is in the period) mainly to the solmization sound 'fa'; it appears first as a
chord of F ('fa' in the naturale hexachord: bar 16),[41] then as B♭ in an altered
repeat (*'fa'* in the molle hexachord: bar 24), and finally on a chord of E♭ ('*fa*'
in the molle hexachord transposed to B♭). The gradual flattening must, to the
late-Renaissance mind, have indicated an increasingly dolorous sound: on the
other hand, the movement towards (and beyond) the molle hexachord would
have suggested growing sweetness. The two ideas form a close parallel to the
sentiments of the text.

Gesualdo re-used the idea (with some additional entries not at the fifth) on
a very much larger scale at the end of *Moro lasso* (1611). It is again 'Ahi' –
mostly set as 'fa',[42] but at times with 'mi' present simultaneously – that gives
rise to the circle of fifths. An unexpected and unaccompanied E♭ early in the
piece ('*fa*' in the molle hexachord transposed) setting 'Ahi' suggests that one
should be aware of such solmization: indeed, 'lasso' in the first phrase has
already used the classic shape, though in a chromatic form;[43] and the first
imitative point ('E chi mi puo dar vita' – 'And who can give me life') is built
carefully around mi–mi–sol–FA–MI–FA. The transposition of the opening up
a fourth at the subsequent repeat may likewise indicate the possibility that
hexachord mutations are in the air. The final passage 'Ahi mi da morte' ('Alas
gives me death') does, indeed, splendidly capitalize on the idea (see Example
28).

Gesualdo starts by moving sharpwards (becoming harder, therefore), but
then reverses the process (becoming softer, sweeter, more dolorous) before
increasing tension greatly by moving both sharpwards and flatwards simultaneously (though at different speeds). The bass E♭ near the close (though not

Example 28

Gesualdo: *Moro lasso*

setting the word 'Ahi') could be considered the end of the flatwards motion: and in a sense it is. Yet, because of the circle of fifths motion already set up, the G♯ leading-note which follows this E♭ might be heard enharmonically as A♭: furthermore, C♯ at the top of the final chord could conceivably be considered as D♭, written enharmonically. Such an approach would, to contemporary thinking, make the music seem much less bright than A major would normally be, for the very extreme note D♭ would be doleful to a powerful degree. By contrast, the D♯ near the end of the upper voice will probably sound sharp (rather than as E♭), since it results from the application of the 'mi fa' semitone (setting 'mi da . . .') to E natural. In other words, the 'mi fa' here suggests a hexachord on B natural. The simultaneous co-existence of another semitone, lower in the choir but in the durum hexachord, emphasizes the instability of the tonality even more. This sense of instability is increased still further by Gesualdo's lack of consistency in the use of 'mi' and 'fa' – a lack of consistency that is presumably intentional. The passage is full of semitones; yet by no means every 'mi da . . .' can be performed as a semitone.

The possibility of an enharmonic interpretation of the end of the circle of fifths may be connected with the fashionable arguments for chromatic and enharmonic music which dated back to Vicentino,[44] and which so much filled the thoughts of the learned academies. Whether or not that is the case, the reason for using a mixture of sharp and flat in *Moro lasso* is to parallel the text in the most vivid manner possible. The idea at the end of the poem is the paradox

> Chi dar vita mi può,
> Ahi, mi dà morte.
>
> (Who can give me life,
> Alas, gives me death):

the paradox of A major being a dolefully flat sound nicely parallels the mixing of life and death. Moreover, a further parallel is drawn by Gesualdo between this paradox and that of the circle of fifths, which moves outwards from B♭ in both sharpwards and flatwards directions simultaneously. Indeed, such is the confusion of tonalities that results from setting this paradox that singers are themselves confronted with a difficulty. The second soprano in the penultimate bar has 'mi da . . .' set to A–G; yet this is in a falling sequence with the previous, correctly solmized, setting, B♭–A (though, as so often, 'fa mi' rather than 'mi fa'). Should the singer make the *musica ficta* alteration A♭–G, so creating a more closely solmized version? There is really no correct answer, for either A natural or A♭ is possible (there are, as mentioned above, occasions in this passage where 'mi da . . .' has to be a whole tone): in a sense the paradox is being passed on to the performers – a procedure which we shall encounter again later.

Dowland's Summary

For a summary of the various techniques of solmization we must turn to an Englishman – albeit one widely travelled and knowledgeable. John Dowland, who probably gained much of his appreciation of these techniques from his acquaintanceship with Marenzio, prefaced his *A Pilgrimes Solace* (1612) with an address 'to the reader' which complains that after his sojourn in and wanderings through Europe, he had encountered much animosity from younger men on his return home. He reports that they say about him, 'What I doe is after the old manner'. Dowland solaces himself after this pilgrimage by producing a volume which contains 'such things as I my selfe have thought well of, as being in mine opinion furnished with varietie of matter both of Iudgement and delight . . .' He addresses the book to the approbation of the skilful rather than – by implication – to those 'who . . . are merely ignorant, even in the first elements of Musicke, and also in the true order of the mutation of the *hexachord* in the Systeme, (which hath ben approved by all the learned and skilfull men of Christendome, this 800 yeares)'. It is known that Dowland travelled to Italy in order to meet Marenzio (who, as we have seen, was a frequent user of the various possibilities of the hexachord in the service of text illustration), and it may therefore have been contact with Marenzio's music that aroused Dowland's interest in those possibilities. However this may be, Dowland uses various methods in order to console himself and disprove the charge of being old-fashioned. *Lasso vita mia*, a piece for solo voice, lute and instruments (possibly viols) is one of the demonstrations: here he summarized the devices of solmization used in his time.

The text of *Lasso vita mia mi fa morire* seems to have been chosen because it contains so many solmization syllables – it is a patchwork of clichés from Italian madrigal verse – and Dowland makes full use of every opportunity presented. It is as if he is forced to use the most obvious solmization treatments so that his audience – many of whom, it seems, were untutored in the art – will be aware of his intentions and thus be made the more ready to follow his quite abstruse uses of the hexachord. The opening line, which is carefully matched to solmization sounds and includes 'mia' set to a note which represents both elements of the word (mi and LA),[45] can scarcely fail to call to mind Willaert's *Amor mi fa morire* (see Example 29). The descending tetrachord results from the close solmization of 'Lasso vita mia' (la–sol–fa–mi): later it also appears to result from 'mille marti[re]', set as *mi–re*–fa–mi–[re], and rising at 'mi fa sof[rir]' given as *mi–fa–sol–*[la]. Even if these correspondences had not obtained, the descending tetrachord (which plays a considerable part in the piece) would have been appropriate, since it was frequently used in passionate music.[46] (The use of this phrase generally in the period will be discussed below.)

Example 29   Dowland: *Lasso vita mia*

Mutating from naturale to molle, Dowland repeats the opening line a fourth higher. The opening descending A–D scale is governed by solmization of the opening phrase; the tonality is virtually D minor (one is justified in calling the mode dorian, for the final is D, and the instruments have no flat in the signature, though the voice part has a key signature of one flat for part of the time). At the repetition, the D–G scale (with B♭) is a move in a flatwards direction – not so much becoming sweeter since the tonality is G minor rather than B♭, but more dolorous. This is not an exact repeat, however, for a change of hexachord takes place during it. 'Mi fa' is this time set first as 'MI FA', then as '*mi fa*': as we have seen, mutation directly from durum to molle was discouraged in conventional theory, since it was inclined to result in tritones and cross-relations. Dowland manages to incorporate both 'MI FA' and '*mi fa*' by the simple process of writing a circle of fifths in the accompanying instruments. He may well, by this, have intended to demonstrate how superior was his own knowledge to that of the musicians whom he castigates in his preface for not knowing about the mutations of the hexachord. The touch of durum introduces a touch of hardness – a very appropriate feeling in view of the mention of death in the text. It is, moreover, rapidly becoming clear that any text which juxtaposed sweetness and hardness, joy and sorrow, life and death – as so many Petrarchan poems did – was bound to call for a juxtaposition of molle and durum, and thus of 'MI' and 'fa'. Only by disobeying the theorists' rule could the texts be set with the expressiveness due to them: and by so disobeying, the path towards a juxtaposition of major and minor keys, characteristic of tonality, was smoothed.

Instead of cadencing the second phrase in G minor, a B natural *tierce de Picardie* moves the music straight into the durum area; this is very appropriate, for the next line of the text begins with the word 'Crudel'. For some time the music veers between passages happily accommodating E-major triads and passages containing G-minor triads: such a pendulum swing between the soft and hard areas is a characteristic feature of the scene in which Eurydice's death is announced in Monteverdi's *l'Orfeo* (1607), and something similar was already present in Peri's *L'Euridice* (1601). The vocal line in *Lasso vita mia*, in fact, contains several other elements which show an awareness of the *nuove musiche*. A different kind of mutation is implied also when the normal semitone rise which sets the words 'mi fa' (B natural–C) is later extended to set these words to a rise of a sixth from E ('mi' in the naturale hexachord) to

C ('FA' in the durum hexachord). A considerable increase in the tension generated by the vocal line is thus also the result of 'learned' writing aimed at confounding the composer's critics. Moreover, Dowland may in addition be alluding to Marenzio's *Mi fa lasso languisce* (1581), where – as mentioned above – 'Mi fa' is set as both 'mi–fa' (or '*mi–fa*') and with the rising sixth '*mi–fa*'.

Dowland also uses solmization syllables in a demonstration of ways in which the system can suggest *ficta*.[47] At the words 'che mi fa [morir]' the written notes A–B♭–C (the B is flat, since the voice part – the only one with this note here – still has a signature of one flat at this point) are clearly to be interpreted as RE–MI–FA in the durum hexachord. Since 'MI' is a tone (not a semitone) above RE, the singer who understands the system will obviously adjust B♭ to B natural: this is sensible because Dowland is moving towards a cadence on A, and because the instruments in any case have an open signature (see Example 30). B natural must be correct here:[48] yet we cannot always take solmization as a reliable guide to the application of unmarked accidentals (indeed, solmization cannot be used to alter the following notes, C–D–E, in Example 30). In Monteverdi's *Ch'io t'ami* (1605), for instance, one could not possibly force a 'fa mi' interpretation (in any hexachord) onto 't'ami'. At the words 'Ahi me' Dowland writes B♭–A, perhaps regarding the second word as being pronounced 'mi'. But this 'fa mi' cannot apply to the sequential repetition of the phrase on the notes C–B♭, for to make the B♭ into B natural ('MI') would involve a clash with a B♭ in the lute part at this point. Towards the end, the ultimate hardness is reached when 'mille mille martire' ('a thousand thousand martyrdoms') reaches triads of B major.

Dowland's knowledge of continental music is clearly evident in this piece: the settings of 'mille mille' and 'mi fa' which are reminiscent of Marenzio, the recalling of Willaert, the references to the 'new music' and the use of hexachords for colour as well as solmization, and the descending tetrachord which recalls such pieces as those in the *Cruda Amarilli* tradition – to be discussed below – are all evidence of the thoroughness of this knowledge, and make *Lasso vita mia* a veritable compendium of devices using the *voces musicales*.

The methods of treating the hexachord outlined above suggest that composers were attempting to communicate with their performers and listeners in a way that went beyond the mere notes. Some of these methods are fairly basic; some are quite abstruse. Those that seek to express the inner meanings of the text have often led to a treatment of tonality that expands a basically modal language. It becomes clear from this that analyses of the music of this period carried out as if modality (and musical style itself) was an unchanging phenomenon – like a building – are ill-advised. We shall return to this matter of the modes later. The abstruse jokes and paradoxes involving *musica ficta*,

Example 30

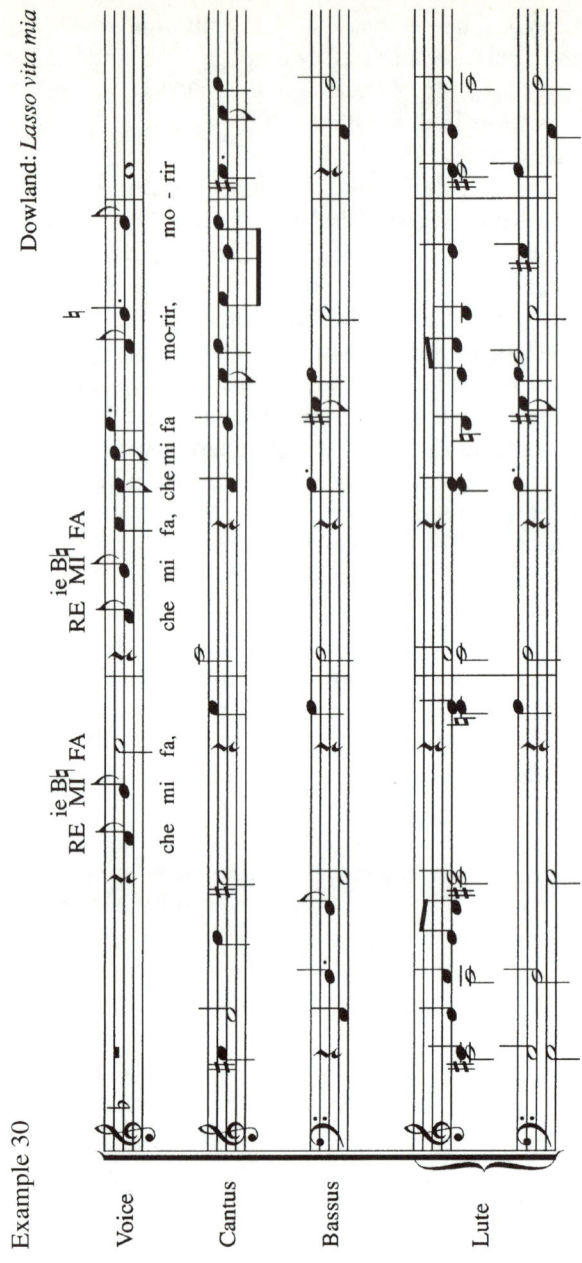

Dowland: *Lasso vita mia*

96

as well as the streams of madrigals which build on a previous idea, must now be discussed at length.

Notes

1. The solmization in this piece frequently leads one to question the editorial accidentals in Einstein's edition (Einstein 1949, Vol. 3).
2. Allaire 1972, p. 29ff, shows that conflicting signatures (which he prefers to call 'contrasting signatures') are not incompatible with a more classically regular style of writing. But Rore generates many tritones, cross-relations, etc, from the conflict. Owens 1990, p. 6, comments that this piece is unaccounted for in the modal system (on p. 8 she remarks that Rore never again used this tonal type), and that after 1550 Rore was increasingly interested in unusual tonal types. As she rightly says, tonal type or mode conveys no information about musical content.
3. It will be remembered that earlier in this madrigal 'mi' and 'fa' were often reversed, perhaps to illustrate the way in which everything has been overturned by Madonna Laura's death. Such 'topsy-turviness' seems to be the reason for using molle at 'Duri' in Marenzio's *Dolorosi martir* (1580).
4. The Eb–D–C♯ cadence figure occurs in several Netherlandish motets of a penitential type; they are discussed in Lowinsky 1967, pp. 11–15. Owens 1990, p. 7, comments on the continuing impact of Rore's music on later generations.
5. Examples are far too numerous to list, but see, for example, 'fieri tormenti' and 'della mia vita' in Marenzio's *Dolorosi martir* (1580). In Monte's *Dolorosi martir* (1558) the descending tetrachord is suggested by the solmization of 'lagrime' – an idea we shall have cause to recall later. The popularity of the tetrachord may be connected with the fact that Ancient Greek musical theory made much use of tetrachords.
6. In the edition in Roche 1974.
7. See, for example, Weelkes's *When David heard*, at the words 'O my son Absalom'.
8. See the comments in Selfridge-Field 1990, p. 54.
9. The piece is discussed in depth in Chapter 3. Lasso uses the idea in *Queste non son piu lagrime* (1560) and *Deh, lascia, anime* (1587); Andrea Gabrieli in *Non vedi o sacr'Apollo* (1570) and the posthumously published *I'vo piangendo/Si che s'io vissi*; and Gesualdo in *Se per lieve/Che sentir* (1594). There are certain similarities, too, in Monte's *Solingo in selve* (1595).
10. Bars 42–50 of the edition in Newcomb 1980. Palisca 1985, p. 379, refers to a similar flowering which depicts the growth of laurels.
11. It is usual to understand the old mnemonic rhyme 'Mi contra fa diabolus est in musica' as referring to the tritone (i.e. 'MI–fa' or 'mi–*fa*'). But since the co-existence of durum and molle hexachords was regarded with suspicion, one could argue that 'MI–*fa*' (a clashing of the major third – durum – with the minor – molle) was also proscribed: nevertheless, the simultaneous sounding of major and minor thirds is occasionally found abroad at this time, and often crops up in England. The combination used here by Luzzaschi ('mi(E) contra fa(F)') is unexceptional, since the resulting semitone is 'diatonic' and merely calls for a normal resolution. Of course, 'mi(E) contra FA(C)' would likewise pose no problem: see Allaire 1972, p. 56f. Tritones are discussed at length in Berger 1987.

See also Stevenson 1961, p. 43. Harmonic tritones are by no means unknown, in fact.

12. A footnote in Poulton 1972, p. 304, deserves quotation in full:

> The importance, and the difficulty of learning solmization in Elizabeth times is illustrated by a quotation in Strachey's *Elizabeth and Essex*, p. 60. Anthony Standen, it appears, thought Essex lacked tenacity of purpose, and that 'he must be continually pulled by the ear, as a boy that learneth *ut, re, mi, fa*'.

See also Hughes 1980: 'mutations . . . were regarded by choristers as a "cross of tribulation"'. The 'hard climb' in *Affliger chi per voi/Nulla da voi* may also remind performers and hearers of the ladder which contemporaries imagined as joining all creation.

13. Einstein 1949, p. 229.
14. Bar 36 of the edition in Newcomb 1980.
15. The bulk of this section first appeared in Pike 1984. Much more detail about the Netherlands during this period can be found in Geyl 1961.
16. Pike 1969.
17. Other elements contribute to the underlying symbolism discussed below: the Marian plainsongs *Salve Regina* and *Veni sponsa Christi* can be shown to be reflected in some of the vocal lines, for example.
18. In fact, *Gaude gaude gaude Maria virgo*.
19. This vital element of solmization suggests that Thurston Dart's editorial textual underlay in his edition of Morley's *Gaude Maria virgo* (in Andrews 1959) badly needs revision.
20. The *Oxford English Dictionary* gives *c.* 1450 as the earliest occurrence of 'solar'; 'lunar' is first noted in 1626, though 'luna' can be found as early as *c.* 1386.
21. Hulme 1976, p. 205. John Taverner parallels the usage described here at his settings of 'ut sol' and 'luna' in the votive antiphon *Ave Dei patris filia*.
22. See Reardon 1981, p. 21.
23. See Nicole Verhaegan, in Martin 1981, pp. 123–30.
24. Burke 1974, pp. 161ff.
25. Guerrero also does this in *Beata Dei genitrix*.
26. Kerman 1981, pp. 96f and 138f, has not realized the solmization background of *De lamentatione* and *Peccavi* in producing points with semitones; the same background occurs in Tallis' *Incipit lamentatio* (discussed in detail in Chapter 5), where the introduction of B♭ into the phrygian mode is ultimately the result of mirroring an ah sound with 'fa': the solmization of the opening four syllables as a series of 'MI' (and 'mi') sounds followed by 'FA' (and 'fa') is quite obvious, though English composers as a whole showed less interest in these processes than did composers working in Italy. (Cf the *seconda parte* of Marenzio's *Se la mia vita*, where a similar thing occurs at 'pur mi dara tanta', but without leading to B♭. The opening of Pietro Vinci's *Mirabile Mysterium* is a continental example of the influence of hexachord sounds on the construction of melodic lines in church music.
27. Probably in 1588 or 1589. The bulk of this discussion appeared in Pike 1986.
28. It was not only the Council of Trent that maintained that words were inaudible in polyphony: Savonarola had already done so in the fifteenth century (see Fenlon 1989, p. 53).
29. Progressions which bear some similarities turn up from time to time elsewhere: for example, in Palestrina's Mass and motet *Dies sanctificatus*, Ferrabosco I's five-voice Lamentations (no. 3) and the six-voice set (no. 4), Monte's *Lasso, Amor* and *Fui presso fui ferito* (1595), and Marenzio's *Baci soave* (1591).

30. Morley 1597, p. 18. See also Berger 1987, p. 144.
31. Yet, in contrast, when a *ficta* flat was added to a note it almost automatically caused it to be thought of as 'fa'.
32. A further pun, on the name Laura, may be intended.
33. See above.
34. Palestrina could, of course, have set the first and last syllables to an F chord rather than A major: the ah sound would still have been given its appropriate solmization sounds. Nevertheless, to have done so would have removed the shift to molle for 'mater'.
35. Palestrina uses the device of repeating F cadences in the fourth and fifth lines of the Sequence, so that 'gementem' rhymes with 'dolentem' musically as well as verbally. This idea – presumably remembered from the madrigal – is extended in the Sequence, so that 'tormentem' (in verse 7) has a lengthy stop on a B♭ chord just such as had appeared at 'gementem'. This provides another reason for the use of the molle hexachord for 'tormenting', mentioned above.
36. The sharp itself (♯) might have been a reference to the cross or to related ideas: it certainly is so in English liturgical music of the period (at 'the sharpness of death' in the *Te Deum*, for instance), and its use for this purpose in the music of Bach is well known. Sweelinck apparently uses the sharp to illustrate 'crucem' in *Qui vult venire post me* (1619).
37. In this connection see Reynolds 1989, p. 95.
38. I use the Latin version of this phrase as a sub-title for Chapter 4 of this book.
39. Palisca 1968, pp. 161f.
40. As is clearly indicated in Maniates 1979.
    I am grateful to Mrs Joanna West (née Collyer) for drawing to my attention Metallo's use of solmization to produce a canon at the fifth. The rubric for several of the verses of his *Magnificat Quinti Toni* (1603) reads 'canon ut supra', meaning 'canon at the next ut above': since he starts on F – *ut* in the molle hexachord – this means 'at the fifth above' (treating C as ut), rather than 'at the tone above' (treating G as UT), for a mixture of molle and durum would not be countenanced by a conservative, *prima prattica*-based composer like Metallo. Moreover, in any hierarchy of hexachords, the naturale was thought of as coming between the molle and the durum. The punning use of the phrase 'ut supra' is not only typical of Metallo's directions to performers, but forms a link with the hexachord games discussed in Chapter 5 below. Metallo produced a 'circolo musicale' and a mutation wheel illustrating movement around the hexachords in *Del Metallo Ricercari a due voci per sonare et cantare ... In Venetia ... MDCXIV*. See Collyer 1987, pp. 112–13, 332, and the edition of *Magnificat Primi Toni*, Collyer 1987, pp. 239–49.
41. The most generally available edition is in Parrish 1958. Bar numbers refer to that edition.
42. It must not be thought that 'ahi' is invariably set as 'fa'. Marenzio, in his *Cruda Amarilli* (1595), sets the words 'Ahi lasso' in such a way that 'Ahi' is reckoned to be 'mi': the passage bears a close resemblance to the one by Luzzaschi shown in Example 19, and may indeed be a conscious parody of it. Marenzio's piece is discussed below.
43. Rore had previously done this in *O sonno* (1557).
44. Berger 1976, *passim*.
45. Examples 14b, 19 and 28 also contain instances of this. Incidentally, in The Third Booke of Songs (1603) Dowland had already set the opening line of *Me, me, and none but me* to nothing but B natural (i.e. 'MI'). Translators of such

English anthologies of Italian madrigals as *Musica Transalpina* and *Italian Madrigals Englished* clearly made no attempt to match solmized syllables in the original language with corresponding vernacular vowels.

46.   The matter is dealt with at length in Chapter 4.

47.   Instances of this in earlier composers have been noted above.

48.   There are similar instances in Josquin's *Missa Hercules Dux Ferrariae*. In the Gloria (O.O. bars 35 and 36, at 'Fili unigenite') both bassus and superius have the line A–G–A–C–B–A, a clear reference to the end of the *soggetto cavato* re–ut–re–ut–re–fa–mi–re, though not one of the absolutely overt references to it. Nevertheless, the performer must be aware that the solmization of B must be 'MI' rather than 'fa' according to the theme in general use, and, despite the B♭s which have been added by *musica ficta* in both parts of the complete edition, sing 'MI' on the penultimate note of the phrase (the text syllable is in any case '–ni–'). In the Credo (O.O. bars 104 and 106) at 'Et in spiritum sanctum Dominum', a similar thing occurs twice in the superius: the notes G–A–C–B*–A–B–A–G–A–C–B*–A–B–A–G–A would seem, by the same token, to require the asterisked B's to be sung as 'MI' and not altered by *musica ficta* to 'fa' (as the O.O. makes them).

3   Emulation and Parody I

The preceding chapters have already drawn attention to treatments of the hexachord and of solmization syllables that could be described as 'emulative'; treatments, that is, in which a composer has tried to improve upon or outdo a previous setting of the same (or a similar) text by applying more extensive or more abstruse uses of the hexachord to it. Indeed, the study of the hexachord inevitably leads to a study of the part played by solmization syllables within the emulative and parody tradition. This chapter and the following one will therefore be concerned with emulation and parody.

The concept of parody[1] has a long history. Reference back to authority is a feature of much medieval work in all the arts: in music, tropes and the addition of new voices to pre-existent material were common. It was a concept that remained in force to a somewhat lesser extent to the end of the Renaissance. Borrowing material from some pre-existent source certainly did not have the stigma that it has today. In other arts, too, borrowings were normal: a young painter, for example, would learn his trade by copying his teacher's work under the eye of the master. Though progress was regarded as a cardinal virtue, particularly in Italy where it was strongly encouraged by the interest in theory and by the academies, parody – the basing of music (or, indeed, other artefacts) on pre-existing material – was common.[2] Parodies were not necessarily emulative; there are, for example, parody masses which do little more than rearrange the sections of their models: but on the other hand there are also parodies whose reorganization of borrowed material exhibits remarkable skill in the writing of additional voices, in contriving new combinations of motifs from the model, or in other ways. Emulation, too, may not involve parody; in some of the madrigals discussed in this chapter and the following one the effort to outdo a previous setting of the chosen poem does not involve any borrowing of musical material at all. Yet emulation and parody quite often go hand in hand, as in many of the pieces discussed below.

101

Parody and emulation can be yardsticks for progress: if each setting was to add something in expressiveness to its predecessor, then a development in musical language was unavoidable. When a composer built a new madrigal on material borrowed from a previous setting of his chosen text, that model became a standard against which the novelties of the later piece could be judged. Emulation in particular forms one of the main paths towards the 'new music' which Monteverdi classified as belonging to the *seconda prattica*. Clearly, for a full appreciation of any parody a thorough knowledge of the model is essential; and to gain such an appreciation elements other than the hexachord must be considered. Only by studying all the elements can we see how great (or how small) a part hexachords and solmization syllables played in the emulative process.

The concept of parody in the French chanson has been dealt with in such exemplary fashion by Frank Dobbins[3] that it would be superfluous to recapitulate the matter here. But the concept is even more applicable to the Italian madrigal, and it is with this area of late-Renaissance music that the present chapter and the following one are concerned. Much of the poetry set builds upon the tradition of Petrarch: as Dobbins says, 'The entire neo-Petrarchist repertoire is emulative'.[4] So it is with settings of that poet that I begin the investigation of parody, and of the tradition that resulted in a series of pieces each of which tried to outdo a previous setting of the same poem.

Mia Benigna Fortuna / Crudele Acerba

Mia benigna fortuna and *Crudele acerba* form the first two stanzas of Petrarch's double Sestina on the death of Madonna Laura. Maniates says of this cycle of poems:

> The poems of the *In morte [di Madonna Laura]* cycle are remarkable for their forceful portayal of agony. Petrarch's sorrow ranges from serene resignation to furious anger, and his images have a particular acidity that fascinates musicians and induces them to invent new techniques. The great double sestina *Mia benigna fortuna/Crudele acerba inesorabil morte* occasions some of the most unusual music in the literature of the radical madrigal because composers respond to the incredible richness of its vocabulary. The last strophe before the *commiato*, in particular, utters a challenge to the legendary affective power of music, and musicians cannot resist meeting the challenge.
>
> O voi che sospirate . . . for si lieto.
>
> The general conceit of this strophe is full of evocative resonances, including a series of ambiguous double meanings (*sospirate, notti, sorda Morte, antico stile*). The lover's entreaty to unnamed poet-musicians receives added import from the references to antique style and the implication that a change or adaptation of ancient style to a modern or contemporary one will gladden the dying lover by making his death a more eloquent one.[5]

The first two stanzas – the ones most usually set to music – are as follows:

Mia benigna fortuna e'l viver lieto
I chiari giorni e le tranquilli notti,
Ei soavi sospiri e'l dolce stile
Che solea risonar in versi e'n rime,
Volti subitamente in dogli e'n pianto
Odiar vita mi fanno e bramar morte.

Crudele acerba, inesorabil Morte,
Cagion mi dai di mai non esser lieto,
Ma di menar tutta mia vita in pianto
E i giorni oscuri e le dogliose notti,
I miei gravi sospir non vann'in rime,
E'l mio duro martir vinc'ogni stile.

(My blessed fate and happy life
The clear days and the tranquil nights
And the dulcet sighs and the sweet style
Which once resounded in verses and rhymes;
You suddenly turn to grief and tears
Making me hate life and long for death.

Cruel, bitter, inexorable death,
Because of you my joy has ceased
All my life is spent in tears
My days in darkness and my nights in anguish.
My heavy sighs cannot be expressed in verse
And my harsh torment defeats every style.)

To trace through the settings of this text is virtually to trace the development of the Italian madrigal. We shall examine Arcadelt's setting for five voices of *Crudele acerba* (1538); Lasso's setting of both *Mia benigna fortuna* and *Crudele acerba* for five voices (1555); Rore's setting of both sections, for four voices (1557); Wert's five-voice setting of both *partes* (1558); and finally Marenzio's five-voice setting of *Crudele acerba* (1599). Monte's setting of the whole Sestina (1562) is not considered here, since it stands outside the emulative tradition.

Anonymous (c. 1508); and Jacques Arcadelt

Nevertheless, before proceeding to discuss the madrigals in detail, it will be as well to examine briefly an anonymous setting of *Mia benigna fortuna* which dates from the early years of the sixteenth century. This four-voice setting – with four stanzas (though the remainder were perhaps left to the performer to supply) – was published by Petrucci in his Ninth Book of Frottole in 1508, and reissued a year later as a solo with lute accompaniment. Its simplicity and its verse-repeating form, characteristic of the frottola, set it apart from the madrigals to be discussed below. There is nevertheless a clear attempt to translate the sound of Petrarch's poetry into musical terms. This is not achieved through rhetorical devices or madrigalisms, for – apart from the hauntingly beautiful sadness of the overall sound – the piece makes no attempt at text illustration of this kind (one would scarcely expect it to at this early part of the sixteenth century): instead it is done by matching the vowels of the first stanza with their solmization syllables. The outside voices, at the line 'e i soavi sospir' e'l dolce stile', provide an example of this (see Example 31). The composer makes his intentions in the matter perfectly clear at the very opening, since the ah sound in 'benigna' is set to a chord of F

Example 31   **Anonymous:** *Mia benigna fortuna*

immediately after a G-dorian opening, the solmization syllable 'fa' (or 'FA') occurring in both durum and naturale hexachords.[6] The solmization, however, works only for the first stanza.

Jacques Arcadelt (*c.* 1505–1568) is an important figure in the early history of the madrigal: though working for much of his life in Italy (Florence, Venice, and finally Rome), he spent his last years in France (of which he was probably a native, though it is by no means certain whether he was French or Flemish). His madrigals are largely a product of his early years, for he seems to have concentrated more on the chanson and on church music after his return to France. His *Primo libro dei madrigali* was enormously popular, and was printed in 45 editions between 1543 and 1654, though the contents vary somewhat. The *Crudele acerba* setting (which appeared even before the first edition of that volume) is for five voices, and it is unusual in that it is strikingly dissonant: the majority of Arcadelt's madrigals are for four voices – the typical number for the early madrigal – and have a much more mellifluous nature.[7]

Arcadelt's setting of the second stanza of the poem, *Crudele acerba*, was first published in Venice in 1538: it occurs in *Di Verdelot le dotte et eccellente compositioni de i madrigali a cinque voci*. It thus dates from relatively early in the history of the madrigal, and before the years of Arcadelt's fame. It is set for five low voices: the clefs are C2 for four voices and F2 for the lowest, and the ranges suggest two tenors, two baritones and a bass. The sombre colour, so fitting for the text, is partnered by a G-dorian modality that places much stress on minor triads.[8] Arcadelt uses several devices to illustrate the harshness and cruelty mentioned in the text. The 'sound' consecutives of bars 2, 10f, 20,

22f, 31, 38f, 44 and 50f [9] are one: even though 'sound consecutives' occur in other works, it is the peculiar density of them here that draws particular attention to the device.[10] The large number of suspensions which sound at the same time as their own note of resolution in another voice (a type of 'English cadence') constitute another of these devices.[11] The use of low voices helps to draw attention to these dissonances, since the vocal strands tend to accentuate the clashes when they are in close position.

It is the first two words of the text that suggest to Arcadelt the character of his setting: he uses the fact that performers would be tempted to apply *musica ficta* sharps to the leading-notes at cadences as part of the expressive design. Almost every cadential suspended major seventh (applied by *musica ficta*) clashes with the minor seventh: yet the composer takes great care that the voice which does not have the cadential suspended leading-note cannot itself be sharpened. The opening of the piece provides a good example (see Example 32). The altus might well sharpen the fifth note: but the quintus cannot make the fourth note anything but C natural, since that note is preceded by G

Example 32 Arcadelt: *Crudele acerba*

natural. (The melodic tritone turns up as part of Marenzio's armoury later, and then only under very carefully controlled conditions which are described below; but it would not be a possibility in Arcadelt.)[12] The same processes are at work two bars later, but with an additional crude complication that what seems (if one considers only the cantus, altus and quintus) to be a D-minor cadence is negated by the other voices. There will be an even greater crudity if the suspended C in the quintus is sharpened here. Clearly a sense of tension – rather than of pure harmony – is built into the voice parts. Bars 6 and 7 take the idea further (see Example 33).

Example 33   **Arcadelt:** *Crudele acerba*

There are two possibilities in this passage, both resulting in some crudity. If the cantus sings E natural so as to conform with the quintus, a tritone ('mi contra *fa*') will be formed with the B♭ of the bass (second beat). On the other hand, if the cantus singer sees the B♭ which is approaching in his part (beat three of bar 4) and modifies the E to E♭ so as to avoid the outline of a tritone, it will conflict with the E natural in the quintus ('mi contra *fa*').[13] Just after this, the tenor may well sharpen his F, making a conflict with the quintus F (on 'morte'): the quintus F cannot be modified, since it follows a leap up from C natural. Arcadelt's setting is so full of such problems that they tumble over one another as the piece progresses. There is crudity without *musica ficta* being applied; but singers who attempt to apply it in this piece must perforce be aware of an even more cruel crudity as they try to adapt their parts to the surrounding polyphony. A further example is at bar 24: the bass E natural has B♭ sounding above it; should the bass singer attempt to change the cadence into a phrygian one, so making a more regular perfect fifth between E♭ and

Bb?[14] (See Example 34). To do so would involve changing a bass line that had previously used the same phrase (it was sung by the tenor, though acting as the lowest sounding part), but with a clear E natural that does not warrant flattening; and to flatten the E in the bassus of Example 34 would also cause

Example 34   Arcadelt: *Crudele acerba*

difficulties with the E in the altus. On the other hand, there is an Eb (so marked) in the bass part only just after this point, and a singer would not have to be reading his part more than a fraction ahead to be aware of its proximity. Again the crudities are set up by Arcadelt, who challenges the performers to resolve the difficulties, only for such resolutions to result in yet worse crudity. (Even *musica ficta* 'ironing-out' is insufficient to counter the dissonant runs of passing-notes that occur on several occasions, however). The processes remind one of the apparent shifting to the performer of the responsibility for discovering the correct application of *musica ficta* perpetrated by Rore and Gesualdo later in the period.[15]

Einstein clearly finds it difficult to accept that this manner of writing could have been part of the composer's design:

> Arcadelt . . . resorts in this piece to a five-part texture that he does not know how to master. And he makes his task more difficult by writing for low voices only: four tenors which are constantly crossing, colliding and obstructing, and a single bass

> ... Arcadelt either handled the five-part texture very awkwardly or was a bold
> master who was not afraid to resort to extremes ... If Arcadelt intended all these
> harsh moments, it would have to be said that, while the brightness and purity of his
> writing make him a forerunner of Palestrina, his boldness and ruthlessness in voice-
> leading make him at the same time a forerunner of Rore or of the Marenzio of the
> *Canzon pietrosa*.[16]

Yet the compositional style is clearly part of the business of expressing the
black cruelty of the text: in particular, the difficulties presented by the various
permutations of 'mi fa' – whether semitones or tritones – account in large
measure for the gritty crudities which so accurately reflect the text.[17]

Orlando di Lasso

Lasso, or Orlande de Lassus (1530–1594), has always been regarded as one of
the few very greatest composers of the sixteenth century: this view obtained
even in his lifetime, and honours were showered upon him. His life was
cosmopolitan, being divided between a Franco–Flemish upbringing, Munich
and Italy (Mantua, Naples and Rome), and his output was equally cosmopolitan. His preferred home, though, was Munich: he was ennobled in 1570 by
Maximilian II, and made a Knight of the Golden Spur by Pope Gregory
XIII.

Lasso wrote his settings of *Mia benigna fortuna* and *Crudele acerba* in his
early twenties (they do not appear as *prima* and *second parte* in *Il primo libro
de madrigali* (1555), but as Numbers 10 and 12): it is the most classical and
neutral of all settings of the poem, with the exception of the anonymous *Mia
benigna* discussed above. This is an early work for Lasso; no doubt he would
have produced something more colourful and extraordinary later in his life,
though it is true that his experimental *Alma Nemes* also dates from this early
period. One cannot avoid the impression that Lasso has failed to realise the
implications of Petrarch's Sestina; and one wonders whether he had actually
encountered Arcadelt's extraordinary setting.

Lasso remains within his chosen G dorian in both stanzas, and in *Crudele
acerba* makes quite frequent use of the descending tetrachord (a phrase much
used for expressive music during the Renaissance, and one to which we shall
return later). There is, in *Crudele acerba*, a fairly wide use of vocal strands
that include a prominent semitone descent at or near the end of a phrase
(sometimes ornamented with a 4–3–2–3 resolution); this idea is, of course,
one found in the descending tetrachord itself. One of the most obvious places
is at the word 'martir' where the descending semitones match their hexachord
syllables ('fa mi') to the sound of the text. The delay in stating the most
expressive interval in these lines – that is, the use of 'mi fa' only after several
whole tones have been sounded – provides a tense quality. But, apart from
this, there is not much evidence that Lasso was intending to outdo Arcadelt.
Mia benigna fortuna has a single set of 'sound consecutive fifths' at 'e'l dolce'

which could scarcely be an emulation of Arcadelt's many versions. Lasso chooses SATTB as his vocal combination[18] – a much less colourful one than Arcadelt's – though Lasso does write a low spacing for 'doglia e pianto' ('grief and tears'), for 'Morte' ('death'), and for 'mia vita in pianto' ('all my life in tears'). 'Sospir' in *Mia benigna* passes by without illustration, but a large number of sighs are indicated by rests which occur at that word in *Crudele acerba* (a device not used at all by Arcadelt): and the occasional cross-relation occurs, though without the far-reaching implications for the performer that are perpetrated by Arcadelt.

Lasso is at his most expressive – and most forward-looking – in his use of unexpected triads and in his wide use of six-four chords in *Crudele acerba*, though these are still relatively close to Palestrina's style in their treatment.[19] The rising minor sixth – one of the versions of 'mi fa' – occurs melodically several times ('odiar' in *Mia benigna*, 'Crudel' and 'in pianto' in *Crudele acerba*), obviously with expressive intent, and the same interval is used harmonically for similar reasons. In *Mia benigna* 'E i soavi sospir' ('and the dulcet sighs') moves from the hard chord of G major round a circle of fifths in a flatwards direction as far as the sweet Eb (on the second syllable of 'soavi'), so that three voices use 'fa' in the Eb and Bb hexachords. But, expressive as it is, it would be idle to maintain that Lasso's piece shows anything like the structural brilliance of Arcadelt's setting.

Cipriano de Rore

Rore (1515 or 1516–1565) was born in Flanders, but spent nearly all his life in Italy, mostly in Venice and Ferrara. As we shall see, he holds a pivotal and extremely influential position in the history of the madrigal: Einstein[20] said of him

> ... all madrigal music of the 16th century that lays claim to serious dignity is dependent upon Rore. Lasso and Monte are inconceivable without him. Palestrina, who began as an imitator of Arcadelt, changed his style after his acquaintance with Rore. But Rore's true spiritual successor was Monteverdi. Rore holds the key to the whole development of the Italian madrigal after 1550.

Rore's favourite texts were sonnets: he normally set these in two *partes*, with the first containing the octave and the second the *sestet*. In view of his predilection for this pattern it is hardly surprising that Rore chose to set two stanzas of Petrarch's Sestina rather than a single one, and that he treated them as an organic pair.

Rore's *Mia benigna/Crudele acerba*, published two years after Lasso's, represents an attempt to outdo it, and to realize the implications of the opening stanzas of Petrarch's Sestina in a much more vivid fashion than the young Lasso had managed. Such value judgements must, however, take into account the fact that Rore was twice Lasso's age at the time when his setting was first published (1557), and a much more experienced composer. On the other hand, Rore's use of a paired setting of these two stanzas – as opposed to Lasso's use of two separate settings, one for each stanza – poses additional problems for the composer, for he is bound to attempt to parallel the subtly different shades of meaning which the line endings have in each stanza. No previous setting had attempted to address this problem.

Rore introduces the idea of conflict – cruelty and crudity – in his use of conflicting key signatures (some voices have two flats, some have only one).[21] This is an entirely different technique from that used earlier in the Renaissance: the conflict of mode implicit in the different signatures is a parallel to the conflicting pitches in Arcadelt's setting. The result, in Rore's piece, is something approaching D phrygian – a very unusual mode. The phrygian was conventionally used for laments: it is a mode where the minor second is available above both the root and the fifth without the use of accidentals, and this factor contributes in no small measure to the phrygian's extraordinary colour and power. Moreover, its transposition to flatter areas – to A phrygian and even to D phrygian – gives it a yet more dolorous quality. Rore used the phrygian mode for similar expressiveness on other occasions: *O sonno* (of 1557) uses A phrygian, for example.[22] In *Mia benigna/Crudele acerba* there is a dichotomy between the phrygian Eb–D and the E natural–D which would be characteristic of an aeolian scale of D. The result of this is that cross-relations are frequent, that tritones (as roots of chords as well as within the vocal lines) occur quite regularly, and that there is some use of three adjacent melodic semitones (see Example 35).[23] As in Lasso's setting, the minor sixth is much used in the harmony to create an expressive sound:[24] but the leaps of a minor sixth, quite widely used by Lasso, are consciously 'capped' by Rore, who also makes a considerable feature of the leap upwards of the forbidden major sixth. This interval, avoided since it was considered difficult to sing in tune (despite the fact that it merely provides the two extremes of a hexachord), is used to illustrate 'Crudele' at the opening of the *seconda parte*: but it had, in any case, been foreshadowed by the last point of the *prima parte* (see Example 36a).[25] The spacing at the start of the *seconda parte* – with one voice high and the others in a rather turgid low spacing – is a texture used elsewhere for grief-laden utterances (Lasso's *Tristis est anima mea* is a good example).

The use of the major-sixth interval emphasizes an important structural feature of the text: since the Sestina form requires that the same line-endings be used in each of the stanzas, though in a different order, it follows that stanzas may contain answering or balancing ideas. (Lasso had also used a rising sixth – though minor in his case – at 'odiar' in *Mia benigna* and at the start of *Crudele acerba* – and this despite the fact that the two madrigals do not form a pair.) In the present case, the repetition of 'morte' ('death') is, perhaps, the most immediately obvious, and it is this that causes Rore to

Example 35   Rore: *Mia benigna fortuna/Crudele acerba*

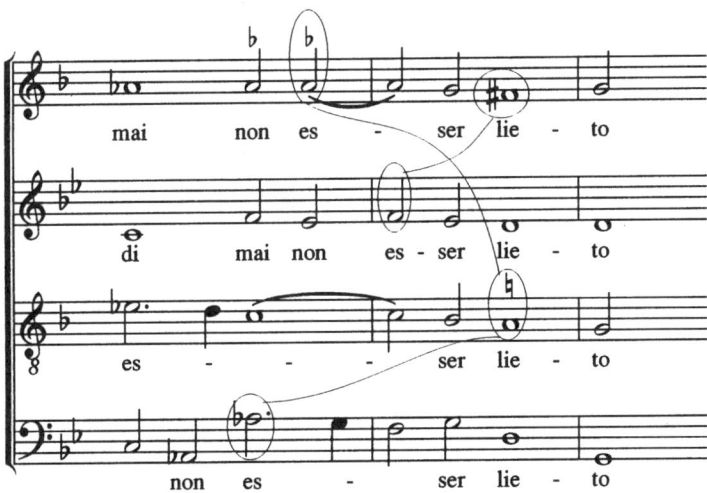

Example 36a   Rore: *Mia benigna fortuna*

follow Lasso in using a similar device in both the lines that include the
word.

But Rore goes beyond simply making correspondences between the rising
major sixths: in a complex pattern that parallels – and, indeed, expands – the
poetic scheme of the Sestina, he makes subtle musical rhymes between the two
partes: these are shown in Example 36b.

Example 36b

The triple-time B♭ cadence on 'lieto' is rhythmically recast in the *seconda parte*, and moved to G minor to illustrate the subtle change of emphasis given to this word in the poem. The mixture of phrygian and plagal cadences at 'notti' in the *prima parte* is echoed by a phrygian cadence that reaches its goal on a weak pulse, only to turn into a form of perfect cadence. 'Stile' and 'rime' come next to each other in both stanzas, and form a real rhyme: Rore therefore makes 'vertical' rather than 'horizontal' connections here in that lines 3 and 4 of *Mia benigna fortuna* have cadences that are closely related (both are phrygian, with some swopping of material among the upper voices), and that lines 5 and 6 of *Crudele acerba* share the same overall chord scheme and highly individual chromatic colouring. But there is also a 'horizontal' connection between the cadences of the two *partes* in that the phrygian tendency of the upper voice in the two *Crudele acerba* cadences derives from the phrygian colour of those in *Mia benigna fortuna*. The repetition of the 'stile' cadence (line 5 of *Crudele acerba*) as the final cadence makes for a most satisfactory ending, giving the impression that the last two lines form a couplet. As Edward Doughtie so rightly says of closure generally

> . . . what is sounded exactly twice, we do not expect to be repeated exactly a third time without some intervening material.[26]

Rore's repetition, then, is a clear signal that the end has arrived.

'Pianto' has a correspondence between the upper voice in each stanza: the phrygian cadence on 'morte' has the canto line of the *prima parte* given to the alto in the *seconda parte*. The treatment of these cadences shows a sophisticated understanding of the literary qualities of Rore's chosen text.[27]

In Examples 36a and 38 the forbidden major sixth, with the frequent cross-relations, makes for a very vivid illustration of bitterness and cruelty ('Crudele'). Nevertheless, apart from one slightly unusual treatment of a six–four chord, the handling of dissonance conforms to that of the classical polyphonic style as seen in the works of Palestrina.[28] It is as if composers feared to make their music *avant-garde* in more than one way at a time: it is only later that chromaticism goes hand-in-hand with novel dissonance treatment.[29]

Solmization also plays a part in Rore's musical interpretation of the text. As the previous discussion has shown, the frequent semitone drops for 'stile' illustrate the 'defeating of every style' by stretching 'mi re' to make the hexachord unconventional – with 'mi' a semitone instead of the normal whole tone above 're', and the expected major third for 'sti–' being replaced by a surprise minor third, so 'defeating the hexachord style': moreover, at times 'E'l mio' is set as 'RE ♭mi' (see Example 17). *Mia benigna fortuna*, starting as if in D dorian, cadences in F, so invoking the sweet hexachord to parallel 'blessed fortune'; 'e'l viver lieto' moves to a yet sweeter area, by being cast entirely in B♭, so that the B♭ hexachord illustrates 'happy life' (an idea emphasized also by setting this one phrase in triple time). In the following phrases ('I chiari giorno e le tranquille notti') it might be thought that Rore has reversed the normal madrigalisms by writing black notes for 'day' and white notes for 'night', but the black notes at 'giorno' illustrate the activity of the day-time, while the slow notes and even slower rate of chord change at 'tranquille notti' are intended to introduce a quality of peace and quiet.

In addition, the tonal colour of the hexachords is worth noting: 'giorno', with its G minor–D major half-close, and 'notti', with its D minor–A major half-close, both have lines that end with prominent falling semitones – a feature we have already noticed in Lasso's setting. Again the delayed use of 'fa mi' makes for a particular kind of tension. The cadence onto an A-major chord is particularly unexpected: one could argue that the flatwards direction set up by the first two cadences (those on F and B♭) is being countered by the half-closes on D major and A major: but the durum nature of the sharpwards motion seems less important here than the use of the very remote A-major chord (considering the number of E♭s already used). The *frisson* that this gives is intended to illustrate 'night': moreover the unexpected major third – as we have seen – would be thought of as the solmization syllable 'mi', so echoing the final vowel of the line of text.

'E'i soavi', with triads of D minor, G minor, C major and B♭, clearly begins to use a circle of fifths to move back towards the molle area; but when C is reached, the expected C–F cadence is avoided, for B♭ occurs at the point where F is expected. The result is to produce a chord even sweeter than the simple – and expected – move back to F would have given. The idea is extended when 'e'l dolce stile' uses chords of C major, B♭, E♭, and D (with a flat six–three above the D), for the illustration of 'the sweet style' moves us to a yet sweeter area which includes an E♭ chord. By contrast, the leaps of a major sixth at the end of the *prima parte*, starting with the C–A at 'in doglia' but then using a much more exposed rising D–B natural at 'Odiar', return the tonality to durum in the most dramatic fashion – by using an interval that, because it is forbidden, draws particular attention to the durum area (and, in particular, to the hard B natural).

Since many cadence points have descending semitones in the melodic lines, it is not surprising that the final cadence of the *prima parte* has the descending semitone writ large – by using a phrygian cadence. There are, however, odd features about this cadence, both of which refer back to Arcadelt's setting (see Example 37). The alto's move down to F on the penultimate chord renders the cadence not quite phrygian because it replaces the bass A♭: instead, the final two chords become 'sound consecutives': though not in breach of any rules, this does help to illustrate death because of its unexpectedness. In addition, by moving down to F and back to B♭, the possibility of a major third sounding in the final chord – usually added by the performers in minor-mode pieces by applying *musica ficta* – is removed. In just such a manner Arcadelt had also posed problems for the addition of *musica ficta* major thirds and sevenths. Moreover, the final F minor–G minor progression is a relatively unusual one: it is not so much that two minor triads a tone apart will contain a tritone (the forbidden *mi contra fa*), for the normal phrygian cadence would also have done this; it is more that that particular progression is found so rarely –

Example 37   Rore: *Mia benigna fortuna*

though it had occurred, again with 'sound consecutives', just after the opening
of Arcadelt's *Crudele acerba*.[30]

The *seconda parte* of Rore's madrigal *Crudele acerba* begins by picking up
the rising major sixth D–B natural which formed such a feature of the end of
the *prima parte*: this is a further use of the G-major sound to illustrate
'crudele' with the hard hexachord. But there are continual clashes with voices
that insist on using flats, and the conflict is aggravated by the fact that, after
the initial upward leap, each voice enters in imitation using the sequence
TONE DOWN–MINOR THIRD UP. This shape is driven through the texture
with a purely musical logic, despite the activity of the other voices with which
it frequently clashes, causing various cross-relations (see Example 38). Such a
following of a musical logic that is not dependent upon a text – that is not
built from madrigalisms – suggests that there was a growing interest in
organizing pure sound: without this interest there could have been no general
shift towards purely instrumental music.

The phrygian cadence on 'morte' that ends the opening phrase of the
seconda parte recalls the much less conventional one at the end of the *prima
parte*: and it is shortly followed by a much more unusual derivation of the
phrygian cadence (at 'pianto', where a ♭6–3 chord over D (in three low voices)
moves to an open fifth on A). This is a much more stark and empty sound
than the A major of line 2 in *Mia benigna fortuna*, and thus contrasts
markedly with the foregoing 'night'. The importance of the descending
semitone at the end of phrases is again obvious, as it is in many subsequent
places not identified in the present discussion. For the rest of the piece it is

Example 38   Rore: *Mia benigna fortuna/Crudele acerba*

sufficient to point out that chords of A♭ – a dolorous sound – illustrate 'E i giorni oscuri' ('my days in darkness'), but that there are no rests to illustrate 'sighs'. The phrygian cadence which Rore leads the listener to expect at 'dogliose notti' is first denied by the basso entering to change the harmonic basis, and then – on a subsequent occasion hard on its heels – by rhythmic means in which the expected resolution onto the final chord of the cadence is placed on a weak pulse, only for the harmony to move elsewhere on the following strong pulse.

As mentioned in Chapter 2, other composers apparently copied some elements from Rore's setting in pieces based on other texts.[31] Marenzio, in *O fere stelle* (1588), also refers to a cruel style, but he illustrates the concept with a wide-ranging circle of fifths that takes the music into D♭: this madrigal forms a companion-piece to Rore's. Indeed, Rore's *Mia benigna fortuna/Crudele acerba* – which is as much an advance on Lasso's setting as Arcadelt's *Crudele acerba* was an advance on the anonymous *Mia benigna* – was widely regarded as an epoch-making piece, and it was much admired and imitated for half a century: it was, however, many years before anyone tried to emulate this setting of the opening stanzas of the Sestina.

Giaches de Wert

Giaches de Wert (1535–1596), although born in Flanders, spent nearly all his life in Italy: he may well have had some early contact with Rore at Parma, and he was later much influenced by the progressive madrigals written in Florence in the 1580s, and particularly by the style which involved the *Concerto delle Donne* – the consort of virtuoso sopranos that affected secular music deeply at that time. Since he numbered Tasso and Guarini among his associates it is hardly surprising that he showed a refined literary taste, choosing madrigal texts of the highest quality.

Wert's five-voice setting of the opening two stanzas was published in 1588, in his *Il Nono libro de madrigali a cinque e sei voci*. Thirty years had elapsed since Rore had written his classic piece: the lack of attempts to emulate that setting of the poem in the intervening years (Monte's setting of 1562 is not part of the emulative tradition) indicates the high esteem in which it was held. Wert must have felt self-confident enough by 1588 to undertake the task of attempting to outdo Rore.[32] The nature of this attempt is discussed by Einstein[33] and Maniates[34]: there are, nevertheless, more elements of interest than are treated in those two accounts.

Although the two stanzas are composed as a pair, the complex rhyme structure which we found in Rore is not matched by Wert (see Example 39a). One could make out a case for the cadences at 'lieto' being related, and the figuration of the end of the *prima parte* (on 'morte') is roughly imitated at the start of the *seconda parte*. The cadence formulae, though, are generally less clear-cut than Rore's.

Wert's *Mia benigna fortuna/Crudele acerba* is cast in the dorian mode, whereas Rore's was composed on the final D using a mixture of signatures with one and two flats: the advantage of using D as a final, for both composers, is that the last syllable of each *parte* of the madrigal can be set to its solmization syllable – 're' in each *parte*, since the final words are 'morte' and 'stile'.[35] Thus Rore ends his two *partes* with G minor (reading downwards, the voices sing *re*, re, B♭ and *re*) and D major (the voices singing re, RE, F♯ and re). Wert on both occasions uses D major (reading downwards, the voices use F♯, re, RE, re and re): he does not, however, start in the dorian mode, for good reasons – reasons which vividly recall those advanced in the

Example 39a

above discussion of the opening of Palestrina's *Stabat Mater*. Wert's ionian-transposed (or rather, F-major) opening – though written without a B♭ in the signature – suggests the molle ('sweet') hexachord in order to illustrate the 'blessed fortune' of the text. Moreover, the ah sounds which begin and end the first phrase of the poem are set to ah sounds in the hexachord, almost guaranteeing the use of F major: indeed, the first note of the topmost voice is set to the note la–mi, so illustrating both parts of the double vowel sound. The semitone 'fa mi' is reversed in the upper part (at '–nigna'). Not since the anonymous setting of *c.*1508 had the *Mia benigna fortuna* text been set with such close attention to the sounds of the gamut: even the shape of the poem is copied by Wert's returns to F-major chords on the internal ah rhymes. This is clearly one of the ways in which he reckoned to outdo Rore (see Example 39b). In fact, it is almost possible to give a reason for the choice of every chord in Wert's setting, just as it was for the chords at the opening of Palestrina's *Stabat Mater.*

Example 39b   Wert: *Mia benigna fortuna/Crudele acerba*

The second phrase, 'e'l viver lieto', moves faster (as it does in Rore's setting), but without calling on triple rhythms: the move into pure A minor shifts the music away from these sweet areas. It might be that this encourages a feeling of dynamic movement which in later music is associated with sharpward tonal shifts, though such an effect is unlikely to have been generally felt at this early stage of the evolution of the major–minor system. However, the long A-major harmony (which is only momentarily interrupted by a G-minor chord in first inversion) set to 'I chiari giorni' is clearly intent on invoking the brightness of the major triad to illustrate 'clear days'. A major does another thing, though: as we have seen, 'mi' was at times paralleled in solmization terms by an unexpectedly sharp major third: here the C♯ is bound to be thought of as 'mi' (setting the various ee vowels that occur in the course of 'I chiari giorni'), and the E and A of an A-major triad might also be so construed, particularly in view of the molle start. This, then, provides a further reason for the F-major opening, so distant from A major. For 'tranquil nights' the voices are placed low and the harmonic pace remains slow; the passage cadences with a half-close in A minor (one degree sharper than Rore's half-close in D minor – Rore ends with a chord of A major, Wert with E major). Like Rore, there are black notes at 'day', but white notes at 'night'.

At 'E'i soavi sospiri' the expected rests illustrate the sighs, while the method of expressing sweetness which calls on a chromatic shift between major chords a third apart[36] is used to illustrate 'soavi' by moving directly from a chord of C major to one of A major. Yet immediately the other means of expressing sweetness is used, for at 'e'l dolce stile' the sweet style is illustrated with a brief move towards the molle hexachord: one might wonder whether the alto and bass singers, knowing of the convention of expressing 'sweet' by the molle hexachord, might be tempted to add *musica ficta* B♭s at this point (they are not indicated by Carol MacClintock in her edition).[37] The B♭ triad which Wert reaches in his illustration of 'dolce stile' is not such an extreme use of molle as the E♭ triad used by Rore at the same point: it has usually been the case that later composers have tried to outdo their predecessors by shifting farther round the circle of fifths which the hexachord system implies. Yet after his excursion into A major – sharper than Rore – Wert makes his point perfectly well by using F. The close solmization of the ending of the *prima parte* – where the text 'vita mi fanno e bramar morte' is almost entirely set to the correct hexachord sounds – results in a double-leading-note: this feature, often thought of as a medieval sound, is very expressive because it is unexpected: but it is just as much to the point that it results from close solmization (see Example 40).[38] Despite the close solmization in both, the outcome, in Wert's piece, is utterly different from that of the anonymous *Mia benigna fortuna* discussed above.

The *second parte*, *Crudele acerba*, opens in a very striking fashion: its parallel six–three chords may derive from 'duro martir' near the end of Rore's setting, and Wert expands the idea by using it in smaller note-values in bars 13–14.[39] The forbidden major sixth leap upwards, taken from Rore's opening, is applied by Wert to 'inesorabil' so as to emphasize its second syllable: this makes it peculiarly expressive. The relationship between the two openings is close, though Wert has rearranged the elements (see Example 41). Moreover, for once the solmization, as marked in the Rore example, is rather forced – one has to search around for the vowels that fit, since the 'right' hexachord sounds do not appear naturally in this piece. One suspects, therefore, that their occurrence in Rore is unintentional. This cannot be true in Wert's opening,[40] where the falling line nicely fits the hexachord so as to produce an illustration of death and a compensating balance for the rising sixth. More-over, the rising sixth as used by Wert fits the text better than in Rore: firstly, it

Example 40   Wert: *Mia benigna fortuna/Crudele acerba*

double-leading-note

Example 41

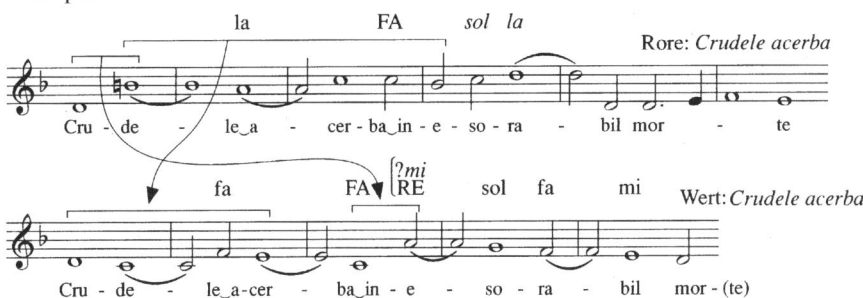

beautifully emphasizes the second syllable, and secondly, it is in a sense explained by the movement from '–ba' (= 'FA') to '–e–' ('RE') with an intermediate 'i–' ('mi', which sounds simultaneously with 'RE'; theorists accepted mutations between durum and molle in chromatic music). In turn, this hexachord setting helps the singer to tune the musical interval correctly.[41] Nevertheless, we have to admit that the hexachord logic does not extend to Wert's tenor voice, which also contains the leap (in the tenor, only the note following the leap is solmized).

Wert applies much more dissonance than does Rore: unconventionally long six–four chords,[42] entries on a dissonance, and prolonged fourths are now found in a piece which also contains chromatic elements. For once, therefore, we have a madrigal which simultaneously extends the treatment of dissonance and uses a chromatic language. It may be that the use of three adjacent semitones is consciously modelled on that illustrated in Example 17. The double-leading-note cadence recurs, but without being suggested by the solmization sounds.

In the passage quoted in Example 42 Einstein does not mark the cantus B with a *musica ficta* flat in his edition, but Carol MacClintock and Melvin Bernstein do in theirs. Who is right? The solution might well indicate the extent to which the performer is a member of the *cognoscenti*. The word 'stile', of course, suggests 'MI RE', or B natural–A in the durum hexachord: so a performer would to some extent be correct in singing B natural. But a more knowledgeable singer would realize that Wert was trying to outdo Rore in this madrigal – the allusions are quite obvious – and would remember that Rore flattened 'MI' in order to illustrate the way in which 'every style is defeated', as shown in Example 17. The leaving of the choice of *musica ficta* to the performer recalls the way in which Arcadelt illustrated the cruelty of the text by his suggestion of *musica ficta* and the difficulties he created for those who attempted to apply it. Perhaps the real *cognoscenti* would sing B♭ in the cantus of Example 42.

Luca Marenzio

Since the *Mia benigna fortuna* setting of *c.* 1508 is anonymous, and since Monte (whose setting is not considered here) came from the Netherlands, Luca Marenzio – 'the Schubert of the madrigal' – is the first native Italian to set the Petrarch Sestina. Marenzio (1553 or 1554–1599) spent much of his life in Rome: it is mainly an accident of history – the delay and confusion in producing a complete edition of his works – that has prevented him from being recognized as the equal of his great contemporary in Rome, Palestrina. Marenzio, indeed, provides the culmination of this line of Petrarch settings with his five-voice *Crudele acerba*, published in *Il nono libro de madrigali a cinque voci* of 1599.[43] It is perhaps his most extreme piece, containing considerable chromaticism allied to a striking use of minim passing-notes (sometimes of a rather unconventional kind) and of a dissonance treatment that is at times rather free. It represents a commentary on Rore's madrigal,

Example 42

Wert: *Mia benigna fortuna/*
Crudele acerba

apparently almost without reference to Wert's intervening – and at least equally impressive – setting of 1588[44] (though a series of parallel six–three chords at 'mia vita in pianto' may perhaps be taken as a reference to the opening of Wert's *seconda parte*). Marenzio chooses to write in the very unusual mode of A phrygian: the A major in which the piece begins is not, on this occasion, intended to sound bright, but to be an expression of hardness or cruelty brought about by using the durum hexachord and even sharper areas. The minor sixth leaps – in ascending and descending form – between C♯ and A refer back to Rore, but do not 'cap' his major sixths; they are, nevertheless, sharper and thus 'harder'. A major is in a phrygian relationship, though, with B♭, and touches of B♭ and other molle areas shortly arrive to illustrate 'morte' by their dolefulness. In a similar way, Rore, who had begun the *seconda parte* in G major, had invoked A♭ – also in a phrygian relationship – to illustrate 'non esser lieto'. Marenzio makes full use of the possibilities of the expressive semitones which are so prominent in the phrygian mode by devising thematic material which rises a semitone and falls back again, and by inverting this figure. Solmization of the final syllable is still possible in this mode, the last chord (setting the second syllable of 'stile') being A major, and the voices having, from top to bottom, C♯, RE, RE, E natural and RE: but there are more voices not solmized than in either Wert's or Rore's setting.

The choice of the phrygian mode seems to have been suggested by the frequent phrygian E♭–D effects which arose from Rore's use of conflicting key signatures. Marenzio's unusual final cadence with B♭–A in the bass strongly supports this interpretation: indeed, it may be copied from Rore's phrygian cadence which ends the *prima parte* (though Marenzio uses a major third in his final chord). But other facets of the writing also suggest that Marenzio had set out to write a commentary on Rore's piece, and in particular on its phrygian tendencies.[45] In view of the traditional associations which the phrygian mode had – and in view of the expressive power of the semitone, along with its prominence in that mode – this is not so very surprising. The semitone rise and fall is a part of this commentary; but there are additional phrygian features. At 'non esser lieto', just after the start, Marenzio makes a very clear allusion to the cadences which end Rore's setting (see Example 17, and compare Example 43). The solmization of Example 43 helps the bass to pitch the tritone accurately, and also helps to ensure that the interval is sung as a tritone rather than turned into a perfect interval by the application of *musica*

Example 43   Marenzio: *Crudele acerba*

ficta (the possibility of this happening is mentioned by Artusi in the controversy discussed below).[46]

Example 43 provides an instance of a phrygian cadence being set up by the composer, but avoided at the last minute. The bass singer, hearing an E♭ in the topmost voice on 'esser', might well feel that E♭ is more correct on the word 'mi', particularly since the perfect fifth leap down would be more usual by far than the tritone (which, as a melodic interval, is very rare). Furthermore, a knowledgeable singer might very well recall the use of E♭ on 'mi–' at the end of Rore's setting, even though it occurs in a different part of the text. If E♭ *had* sounded in the bass on the word 'mi', the soprano part would presumably have used the normal D–C suspension and resolution characteristic of phrygian cadences. The E natural marked in the bass avoids the expected phrygian cadence, creates a tritone (a feature we have noted in Rore, though always with some intervening notes), solmizes 'mi' accurately, and makes it possible for Rore's cadence of three descending semitones in a row to be imitated. Furthermore, we have an illustration in solmization of *mi contra fa diabolus est in musica*, for the bass has sung a B♭ ('*fa*') to 'cagion' so paralleling the first syllable, and 'mi' to the word 'mi': a certain expressive *frisson* again results from 'mi fa'; the 'diabolical' will engage our attention again in the following chapter.

But this is not the only phrygian cadence to be set up and then avoided. Two others are quoted in Example 44: again it is the movement of the bass away from the expected ♭II–I that causes the expected phrygian cadence to be aborted. We have already seen that Rore set up such phrygian cadences only to disappoint the listener's expectations. Other phrygian cadences do, in fact, occur normally; and all-in-all both sorts – those aborted and those used in the normal fashion – help to prepare for the final phrygian cadence.

The intermingling of sharp and flat hexachords plays a considerable part in this madrigal, as in its predecessors in the emulative series. The avoidance of expected phrygian cadences and the chromatic inflections show such an intermingling of the sharp and flat on the smallest scale: on a larger scale, and particularly noticeable at 'ma di menar tutta mia vita', is a mixing of various hexachords, some of them quite conventional (there are several naturale hexachords, but some quite unusual). An A and an E hexachord both place a semitone (rather than the normal whole tone) at the top, the hexachord on E (it is in the bass voice) changing at its top note – C natural – to descend through B♭, A, G, F, and E natural. There is a phrygian nature about the end of this descending hexachord – it suggests A phrygian, of which I have had something to say already: and this nature is reflected in other descending hexachords, many of them in the final section of the madrigal (though at that point they often result from appearing in parallel thirds or tenths with conventional hexachords). The use of phrase endings which descend by a

Example 44   Marenzio: *Crudele acerba*

semitone had been characteristic of both Lasso's and Rore's settings, and is one of the phrygian elements being built upon here.

In addition, one is tempted to suggest that the use of hexachords on unconventional tonics (and with an unconventional make-up of intervals) may be an illustration of the life spent in tears – the anguish of learning one's gamut, as seems to be illustrated in Marenzio's *Affliger chi per voi/Nulla da voi* (1588), discussed in Chapter 1. Moreover, the ascent on hexachords based on E and A seems to be a conscious device to 'defeat every style' even in advance of the mention of that concept in the text: it helps Marenzio to build a certain amount of tension into the piece as the music moves away from conventional hexachords into remote tonalities, and finally to release that tension as the more regular (if not quite conventional) hexachords are regained. Yet even this release is somewhat uneasy, because A phrygian (on which the final section is based) is itself such an unusual modality, because the phrygian cadence makes such a rare ending, and because the 'hexachords' do not always conform to the conventional pattern. The phrygian colour has given rise to many semitone phrase-endings in which the listener is kept in some suspense as he or she waits for the arrival of the ultimate expressive interval. It is a technique to which we shall have cause to return later.

The hexachords based on E and A might well indicate a growing awareness of major–minor tonality, for they are used on the final and dominant of the madrigal, suggesting a feeling for tonic–dominant polarity. Such a feeling balances the old-fashioned appeal to the 'aria' of the phrygian mode. The use of a 'hexachord' on E with a semitone at the bottom similarly indicates a trend away from modal theory: Marenzio may have realized the irrelevance of the gamut to chromatic music and – in a sense – to music whose final does not coincide with one of the conventional pitches for 'ut'. Indeed, the hexachord style has in a very real sense been defeated, so expressing the last idea of the second stanza of the Sestina. By hindsight we can see that the hexachord system was doomed: yet it was still to have some effect on composition before its ultimate demise. Some of this effect will be evident in Chapter 4, which discusses other pointers towards the bringing in of the new Baroque style, with its major–minor tonality. Here, too, the concepts of parody and emulation will act as useful measures of progress.

Notes

1. Discussion of the term may be found in Lockwood 1967 and Falk 1979. Bentmann 1979, p. 84 (*inter alia*), deals with the same phenomenon in architecture. See also Chater 1981, p. 23.
2. See Bianconi 1973: Haar 1966: Tilmouth 1980: also Petrobelli 1968. On the other hand, Arcadelt's setting of *Dormendo un giorno* borrows material from Verdelot's, but simplifies it. (It is, of course, possible that Arcadelt, second to Verdelot in publishing his setting, may in fact have written his first.) Marenzio wrote his *Vezzosi augelli* before Wert, yet he is more expansive: in this instance, it is possible that the two settings were conceived independently. (Marenzio is much more inclined to use contrast of long and short notes, and this holds up the sense of forward motion much more than in Wert's piece.) Vecchi quotes the opening of Palestrina's *Io son ferito* in his canzonetta *S'udia un pastor*: but this could scarcely be counted a serious attempt at emulation.
3. Dobbins 1969. Examples of settings of the same text by various composers are printed by Dobbins in *The Oxford Book of French Chansons*: the texts are: *Petite camusette*; *Je suis déshéritée*; *Douce memoire*; *Un doux regard*; *Bonjour mon coeur*; *J'espère et crains*; *Une puce*.
4. Dobbins 1969, p. 85. In a sense the English *In nomine* settings are also emulative.
5. Maniates 1979, p. 65.
6. A minim anticipation of the final note of the piece is likewise suggested to the composer by the close solmization of the textual syllables in the top voice.
7. Boorman 1990 shows that such dissonances were not so very unusual at this time.
8. Berger 1976, p. 30, shows that the minor third was gradually being accepted as a suitable equivalent to 'sad'.
9. Of the edition by Seay in Arcadelt O.O., Vol. 7. The large number results from the fact that some belong to passages of music that are repeated. Bar 24 has direct consecutive fifths, however. Arcadelt's *Chi portrà dir* and *Nova donna m'apparve*

(both *c.* 1538) have two adjacent minor chords, the second example (D minor – E minor) also with 'sound consecutives'.

10. Real consecutives are found in the lightest forms of secular music as a joke. 'Sound consecutives' are used in great numbers for a particular effect in Wert's *Ascendente Iesus in Naviculum* (there are also real consecutive fifths in bar 30): the well-known set in Byrd's *Laudibus in sanctis* illustrates 'sharp-toned strings'. It is clear that in these instances the device is unusual enough to be employed to give a certain 'off-beat' effect. Yet it is also used without, apparently, any Rhetorical or illustrative purpose. Even Palestrina uses the device from time to time: the *Missa Dies sanctificatus* has several examples, including both fifths and octaves in the *Benedictus*. There is a very striking set towards the end of the *Christe* of his four-voiced *Missa de Beata Virgine*: also at 'altissimus' in the *Gloria*. See also Chew 1989. There is one set of direct consecutive fifths between the alto and tenore at 'pianto' in Arcadelt's *Crudele acerba*.

11. The piece is discussed, along with others, in Boorman 1990: Boorman, however, only discusses one of these cadences (his Example 8c) without mentioning the density of their occurrence.

12. The avoidance of tritones is discussed in Allaire 1972, p. 58; and Bent 1984, pp. 18, 23ff. See also Berger 1987, Chapters 4 and 5.

13. The melodic use of the tritone is discussed in Bent 1984, especially pp. 18 and 23.

14. See Tye, *Cantate Domino*, EECM Vol 33, p. 60.

15. The processes were discussed in Chapter 1.

16. Einstein 1949, p. 559f. In the same collection of madrigals, Arcadelt's *Qualor m'assal'Amore/Ma quell'in un momento* presents similar problems, but without quite the density of *Mia benigna*.

17. Boorman 1990 likewise argues that composers conceived their music in such a way as to cause performers to sing cross-relations.

18. The clefs are C5, C4, C3, C2 and F2 for *Mia benigna fortuna*, and C5, C3, C3 (Quintus), C2 and F2 for *Crudele acerba*; the Quintus in the latter has a fair number of top G's.

19. 'The Palestrina style' is a slightly anachronistic term to give to the classical technique of dissonance treatment in which each essential dissonance is carefully prepared on the previous weak pulse and resolved by a step downwards on the following strong pulse, the three elements – preparation, dissonance, and resolution – being of equal length. Yet it is a term which is useful and easily understood, so long as the caveat is made that it *is* a little anachronistic as far as the early madrigal is concerned.

20. Einstein 1949.

21. See Berger 1987, pp. 65f.

22. Gagliano's 1604 setting of *O sonno*, though aeolian, also invokes phrygian from time to time: Wert's *Giunto alla tomba* (1581) uses touches of A phrygian in an otherwise E-phrygian piece.

23. The piece presents a conflict between E♭ and E natural that Rore may well have learned from Animuccia's *Infinita beltà* (1547).

24. Berger 1976, p. 30, makes the point that the minor sixth (as well as the minor third) was used to illustrate sadness.

25. The major sixth does occasionally crop up before this: a good example is in the Kyrie of Ockeghem's *Missa Mi-mi* (G leaping up to E natural). Monteverdi, obviously seeing the relevance of the rising major sixth to 'crudele', used the D–B natural leap for 'crudel' in *Vattene pur, crudel* (1592): he repeated the idea in

Piagne e sospira (1603) with 'in dura' set to a rising major sixth (C–A) and later to its inversion (E down to G and A down to C). There is a major sixth leap down in *Luci serene e chiare* (1603) at 'Voi m'incendente', and in *Longe da te cor mio* (1603), at 'moriro': and *La piaga c'ho nel cor* (1603) has rising leaps of a major sixth at 'e sola pena mio'. Sometimes a major sixth is used rising in the bass at cadences, ending so that the bass sounds the major third in the final chord: examples may be found in the *Eton Choirbook* and in Tallis's *Sancte Deus* (at 'quaesumus'); see Benham 1977, p. 66. Tye uses a rising major sixth to illustrate 'Exurge' in *Miserere mei Deus*.

26. Doughtie 1986, p. 10
27. This is an example that one might expect Monteverdi, of all Rore's descendants, to follow. No such scheme, however, obtains in the Sestina *Lagrime d'amante* in Monteverdi's Sixth Book of Madrigals. Nevertheless, Monteverdi clearly recognized that (with one exception) the lines of the Sestina's strophes were so arranged that the end of line 6 of each stanza becomes the end of line 1 in the following stanza. The exception is the second stanza, where the end of line 5 (rather than line 6) is the one that is used for line 1 of the third stanza. In order to make this join conform to the others, Monteverdi repeats line 5 after line 6 in his setting of the second stanza, so making the end of the *seconda parte* conform to the first line ending in the *terza parte*.
28. See note 19.
29. Cf. the discussion of Vicentino's *Hierusalem convertere* in Maniates 1979, p. 189.
30. Arcadelt had also used two minor triads a tone apart as consecutive chords at the opening of *Chi potrà* (*c.* 1538) and at 'honore' in *Nova donna m'apparve* (also *c.* 1538) – the latter with sound consecutives and a tenor part that, by rising a fourth, likewise prevents the use of the major third in the final chord of a cadence (Lera 1989 makes the leap a tritone by altering the second note by *musica ficta*, so that the final chord can be major). Indeed, Rore might well have had the *Nova donna* cadence in mind when writing his own at 'bramar Morte'.
31. See Chapter 2, pp. 67–70, and notes 4 and 5.
32. Wert and Rore may for a time have worked together: see Fenlon 1980, p. 107.
33. Einstein 1949, p. 561.
34. Maniates 1979, p. 349.
35. For other uses of solmization in Wert, see MacClintock 1966, pp. 90, 94, 193 and 199.
36. See Chapter 1, pp. 39–41.
37. *CMM* 24.
38. Luzzaschi does something similar at 'd'ira' in *Quivi sospiri*. See also the discussion of Marenzio's *Cruda Amarilli* below. Not all double-leading-notes of this period can be explained by solmization: the example at 'Virgo virginum' in Palestrina's eight-voice *Stabat Mater*, for example, cannot.
39. Of either MacClintock's or Einstein's edition (*CMM* 24, or Einstein 1949).
40. Wert's opening seems to have suggested to Luzzaschi the point he uses for 'Duri cepi' in *Dolorosi martir* (1594).
41. One of the reasons for avoiding the major sixth was that it was considered difficult to sing in tune.
42. Wert uses the same idea in *Amen, amen dico vobis* at 'sed tristitia vestra'. Monteverdi seems to have copied this device in *Luci serene* (1603), at 'Alma ch'e tutta foco e tutta sangue'.

43. Marenzio published a setting of another stanza of the Sestina, *Fuggitò è'l sonno*, in 1588.

44. Marenzio may have known Wert's setting: at the very least, he is at pains to outdo Wert in his own use of dissonance and its unconventional treatment. He outdoes both Wert and Rore in his use of 'cruel' melodic intervals: not major sixths (he uses only one, in a not very prominent place in an inner voice), though minor sixths are frequent. Instead, he uses tritones and a minor seventh. The tritone is made easier for the bass singer (see Example 43) by having the note after the leap carefully solmized.

45. In this connection, see the discussion of Gesualdo's *Languisce al fin* in Finscher 1972, p. 7.

46. Cf. Bent 1984, and Berger 1987.

4 Emulation and Parody II
Ut Oratio Sit Domina Harmoniae

The freedom achieved by composers in their expressive music was bound to lead to the eclipse – if not the outright abandonment – of the hexachord system, for such a system could no longer cope with the increased range of chromatic notes and tonalities. The modal system, too, could no longer be relevant because of the multiplication of pitches now available within a single work. And so, as music became more chromatic, hexachords were at first stretched in an attempt to include the more extreme chromaticisms – a process already encountered in some of the examples discussed above – and then they gradually lost their relevance: yet the system was so much a part of every musician's training that its effect lingered on even when almost everything else in music had changed. We have already seen how Monteverdi's music was at times governed by hexachord colour; and it is clear that, even in a piece hailed as the harbinger of the new music, solmization and the hexachords still had a part to play. But before discussing this epoch-making piece – *Cruda Amarilli* – the whole emulative tradition that lies behind it must be examined. The emulative tradition that is discussed here carries the preceding investigation of parody forward into the early baroque period.

Claude Palisca begins his treatment of *The Artusi–Monteverdi Controversy*[1] with the words

> The debt music history owes to Giovanni Maria Artusi is only grudgingly recognized. Yet it is a great one, for he focused attention on one of the deepest crises in musical composition and stimulated the composer who most squarely confronted it to clarify his position. Without Claudio Monteverdi's letter in the Fifth Book of Madrigals and his brother's glosses upon it in the *Scherzi Musicali* (1607), Monteverdi's youthful creative thought would have left a blunter mark in history. His stylistic profile without Artusi's criticism would be set less boldly in relief.

131

This passage codifies the matter just as clearly as Artusi did, and perhaps more clearly than Monteverdi and his brother Giulio Cesare did, in the early years of the seventeenth century.

Artusi was a very good, thorough theorist, who was by no means an arch-conservative:[2] he was, however, genuinely concerned that the whole basis of music was being turned upside-down by the moderns. As 'Vario' (one of the interlocutors in Artusi's discourse) puts it,

> these composers may perhaps so exert themselves that in the course of time they will discover a new method by which dissonance will become consonance, and consonance dissonance.[3]

Artusi published his tract, *L'Artusi, over Delle imperfettione della moderna musica* at Venice in 1600. In it he describes a meeting at a nobleman's house at which some madrigals – by Monteverdi, though Artusi does not name him – were sung and repeated. The fact that he says Luzzaschi (one of the foremost *avant-garde* composers) was present suggests that the meeting was of concern and interest to the *avant-garde*; and the setting – Ferrara – also places the meeting in a city noted for its modern tendencies in the madrigal. (Rore, Wert and Marenzio, each of whom became additional butts of Artusi's criticism in a further attack on the new music three years later, all had links with the court of Ferrara[4].) It was, one presumes, a gathering of *cognoscenti*, just such as might occur at a meeting of an Academy.

Artusi took particular exception to Monteverdi's *Cruda Amarilli*: and though he also makes criticism of *Anima mia, perdona*, it is upon *Cruda Amarilli* that he most vents his spleen.[5] A man of Artusi's knowledge can scarcely have been unaware of recent – and not-so-recent – trends in the madrigal. The narrowing spiral of increasing chromaticism and ever more pungent dissonance, starting in mid-century and accelerating into a fast spin by the time of Marenzio's *Crudele acerba*, Luzzaschi's *Dolorosi martir*, and the later works of Gesualdo,[6] can scarcely have passed him by. Why, then, is it Monteverdi rather than, say, Marenzio or Gesualdo, who is singled out for criticism in the 1600 discourse?

Theorists codify the compositional practice of their time – or, more frequently, of the music just before their time;[7] and Artusi has taken as his ideal the music of a much earlier generation, and a style more generally characteristic of church music than of the contemporary madrigal (though the madrigal itself has a stream of compositions which do not breach what we now normally think of as 'the Palestrina style'). He refers to the authority of Zarlino, whose treatise is a very model of correctness of the *prima prattica* idiom:[8] among composers worthy of emulation Artusi cites Willaert, Rore, and Palestrina.

Claudio Monteverdi, without going into detail, wrote a short defence of his position, and published it as a Foreword to his Fifth Book of Madrigals (1605);[9] his brother Giulio Cesare annotated this with additional explanations, and printed them alongside Claudio's 1605 letter as a Preface to the *Scherzi Musicali* (Venice, 1607).[10] Giulio Cesare was quick to point out that Artusi could well have made his criticism against composers earlier than Claudio: clearly he felt there was an injustice in singling out Monteverdi when he merely stood in a line of development going back many years. The Monteverdi camp, in fact, also claimed Rore as a member; Giulio Cesare may have been attempting to cut the ground from under Artusi's feet when he maintained that his criticisms might well have been made against Rore,[11] an acknowledged pioneer of the *seconda prattica* style, yet nevertheless included in Artusi's list of composers to be admired. Giulio Cesare omits Rore from his own list of *prima prattica* composers: when he includes him in his *seconda prattica* list it is with the statement that 'my brother' (Claudio Monteverdi) will make clear – presumably in his promised tract on the *seconda prattica* – that Rore belongs to the 'new music' camp.[12] He pointed out that Zarlino admitted to not dealing with all aspects of music,[13] and implied that he dealt with only one side of music theory – that relating to *prima prattica*, and not to that of the emerging *seconda prattica*.

Artusi stood for theory, and could not comprehend the idea of a composer daring to write at the dictates of his feelings and inspiration regardless of received theoretical knowledge. The dispute between Monteverdi and Artusi is one between the romantics – as at other periods of music history, avowedly interested in extra-musical inspiration (in this instance, text) – and the classicists, who, while they themselves may have had similar interests, nevertheless insisted on the traditional musical virtues.[14] Artusi makes the point very succinctly in his own discourse, which is cast in the form of a dialogue between 'Luca' and 'Vario'. He contrives a defence of Monteverdi in the dialogue, though it is rather a weak one: it presents the same kind of difficulties as are presented to a man playing himself at chess, though it is true that Artusi may have picked up some of his 'defence' of Monteverdi at the meeting where the music was sung, for it would seem likely, with Luzzaschi (and presumably Monteverdi and others) present, that some discussion of the new music would have taken place. 'Luca' in fact states the usual objection to the new music most succinctly when he says,

> They [that is, the moderns] think only of satisfying the sense, caring little that reason should enter here to judge their compositions.[15]

Monteverdi stood for practice, and the practice of his art meant that he never found time to write a detailed reply to Artusi. The short letter in his Fifth Book of Madrigals (in which *Cruda Amarilli* is placed first), though, claims that Monteverdi has coined a name for the new music – the *seconda prattica*.[16] As Palisca points out, the term had first been used by 'l'Ottuso Academico' in his defence of Monteverdi made in letters to Artusi after the

1600 discourse, and prior to Artusi's 1603 *Seconda parte.* . . .[17] By implication, therefore, the older style, advocated by Artusi and Zarlino, is the *prima
prattica*. Monteverdi clearly considered his talents better employed in writing
music than in pamphleteering: the treatise on the *seconda prattica* which he
promised in his letter in the Fifth Book of Madrigals, and which would have
focused his reply to Artusi, never materialized. Giulio Cesare Monteverdi tells
us that in that treatise

> he promises to show, in refutation of his opponent, that the harmony of the
> madrigal *Cruda Amarilli* is not composed at haphazard, but with beautiful art and
> excellent study, unperceived by his adversary and unknown to him.

Such a piece of work, had it ever appeared, would indeed have been
fascinating: we can only regret that it was never written, imagine what the
arguments might have been, and – on the other hand – rejoice that Monteverdi was practical and confident enough to continue to write more music of
his own kind instead. In any case, it is true that composers have almost
invariably been reticent about analysing and explaining their own works.

In spite of Giulio Cesare's glosses to Monteverdi's letter and the weakish
defence of the new style put up by Artusi himself, the argument is an uneven
one, since the case for the new music has scarcely been put in any depth. This
being so, Artusi must have realized that his own case had been more
thoroughly argued than Monteverdi's, and no doubt he considered that he had
won a mighty victory. Yet it might be said that Monteverdi's reply, advocating
a new category of *seconda prattica* (or perhaps, codifying as two practices the
division into two streams that had already been part of madrigalian history),
hardened attitudes into two groups. Even so, Monteverdi continued to write
in both practices, composing severely old-fashioned church music right to the
end of his life. This division of music into two practices, however, is a piece of
post facto theorizing, for there had been a divergence of style between the
madrigal and church music (and to a lesser extent within the madrigal itself)
for fifty years – a divergence growing ever wider.[18]

One of the arguments used for the Monteverdi camp is that

> the harmony . . . becomes the servant of the words, and the words the mistress of
> the harmony.[19]

Words describing cruelty will, naturally, call for cruel dissonance; but, equally,
words not calling for abnormal dissonance should not be set to abnormal
dissonance. It follows that church music might well be in the *prima prattica*
style, if the words are themselves neutral rather than highly emotional.
(Indeed, as I have said, Monteverdi himself wrote in both the *prima* and
seconda prattica.) The corollary to this position – one which, by implication,
Giulio Cesare Monteverdi assigns to Artusi and Zarlino – is that in classical
polyphony the harmony is mistress of the words. The truth of this is shown by
Artusi's failure to concern himself with the text at all in his criticism of *Cruda*

Amarilli: his ignoring of the texts constitutes one of the greatest weaknesses in his case.

The means of text illustration that most upset Artusi was dissonance: not dissonance *per se*, for he had himself written a treatise on dissonance, but the handling of it. Artusi appealed to the fundamental laws of acoustics – as demonstrable on the monochord – to prove that dissonances *are* dissonances.[20] This, however, was scarcely the point at issue; Monteverdi did not deny the dissonant nature of a dissonance: dissonance does not become consonance or vice versa, as Artusi fears.[21] If this had been the case, the primacy of the expression of the text could scarcely have been put forward as a logical argument for Monteverdi, who specifically employs dissonance as part of his armoury in illustrating certain types of text. It is the increasing freedom of dissonance treatment that concerns Artusi: he expects suspensions to be correctly prepared and resolved according to what he takes to be universal laws,[22] and he is also concerned about the correct placing of dissonances on the strong and weak pulses of the tactus.[23] Since Monteverdi never wrote his promised tract on the new music, we are forced to rely on our own analytical investigations of his work in order to discover his views on the matter. It would be quite logical to use *Cruda Amarilli* for this purpose, since this piece was Artusi's main target, and since Monteverdi's brother maintains that Claudio was intending to write a defence of this particular madrigal, showing that it is not 'composed at haphazard, but with beautiful art and study'.[24] But in order to understand the procedures used by Monteverdi, and to understand why it was he and not some other composer who was initially singled out for criticism, we must first look at the three previous settings of *Cruda Amarilli* in some detail.[25]

Cruda Amarilli

Guarini's *Il pastor fido* was complete by 1583, though the definitive edition did not appear until 1601.[26] Mirtillo's soliloquy from the pastoral, *Cruda Amarilli*, became a favourite among composers: its treatment of (apparently) unrequited love and its involved language (full of puns)[27] were much to the taste of the times. It was during the 1580s that a change in taste for poetry occurred among madrigal composers generally.[28] Despite the claims of Petrarch, there had been a strong tendency towards the open-air pastoral atmosphere of Arcady that took root after the publication of Sannazaro's *Arcadia* in 1502. But in the 1580s two composers working at Mantua – Monteverdi and Wert – began to show a new interest in the more intense emotions found in the poetry of Guarini and Tasso: indeed, such poetry was the more likely to provide opportunities for writing expressive music, and more opportunities for experiment. As Denis Arnold puts it

... they preferred poetry with a far more intense emotional atmosphere than that of smiling Arcadia. The 'new' verse is full of sexual overtones (simple words such as 'death' acquire another, erotic, significance); there is no feeling of inevitable contentment or even resignation. The poetry smoulders with intense desire.[29]

The poem reads

> Cruda Amarilli, che col nome ancora.
> D'amar, ahi lasso! amaramente insegni:
> Amarilli, del candido ligustro
> Più candida e più bella,
> Ma de l'aspido sordo
> È più sorda
> È più ferra e più fugace;
> Poichè col dir t'offendo,
> I'mi morrò tacendo.
>
> Ma grideran per me le piagge e i monti,
> E questa selva, a cui
> Si spesso il tuo bel nome
> Di risonar insegno.
> Per me piangendo i fonti,
> E mormorando i venti,
> Diranno i miei lamenti.
> Parlerà il mio morire,
> E ti dirà la morte il mio martire.

The following is a translation of the poem.[30]

Prima parte
Cruel Amarillis, whose name, alas! subjects me still to the bitterness of love; Amarillis, fairer and whiter than the whitest jasmine, but more deadly, deaf, and elusive than the most venomous serpent: since by speaking I offend you, I will die silently.

Seconda parte
But the hills and dales will roar for me, and also this forest, which I instruct so often to resound with your dear name. For me the weeping springs and murmuring winds will lament; and in my face, devotion and sorrow will speak; and, if all else is silent, lastly Death will speak to you and proclaim my suffering.

Giaches de Wert

Wert seems to have been the first to write a setting: this was published in his *L'undecimo Libro de Madrigali, a Cinque Voci* of 1595, and was probably written before 1592, for a projected dramatic performance of Guarini's pastoral at the Mantuan Court.[31]

The classic madrigal combination is a five-voice one: the early madrigal was normally written for four voices, and in the late years there was a tendency to use six parts. There was a special liking for combinations with two soprano parts – a combination that church music composers also used very widely: in Wert's *Cruda Amarilli* this choice of CCATB reflects the fascination among composers at the very end of the sixteenth century with high-spaced sonorities – a fascination which has much to do with the presence of the consort of superb sopranos at Ferrara known as the *Concerto delle Donne*: one would certainly expect the poem to be set in darker, rather than brighter, colours. (The C ionian also makes for a bright, open sound.) Wert's madrigal begins with a descending tetrachord (see Example 45), which will be referred to as 'x' throughout this discussion. The second entry – in the quinto – is on an unprepared fourth which, by breaking the *prima prattica* rules about the preparation of dissonances, illustrates 'cruel'. In order to resolve this fourth, the quinto voice turns the fourth note of the phrase up (C–B–A–B), and so does not state the tetrachord (I shall refer to this shape as 'x^2'): there are thus two versions of the opening, one of which ('x') states the descending tetrachord, the other of which turns back on itself.

The first entry of the quinto raises some points of interest. First, the progression would obey classical rules if preceded by D or B natural in the quinto, for then bar 2 would simply be a conventional consonant fourth idiom. But such an explanation would not have satisfied the upholders of *prima prattica* procedures: Artusi, for example, did not accept the idea that the mind can hear something which does not in fact sound.[32] Wert's progression is a forerunner of Monteverdi's 'Ahi lasso', to which one of Artusi's objections was that the rest was treated as a consonance: 'especially after the rest', he says, 'how much more evident is it to the ear that the soprano sings a sixteenth and then a fourteenth?' Later he says, with disgust, 'They imply that the minim rest serves as a consonance.'[33] Nevertheless, the development of Wert's opening from the consonant fourth is very plain (see Example 45). Second, the six–four chord in bar 2 is unprepared, since the fourth is itself unprepared: this breach of accepted convention again helps to illustrate 'cruel'. Finally, in view of the fact that one might expect the quinto part to be a second tenor or second bass (in order to supply a darker choral colour), one might note that the dissonance here results from the high placing of the quinto: if it had been below the alto and acted as the lowest voice at the opening, the dissonance treatment would have been quite normal.

Wert next introduces the self-same line in the bass, though this does not solve the problems of dissonance, for in bar 5 a suspension in this bass part resolves on a tritone (here it is 'MI contra fa' – the extension of the 'mi fa' interval again used for a particular kind of expression). Two points arise from this: first, the tritone is itself gradually becoming accepted as a viable harmonic sound, acting – as we should say – like an inversion of the dominant seventh chord (even Palestrina occasionally resolves a 4/2 dissonance onto a triad on the leading note). Artusi still regards the tritone as a dissonance, though he does not appear to think it too obnoxious: it has lost some of the sting that caused it to be designated *diabolus in musica*. Discussing Monteverdi, he says

> After a minim rest, the lowest part clashes with the highest in a semi-diapente [tritone] which leaves the singer in doubt whether he is making an error or singing correctly. All composers have employed this interval [above the bass], but in a different way. I say 'in a different way', because although they employ it in the first and second parts of the measure, called arsis and thesis, they do not use it in either case after a 'privation' of sound [a rest];

as Artusi demonstrates in his *Art of Counterpoint*, a sixth or some other consonance precedes it.[34]

Second, if the quinto in Example 45, bar 5, is thought of as being lower in the choir and sounding beneath the other voices, the result is compatible with classical ideas of dissonance treatment.

One of the features of Guarini's language is the use of conceits and puns: the name Amarilli gives rise to 'amar' and 'amaramente', and this facet of language is emphasized by Wert through his use of a parallel musical device – the very thorough development of the opening tetrachord 'x'. He uses the phrase in ascending form for 'D'amar' and descending for 'amaramente': in addition, between the two, the word 'lasso' gets its customary solmization setting, even if 'ahi' does not (see Example 46). It may be that the elusiveness of Amarilli ('E piu ferra e piu fugace') is illustrated by using the tetrachord ('x') in *recto* and inverted form[35]; it is certainly illustrated by making the quinto part erupt into virtuoso runs. The rising tetrachord is now used in imitation for 'Poiche col dir t'offendo'; and the *prima parte* ends by using the descending tetrachord to the words 'I'mi moro', though with the second note changed so that it becomes a chromatically altered version of the third note (see Example 47). This chromatic ending lies very uneasily in a madrigal full of bright, high vocal spacings involving diatonic major triads: the dichotomy is a vivid illustration of the historical position of this madrigal, for the pastoral associations of the title *Il pastor fido* have given rise to musical passages of much more Arcadian nature than is suggested by the actual soliloquy chosen. Wert has not at this stage wholly gone over to the new style.

The final bars of the *prima parte*, which set the words 'I'mi morrò tacendo' ('I will die silently'), include – besides the chromaticism already mentioned – a dissonance which Monteverdi copied in his own setting (see Example 48). Here the cadence is basically the conventional consonant fourth, albeit with a chromatic treble part. The extra dissonance in Example 48 arises because the canto and tenore do not fit with each other: either will fit according to classical principles of dissonance treatment if the other is omitted, and both voices are without blemish if compared against the basso, alto or quinto. Dissonances were calculated against the lowest sounding part during the sixteenth century, and since the fifth and sixth were both reckoned as consonances, they can theoretically sound together. The six–five chord is thus

Example 45

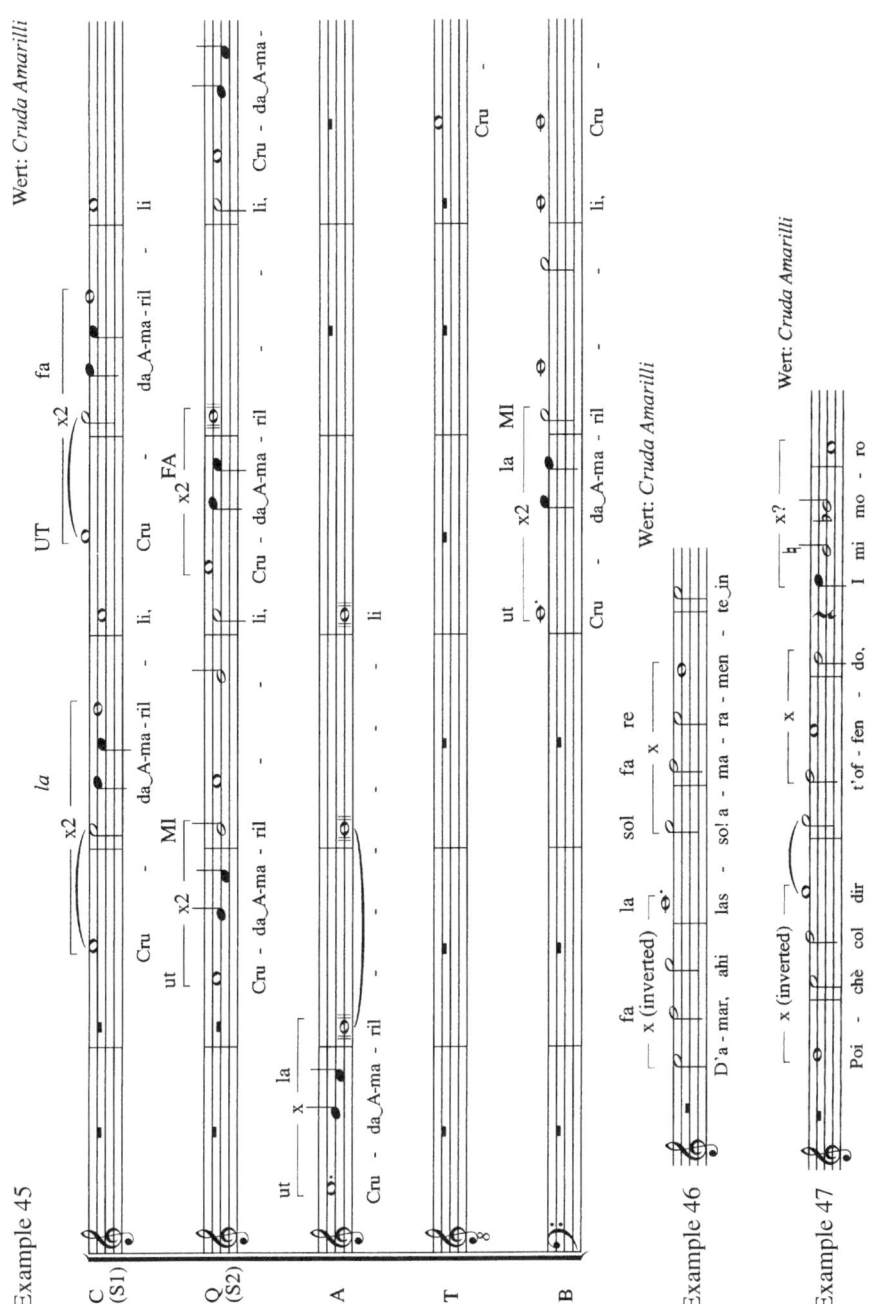

139

Example 48   Wert: *Cruda Amarilli*

found frequently, though the interval of a second that results from this is nevertheless still carefully treated, with the sixth remaining stationary and the fifth moving down by step to resolve in most instances.[36] The voices obey the classical precepts for treatment of the six–five chord if the alto is ignored, save for the fact that the sixth (B♭) rather than the fifth 'resolves'. But the alto uses the consonant fourth idiom (one that, while requiring normal resolution on a weak pulse, is by convention rather freely approached on the preceding weak pulse); and the consonant fourth idiom is an accepted cadential formula, frequently sounding – above a dominant pedal – against either the fifth or the sixth. In Example 48 it sounds against *both* intervals at the same time, so producing a logical extension of the *prima prattica* techniques, and one in which each part is quite acceptable from the classical point of view, so long as the others are not considered. Artusi approaches a description of this state of affairs when he says

> These [avant-garde] musicians observe the rule that the part forming the dissonance with the lowest part has a harmonic correspondence with the tenor, so that it accords with every other part while the lowest part also accords with every other part. Thus they make a mixture of their own.[37]

Yet Wert's procedures are more modern than those envisaged by Artusi. He makes every part compatible with the basso; but he shows up the anomaly by which the cadential consonant fourth idiom can treat the fourth virtually as a consonance, while in addition both the fifth and sixth are also consonant, by sounding all three together. Artusi's formulation would hold good, however, if we substituted 'alto' for 'tenore': both canto and tenore are viable by themselves against alto and basso.

The *seconda parte* (Wert does not set the final couplet quoted above) begins with all the voices roaring at the top of their compass, illustrating the roaring of the hills and valleys: they then plunge down and leap up a tenth – a forbidden interval in the *prima prattica* – in illustration of the topographical features of the landscape. Wert ends at 'lamenti'[38] and illustrates that word with double suspensions in minims[39] and also, in the same bar, with double suspensions simultaneously at two speeds, in crotchets and in minims (see Example 49).

Example 49   **Wert:** *Cruda Amarilli*

The chromatic nature of the end of the *prima parte* and the wide-ranging tessitura of the lines that so vividly illustrate the roaring of the hills and valleys are the sole difficulties for the performers in this piece: the clear texture and C-ionian mode make for an easily approachable and singable madrigal, and one well suited to stage performance. The subsequent settings of the poem present many more *avant-garde* techniques, and their greater subtlety makes them better tailored to performances of the type found in the learned academies rather than those intended for the stage. Nevertheless, we cannot leave Wert's setting without noting the use of regular expressive devices (the chain of rising five–six progressions – so often used to illustrate passionate ideas – at 'D'amar ahi lasso'; the minim dissonances which – as Morley quaintly put it – 'exasperate the harmony'; the high-spaced six–three chords descending slowly by step against a pedal – another common expressive device – at 'amaramente' as well as the unexpected low B♭ in the bass at 'sorda' ('deaf'). But we cannot maintain, as it was possible to maintain in the discussion of Wert's *Mia benigna fortuna*, that the setting is so intricately matched with the text that virtually every chord can be explained.

Luca Marenzio

This is much more the case with Marenzio's setting of *Cruda Amarilli*, which was published in the same year as Wert's (1595): it appears in *De Luca Marenzio il Settimo Libro de Madrigali a cinque voci*. It is not possible to be certain which composer wrote his setting first, though the fact that some of Wert's ideas are present in Marenzio's piece in a more highly developed form suggests that Wert was first in the field. The following discussion assumes this to be the case.

Marenzio begins by employing only one of Wert's two versions of the opening point: recognizing the importance Wert attaches to the tetrachord later in the piece, it is this outline that Marenzio adopts (see Example 50). The differences in treatment are, however, significant. Marenzio chooses to use two tenor voices rather than two sopranos, and the darker colour is emphasized by the choice of a minor-sounding mode (the modality is unstable, but there are strong aeolian elements) instead of the brighter ionian which Wert had used. Wert's opening alto line is transferred to Marenzio's tenore (where a small amount of solmization is evident, C being 'ut' and A being 'la' in the naturale hexachord), but it is shadowed a third higher by the quinto, whose line now gives different syllables their correct solmization notes ('FA' and 'MI' in durum). There had been only a small amount of solmization in Wert's opening, and what there is might easily have occurred by chance – the setting requires much mutation between hexachords, and is far from obvious (see Example 45). One's first reaction might be to suggest that Marenzio's choice of a low-sounding consort was the result of a desire to 'correct' Wert's dissonances, most of which would have been without blemish if the quinto had sounded in the bass. (In Wert the dissonances, in a sense, result from the kind of thing that happens when voices are inverted, by chance, at the octave. We know from Praetorius' *Syntagma Musicum* that such chance dissonances occurred at times.) But the idea of Marenzio setting out to 'correct' Wert's deliberate writing of such dissonances is inconsistent with the musical philosophy of the period, since it would involve a process of regression rather than of emulation.

Example 50

Marenzio: *Cruda Amarilli*

Progress is in fact made in Marenzio's setting by the production of a more far-reaching chromaticism and by a studied use of the unexpected, giving a hot-house atmosphere. The double-leading-note cadence at the end of Example 50 is an instance: this old-fashioned cadence, which in earlier music had been merely the result of part-writing, is sometimes used in the sixteenth century for its shock value – for there is an emotional effect to be gained by doing the unexpected.[40]

Here, as in Wert's *Mia benigna fortuna/Crudele acerba* (see Example 40), solmization has suggested the cadence. As mentioned in Chapter 1, 'mi' indicates a major third; and C♯ and G♯ can quite easily be construed as the major thirds above A and E (see Example 50). This construction is the more convincing when one notices that –fa– (the second syllable of 'cruda') is set to D in the canto, and (as the second syllable of 'Amarilli') to A in the quinto, so that in both voices a semitone – though sounded 'at a remove' – sets the vowels 'fa–mi'. The canto is more complex since the 'fa mi' appears on two levels which overlap: the durum setting of 'Amarilli' (C–B) is held within a frame provided by an unconventional setting of 'Cruda Amar*i*lli' (D–C♯). Such stretching of the hexachord system need not surprise us in a musical world where chromaticism was gradually being accepted. On the last minim of bar 4 of Example 50 every voice is correctly solmized (if not in the basic three hexachords); the use of sharp hexachords – those beyond durum on the sharp side – would cause contemporaries to think of the tonality as even harsher than the hard durum. In addition to this use of solmization, it may be that the A–G on '–maril–' in the quinto of Example 50 presupposes that the G will be sharpened by *musica ficta* so as to produce 'fa? mi?': yet the same cannot be applied to the tenore's first phrase, for A–G♯ (the latter altered by *musica ficta*) on '–maril–' would cause a clash with the opening G natural in the alto.

Marenzio, then, has already sought to improve upon Wert by his close use of solmization. He next sets 'D'amar' with its second syllable solmized as 'FA' and 'la': and he proceeds to set 'ahi lasso' in a much more dramatic manner than did Wert. Marenzio appears to owe something to the setting of these words in Luzzaschi's *Quando io miro* (1594: see Example 19); but apart from this, there are other notable features. 'Ahi' is usually set as 'mi' in this madrigal, though the word is often set to 'fa' or la–mi by composers of Italian madrigals. Marenzio uses 'fa' once, and on some occasions he writes la–mi or la–mi–re. The customary 'lasso' shape also appears (see Example 51), as it had done in Wert's setting. Another double-leading-note cadence is used,[41] (this time setting the last syllable of 'insegni' as 'mi' – the major third – in the same two hexachords as in Example 50); and the slowly resolving bass suspension is an obvious precursor of the one so effectively used by Monteverdi in the *Lament of Arianna* (Marenzio copies the idea – in diminution in the quinto – later). The extension of 'lasso' in the canto through *inganno* (in the first phrase of Example 51) so that a large expressive leap down results, is a parallel to the extensions of 'mi fa' and 'fa mi' that we have already encountered. It seems to prefigure the 'deh non languire' of Caccini's *Le nouve musiche* (1602)[42] – a motive that became a favourite expressive device during the early seventeenth century.

As in Wert, the treatment of the consonant fourth idiom extends that of the classical *prima prattica*. The idea is used as early as the cadence of the second statement of 'Cruda Amarilli'; the first statement (in the lower voices) ends with a II–I cadence onto A minor; the answering phrase ends with a consonant fourth idiom over E whose goal is clearly another cadence on A. But Marenzio replaces the expected A chord with D major: the expected V–I cadence is converted to II–I so that the bass in phrase 2 is an exact transposition of that in the first phrase, in addition providing the *frisson* which the unexpected always gives. Another development of the consonant fourth – one often used in *avant-garde* music at this time – is to be found at 'dolore' in the *seconda parte* (see Example 52). The classical consonant fourth is often approached

Example 51

Marenzio: *Cruda Amarilla*

145

Example 52   Marenzio: *Cruda Amarilli*

with a ♭6/♭3 or ♯6/♯3; mixing the two up so that the augmented triad ♭6/♯3 occurred became one of the frequent ways of extending the classical musical language to produce new sounds. Two instances of a different type are quoted in Example 51. In the first of these (bar 1 of Example 51) the fourth resolves incorrectly (from the classical point of view) on a weak crotchet in the alto, before the pitch which provides the correct resolution – in a different voice and not actually stated as a resolution at all (G♯ in the canto) – arrives. The following instance (bar 2 of Example 51) sets up a consonant fourth in the quinto, but at the strong pulse (on the third minim of the bar where the dissonance would normally occur) the bass moves down by step, making the interval of a fourth into a fifth. The fifth is not a dissonance, so it does not need to be resolved by step downwards: nevertheless, having set up the melodic pattern of the consonant fourth, Marenzio continues the shape, and the 'resolution' downwards by step then occurs on a dissonance (another fourth). The minim passing-note G in the tenore at the end of Example 51 provides a dominant seventh sound in first inversion – a sound that had appeared in the opening point of Wert's setting.

'Amaramente insegni' has a closer solmization setting than does Wert's – though in fact this still does not amount to much. It will be evident, though, that Marenzio's purely musical processes have taken over from the simple use of the descending tetrachord and its inversion which Wert had used to parallel the puns in the text: such a use of purely musical processes – as opposed to processes suggested solely by text-illustration – is an indicator of a desire among some composers to make their works hang together in a purely musical fashion.[43] This interest in purely musical processes inevitably points towards a growing interest in music that can survive on its own terms, without a text to act as an inspiration or as a formal trellis-work. Thus Marenzio inverts the opening descending tetrachord for his setting of 'I'mi moro', which ends the *prima parte* (see Example 53): we shall see further examples of such purely musical processes in the following chapter.

Example 53

Marenzio is much less concerned about vivid text illustration at the opening of the *seconda parte* than is Wert: it may well be that he considered Wert's literalness naive, preferring himself to set a general mood.[44] Marenzio shows his intention of outdoing Wert, though, when he uses slow suspensions and the doleful sound of the molle hexachord for 'piangendo' ('weep'), a *sospiro* (though a crotchet rather than the normal minim rest) before 'lamenti', close solmization of 'venti Diranno i', and when he avoids an expected cadence.

Then follows a final passage, not set (as far as is known) previously – the passage from 'Parlera nel mio volto' to the end. The opening word of this passage is set with its ah sounds matched to hexachord syllables ('la' and '♯fa') in molle and naturale hexachords, resulting in a D-major chord: when the word reappears (at 'Parlera il mi morire') there is a swing towards the molle hexachord (only the quinto uses the naturale hexachord), so that the resulting B♭ chord represents a move to the more doleful flat areas.[45] At 'La pietade e'l dolore' the solmization of the ah sounds as 'LA' and 'FA' in the canto suggests the descending tetrachord 'x', and a free inversion of this line in the lower voices results in grinding minim passing-notes. The final phrase 'E ti dira la morte il mio martire' follows up the previous unconventional treatments of the consonant fourth idiom; it uses that idiom, but then avoids the expected tonic and sounds, instead, a note a semitone higher than the one expected. We have here, then, a further – and even more unconventional – use of the semitone for expressive purposes. The unusual final cadence is prepared by several previous statements of the same unconventional melodic idea: each one of these is unusual in its own way, though none of them would have caused Artusi to complain about irregular dissonance treatments (see Example 54).

In Example 54a the chord above the first bass F♯ is a dominant ninth in first inversion – though it is conventionally approached and (on the whole) quitted conventionally (the C which appears above each bass F♯ is, however, outside the classical style). There is also an extension of the consonant fourth idiom somewhat similar to that used by Wert. The bass G (last minim of the first bar of Example 54a) could be one of two things in the classical polyphonic style. Firstly, it could be the consonant fourth over (or in this instance, *under*) the root D, which would conventionally have either B or A sounding against it. Like Wert, Marenzio chose to sound both notes against it. Alternatively, since the figure is in the bass, one could imagine G as the root of a G major chord. The passage in Example 54a appears to combine these possibilities. The tritone above the bass on the second minim beat of bar 2 of Example 54a would be quite regular if the tenore were in the bass, an octave lower – another feature we have noticed in Wert's setting, and one to which we must return later.

Example 54b provides a consonant fourth idiom combined with double minim suspensions in the two lowest voices: Example 54c extends the normal consonant fourth to make the somewhat less regular consonant seventh; the final example does the same, in an impressive and unexpected cadence which has nevertheless been carefully prepared. The use of the unexpected in this final passage recalls the prescription of Zarlino for avoiding the cadence – though Zarlino does not suggest that this has any emotional value. Moreover, the unconventional use of the consonant fourth had been the starting-point of the Wert setting: at the end of his own setting (as well as earlier) Marenzio has taken over this idea and extended it.

In Chapter 1 I showed that 'fa mi' in the hexachord system stands for a semitone – the only one in the system; and that semitones, rising or falling, became associated with those syllables, whether they occurred in a text in the order 'fa mi' or in the order 'mi fa'. It is scarcely surprising, therefore, to find that in the final point the word 'martire' is set with the first two syllables to a semitone (which happens to be ascending rather than descending). It may be more than just pure coincidence that, after returning to the original pitch (the sound still being 'mi', setting the second syllable of 'martire') Marenzio writes an ascending whole tone: for the distance between 'mi' and 're' is a whole tone. Just as 'fa' and 'mi' are inverted, so are 'mi' and 're': the figures in question are marked 'a' in Example 54. It would seem that we have a rare example of a composer realizing that each hexachord is invertible: in other words, that the TONE–TONE–SEMITONE–TONE–TONE sequence represents the same intervals whether read forwards or backwards. Such a concept of inversion is the more convincing when we recall that 'sol' might well be used for the word 'mio' (it matches the oh part of the double vowel sound) – and that 'mio' ('sol') is given as a tone below the ah vowel of 'martire' (rather than a tone above it as one would expect in a *recto* hexachord) in figure 'a'.

Example 54

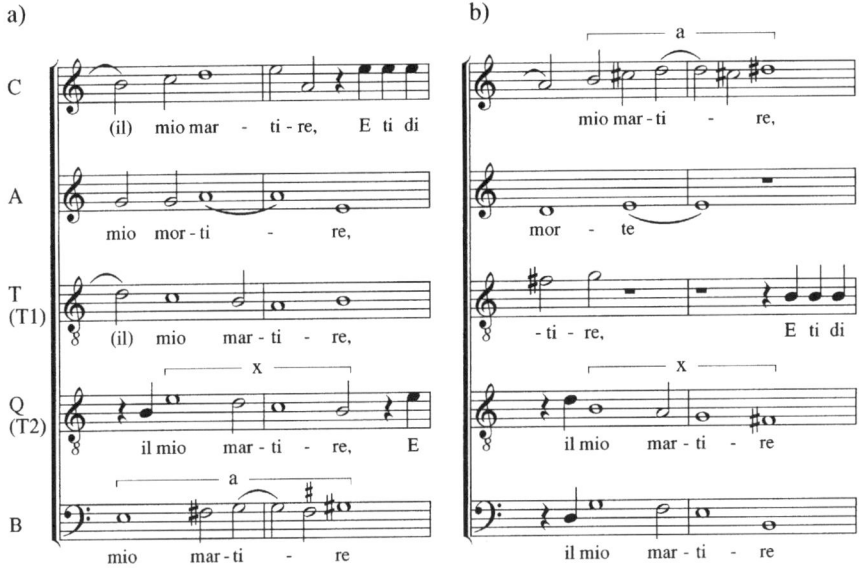

Moreover, Marenzio clarifies the idea by sounding the syllables in their *recto* form (figure 'x' in Example 54), with the solmization syllables in their correct hexachord order, though with the semitone in the 'wrong' place. The composer has, furthermore, already suggested the idea of melodic inversions in his setting of the passage 'La pietade e'l dolore' (the passage is quoted in Example 60a: the musical material at this point bears a striking resemblance to the figures 'a' and 'x' of Example 56; figure 'x' is, of course, none other than the descending tetrachord which plays such a large part in the setting).

The handling of the semitone is yet again of interest here, and again tension results from its treatment. It is not, however, the delaying of the 'mi fa' or 'fa mi' until the last moment that creates the expressive *frisson* here, but the failure to state that interval when all the world expects it to occur – as the final element of a perfect cadence that has been very clearly prepared.

There seems to be a connection between Marenzio's ending and the *Mia benigna fortuna/Crudele acerba* settings already discussed: the topsy-turviness occasioned by the suffering in *Cruda Amarilli* is illustrated by a particular upsetting of the hexachord system – in this instance by inverting it and making a semitone (rather than a whole tone) between 'mi' and 're'. One has to go back to the Rore passage quoted in Example 17 to find a comparable setting. Such pyrotechnics justify the description 'metaphysical' for Marenzio's processes in *Cruda Amarilli*. It is clear that this setting inhabits a completely different world from that of Wert's piece discussed above: the hot-house atmosphere indicates a piece intended not for the relatively large spaces needed for a dramatic production, but for the delectation of the *cognoscenti*.

Benedetto Pallavicino

The next setting of the poem to be published was a five-voice one which appeared in Benedetto Pallavicino's *Il sesto libro de madrigali* (Venice, 1600). In other ways than this Benedetto Pallavicino (1551–1601) provides a neat link between Wert and Monteverdi. He was employed by the Gonzagas in Mantua from 1584 until his death, succeeding Wert (with whom he must have had almost daily contact) as *maestro di cappella* in 1596: it was with this Sixth Book of Madrigals that Pallavicino turned his back on the pastoral madrigal of his earlier years and assumed a mannerist style that he clearly picked up from Wert. In turn, Monteverdi succeeded Pallavicino in the Mantuan post: if the latter admired his predecessor at Mantua, the same is not true of Monteverdi, who seems not to have had a high opinion of Pallavicino.[46]

Pallavicino must have known the Wert and Marenzio *Cruda Amarilli* settings, for certain aspects of his piece parody both. He recognizes the implications for producing suspensions inherent in Wert's opening theme, though the 'x' shape (and its characteristic rhythm) is less useful for this purpose than 'x^2', because it cannot fulfil the *prima prattica* requirements for resolving dissonances. The 'x^2' shape, however, is ideal, and with it Pallavicino provides an opening in which the *stretto* entries of the theme make suspensions crowd in upon one another; in which the rhythm of 'x^2' at times delays the arrival of an expected tonic (such delays result in an expressive tension which is akin to the sort we have already encountered in the delayed use of the semitone); and in which a suspension sounding simultaneously with its note of resolution, together with an augmented triad, give added spice to the harmony. The dissonance which opens Wert's setting – an unprepared fourth – is replaced by an unprepared major seventh in Pallavicino's: in two voices one always feels the seconds and sevenths as more pungently abrasive than the fourth (see Example 55). Moreover, by using the seventh Pallavicino has in fact introduced the most expressive interval, 'mi fa', as a vertical sound; the result has a much more powerfully dissonant grittiness than was evident in Wert's opening.

Suspensions are here much more than a by-product of the part-writing: they have become powerful agents for expressing emotion. This new feeling for suspensions is one that grows considerably at the end of the sixteenth century and at the start of the seventeenth. In the present *Cruda Amarilli* setting, however, it is the number of dissonances rather than their treatment that illustrates the text: apart from the opening major seventh the *prima prattica* rules are obeyed.[47] In this Pallavicino is more old-fashioned than Wert (yet more expressive), and equally expressive as Marenzio (though much more dissonant and expansive). Wert and Pallavicino manage a limited amount of solmization: Marenzio uses the technique widely and with brilliance. Pallavicino has used a relatively flat tonality, presumably feeling it to be doleful (for such an opening could scarcely be thought sweet), whereas Marenzio's opening had tended towards the durum side of the hexachord system.

Pallavicino may well have set himself to emulate his predecessors by applying more dissonance to their material. At 'ahi lasso' an entirely different technique is used in an effort to outdo them in expressiveness. The conventional solmization setting (*mi–la–sol* = A–D–C in molle, with 'ahi' often set to the note la–mi or la–mi–re) appears, but it is used in double-harness with the point setting the remainder of the phrase ('amaramente insegni'), a melodic line which also has a closely solmized setting. Pallavicino inverts note-for-note the carefully solmized melodic line 'ahi lasso amaramente insegni' in the tenore and basso: this idea may be derived from Marenzio, though one could scarcely argue that Pallavicino's melodic inversion emulates the metaphysical brilliance shown by Marenzio. The expressiveness of the opening is also due to several other elements; an augmented triad, for example, and a simultaneous combination of passing-notes some of which are of a minim's length and

Example 55

Pallavicino: *Cruda Amarilli*

some of a crotchet. This combination of lengths of dissonances expands an idea of Wert's, shown in Example 49, suggesting – as do other elements of the composition – that Pallavicino was attempting to outdo him. A consonant fourth idiom, with ♭6/♯3 as its first element, occurs during this opening section (and is used again at 'ahi lasso' and twice in the *seconda parte*). This formula may also have been imitated from Marenzio's setting, though it is relatively common in expressive music at the end of the sixteenth century and the beginning of the seventeenth. In spite of the extremely expressive quality of this opening, Pallavicino's processes are firmly rooted in the classical Renaissance techniques. It is the number and proximity of dissonances (rather than unconventional handling), and the occasional augmented triad, that provide the emotional quality (see Example 56).[48]

At 'aspido sordo', however – a passage which invokes the hard areas of the hexachord system – Pallavicino breaks the bounds of the classical Renaissance style. In an attempt to outdo Marenzio's double-leading-note cadence he uses unconventional resolutions, cross-relations, unexpected chords and a suspension in the bass. There is a pure dominant seventh on 'fera' (see Example 57), a feature copied by Monteverdi and singled out by Artusi for particular criticism. The answer to this criticism (made of Monteverdi's setting, not Pallavicino's) is given, not by Artusi's 'Luca' nor by Giulio Cesare, but by 'l'Ottuso', whose defence of Monteverdi in letters to Artusi caused the theorist to issue *Seconda parte dell'Artusi overo Delle imperfettioni della moderna musica* in Venice in 1603. 'Ottuso' suggests, quite correctly, that the seventh is used where the ear expects an octave: invoking ideas associated with rhetoric, he says, 'you allow an excellent poet the metaphor purposefully used; similarly the seventh is taken in place of the octave'; and he refers to the precedents in Marenzio's *E so come in un punto* and *E cosi nel mio parlare*.[49] This is fair enough as far as it goes, but it is also true that the dominant seventh chord was gradually becoming an acceptable sound in its own right: not a consonance – it still required resolution on most occasions – but a chord occasionally introduced without preparation and obviously creating a *frisson* which was of value in illustrating certain types of text. On the other hand, to pursue an argument used elsewhere in this chapter, the cadence merely combines two forms of what we might call a 'perfect cadence' – the V–I form and the II–I form.[50] The upper three voices, taken alone, present an unblemished II–I cadence: the alto, tenore and basso, considered without the canto, are also unimpeachable. All voices are consonant with the tenore – an idea to which we shall return later: it is the combination of the two types of cadence that takes it beyond the *prima prattica* style.

The dominant seventh is bound to introduce the tritone as a harmonic sound. *Mi contra fa* may have seemed demonic to the old-fashioned theorists, but there must have been a growing realization that this interval was the active ingredient of the dominant seventh – the interval that called for

Example 56

Example 56 *concluded*

resolution, and that produced a feeling of goal-directed motion towards that resolution. The tritone 'mi fa' has become a powerful extension of the ordinary 'mi fa' which was so expressive in earlier years; and just as the 'mi fa' semitone was used as a vertical sound earlier in the piece, so the same now applies to the 'mi fa' tritone.

Pallavicino ends his *prima parte* with a double-subject section like Marenzio's: indeed, 'I'mi moro' is an exact inversion of Marenzio's subject shown in Example 53.

The *seconda parte* begins by copying Marenzio's point, but transposes it a tone higher. Marenzio had himself already used a similar process in transposing Wert's opening of the *prima parte*, and Monteverdi was in his turn to transpose Marenzio's opening to a new pitch. At 'E mormorando' Pallavicino attempts to emulate Marenzio's sigh and extended cadence illustrating 'lamenti' by using a descending melodic seventh: this melodic seventh is another feature which Monteverdi also used. At the same place an abnormally long suspension (a semibreve) results in an abnormally long six–four chord, almost immediately followed by a seventh in the canto which is given a shortened preparation (see Example 58).

Pallavicino, then, has begun to break the rules of the classical style in his *seconda parte*. We may see this as an attempt to emulate Marenzio who, despite his use of dissonance and chromaticism, more or less belongs within the classical school of contrapuntal writing. He attempts to emulate Marenzio

Example 57   Pallavicino: *Cruda Amarilli*

also in his illustration of the roaring of the hills and dales at the opening of the *seconda parte*: while being less extravagant than Wert's extremely angular setting, it is much more vivid than Marenzio's. Nevertheless, Pallavicino is content simply to copy Marenzio's homophonic rhythm at 'Si spesso il tuo bel nome Di risonare insegno', as he does again at 'Parlera nel mio volto', though here he replaces Marenzio's molle and naturale hexachord settings with durum and naturale. Similar processes follow, for at 'E, se fia muta ogn'altra' Pallavicino again copies Marenzio's rhythm: then, at the following 'Parlera il

Example 58 Pallavicino: *Cruda Amarilli*

mio morire' he adopts Marenzio's idea of drawing attention to the ah sounds by using 'fa', though he moves one degree further round the hexachord system, with E♭ replacing B♭. The difference is clear when the two settings, both solmized, are placed together (see Example 59). The consonant fourth introduced by a ♭6/♯3 chord in Example 59b is an idea already discussed above.

We may take this illustration a stage further by examining the two settings of 'La pietade e'il dolore' (see Example 60). Here Pallavicino's attempt to outdo Marenzio in solmization is very evident, but Pallavicino, who may have been aware of Marenzio's use of melodic inversion since he himself used it at 'ahi lasso amaramente insegni', apparently fails to see that Marenzio has also posited an inversion of hexachord syllables and – not content with that – simultaneously made reference back to Rore's *Crudele acerba*. It will take a greater composer than Pallavicino to outdo Marenzio. Pallavicino adopts Marenzio's point – perhaps because he too follows the hexachord syllables – without adopting his model's device of inversion. It is at 'dolore' that Pallavicino decides to use inversion on his own account: the word has its solmization setting (as does the model), but by use of mutation from the durum to the molle hexachord, and by leaping upwards instead of down-wards, Pallavicino draws especial attention to the word, and makes it the

Example 59

a)

Marenzio: *Cruda Amarilli*

b)

Pallavicino: *Cruda Amarilli*

more effective – and, indeed, affective. Both composers write minim passing-notes, and Pallavicino includes a simultaneous cross-relation.

Pallavicino did not attempt to match the end of Marenzio's setting, in which cadences were avoided by unexpected chromatic shifts: instead, he set the text carefully to solmization syllables (but using only the *recto* form, without inversions). He uses multiple minim suspensions (one of them sounded again at the point of dissonance)[51] and 'passionate' five–six progressions (strings of such five–sixes in rising stepwise sequence are a conventional way of producing a 'passionate' sound); the latter may derive from 'I'mi moro' and 'morte il mio' in Marenzio's setting, or perhaps come direct from Wert's 'D'amar, ahi lasso' (which may in any case have been Marenzio's inspiration). Pallavicino's transposition of the opening of his final section ('E se fia . . .') down a fourth at the repeat was an idea later re-used by Monteverdi.

The wandering chromaticism of Marenzio's setting contrasts very vividly with the conservative ionian of Wert and G dorian of Pallavicino; and Pallavicino, demonstrating considerable contrapuntal skill, is also careful – for the most part – to use approved methods of dissonance treatment. But there are occasions on which he finds the received musical language inadequate for improving on Marenzio, and he is forced to use innovatory means of expression such as simultaneous cross-relations, melodic sevenths, a dominant seventh, and unconventional dissonance treatments. It is clearly in the realm of dissonance treatment (and in the sheer density of the number of dissonances) rather than in chromaticism that Pallavicino finds one of his means of advancing the musical language. No doubt he imagined that he had outdone Marenzio in setting the text to the corresponding solmization syllables; but he was unable to emulate Marenzio's brilliance either in his manipulation of the hexachord shape or in the preparation of the unusual final cadence. As a result, Pallavicino's piece – expressive as it is, and appealing to the intellect as it is up to a certain point – lacks the depth of Marenzio's.

Claudio Monteverdi

Monteverdi's *Cruda Amarilli* (a setting of the *prima parte* only) was first published in 1606. It stands, a herald of the new style, first in his *Il quinto libro de madrigali a cinque voci*, though it is true that the composer had already issued *Anima mia, perdona* – another piece criticized by Artusi – in his previous book of madrigals. Composers liked to choose something special to open their madrigal books, and *Cruda Amarilli* does this in open defiance of the criticisms already publicly made by Artusi. Since Artusi published these in 1600, the piece must have been circulating in manuscript copies for at least six

Example 60

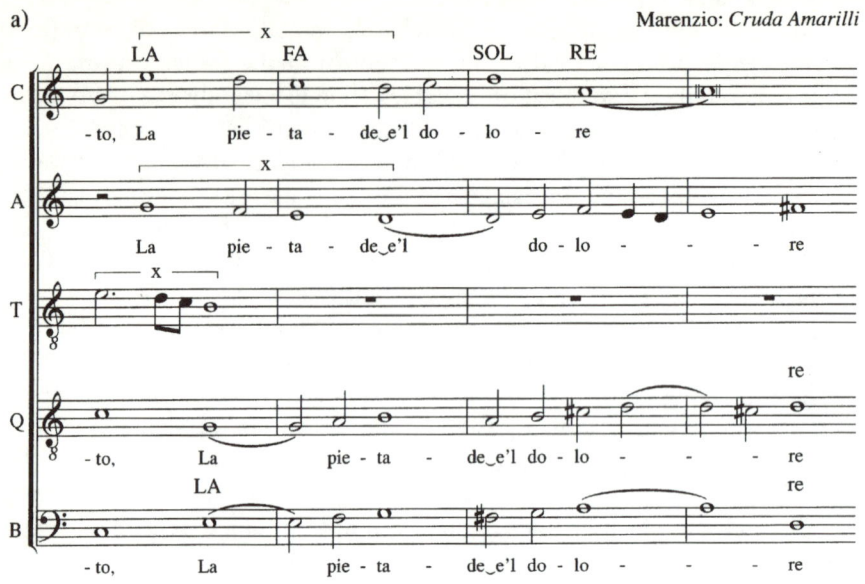

years before it was published – indeed, it is quite possible that it was written before the setting by Pallavicino. Nevertheless, since one or two elements in Monteverdi's piece apparently seek to improve upon that setting, I shall assume that Pallavicino's *Cruda Amarilli* pre-dates Monteverdi's. Monteverdi's setting is, however, very much more a parody of Marenzio's *prima parte*, though it differs markedly from it.[52]

Monteverdi's setting is almost a Ricercar based on Marenzio's first phrase ('x'): he starts by adopting Marenzio's opening descending tetrachord phrase in parallel thirds. Since the *cognoscenti* will recognize the derivation of the tetrachord from earlier settings, there is no need for Monteverdi to adhere rigidly to solmization syllables: a performance of the shape itself would be sufficient for the hearer to associate the setting with its precursors, and thus for the solmization background of the shape to be recognized. By shifting his opening to G, Monteverdi equates the hard hexachord with the hardness, or cruelty, of Amarillis. The descending tetrachord is not set imitatively, but is provided with a harmonic background. Instead of calculating dissonances above the bass, Monteverdi may have worked them out from the tenore – for if one compares the other voices against that part and accepts descending accented passing-notes (and in one case an ascending accented passing-note) the passage is consonant. Yet with all the voices sounding together the result is quite dissonant, with sevenths resolving on ninths, and unprepared sevenths.

The discussion of Wert's passage quoted in Example 48 has already shown that composers were stretching the possibilities of dissonance treatment without going outside the conventions governing classical polyphony: and Pallavicino (see Example 57) has shown how a dominant seventh can result when all voices fit in *prima prattica* style against the tenore, but not necessarily against each other. Both Wert and Pallavicino offer Monteverdi possibilities of a logical extension of the *prima prattica*, in which all voices are consonant with the tenore, yet not with each other and not necessarily with the bass. Palisca[53] makes the point that consonance with the tenore rather than the bass is made when singers improvise around a *cantus firmus* in the tenore. The resulting dissonances were clearly enjoyed by some people: Banchieri wrote glowingly about them, and Vincenzo Galilei – admittedly, like Banchieri, a member of the *seconda prattica* camp – made prescriptions for writing such harmonies in his manuscript counterpoint treatise of 1589–91. In Monteverdi, the result has the advantage of producing pungent dissonances which illustrate the cruelty of Amarillis yet more vividly than any of the previous settings (with the possible exception of Pallavicino's). The lack of a suspension in the cadence helps the alto voice to draw attention to 'x', since it is possible for that voice to use an exact descending tetrachord in the by now accepted rhythm so long as there is no suspension; and the exactly parallel

thirds make clear the reference back to the exactly parallel thirds of Marenzio's opening. Moreover, the suspension would have been a normal way of
cadencing; by avoiding the usual procedure, Monteverdi creates a certain
frisson.

The immediate transposition of the first phrase up a fourth from the durum
hexachord into the naturale (G to C) makes the opening exclamation the more
piercing, for it is placed higher in the voices. The mixture of G and C,
characteristic enough of the mixolydian mode, prefigures the tonal scheme of
the piece as a whole, and the movement up a fourth is a shift in the opposite
direction to that used by Pallavicino at the end of his setting. Monteverdi was
presumably aware of this, for he balances his opening upward shift of a fourth
(see Example 61) by closing the piece with a transposition of material back
down a fourth. Artusi could have found much to object to in the dissonance
treatment of this opening, but in fact he did not criticize it. Perhaps his
avoidance of quoting the first phrase was connected with its unmistakable use
of 'x' in the rhythm already used by other composers for *Cruda Amarilli*:
quoting the opening might have seemed just as sure a way of identifying the
composer as actually naming him in the diatribe.[54]

As we have seen, Monteverdi adopts Marenzio's rhythm for 'Che col nome
ancora D'amar', though this is more than a mere copying, for he develops the
material by building the passage over the descending tetrachord 'x', so that it
is integrated more fully with the rest of the madrigal.

If the opening passage contains pungent dissonances, the setting of 'ahi
lasso' contains more (see Example 62).[55] Here again the progression, strongly
objected to by Artusi, can be justified by comparison with the tenore: if one
imagines a bass part F–D–C in parallel with 'ahi lasso' in the canto (more or
less what the quinto has, but an octave lower and without the semiquavers),
the upper three voices are quite acceptable: the lower three voices, taken
alone, are also within the rules of the *prima prattica*. In *combination*,
however, the result is an unprepared dominant seventh preceded by an
unprepared and unresolved ninth: the seventh may have been suggested to
Monteverdi by Pallavicino's use of the chord quoted in Example 57. Artusi
would have been quite content with the canto F if it had been a passing-note
following a crotchet G rather than an A (this re-drafting is suggested by 'Luca'
to regularize the dissonance treatment): he implies that the seventh passing-
note will occur on the weak fourth crotchet. 'Vario' says

> [It is] one thing to hear two crotchets taken by step in the natural way, another to
> hear a minim, and that taken by leap, in place of the dissonant crotchet. This last
> offends the ear; the others do not, for the movement is by step.[56]

One can, of course, justify Monteverdi's processes on purely musical grounds:
the seventh was gradually beginning to be more widely used, and while
normally requiring resolution, was not always prepared and was sometimes

Example 61   Monteverdi: *Cruda Amarilli*

irregularly resolved. Moreover, the music is – as mentioned above – consonant when judged against the *tenore* rather than the bass part. Yet we are not only concerned with purely musical procedures, but with music as an expression of the text. It is the lack of any attention to the text that invalidates Artusi's criticism of the music.

If the upward graph of progress[57] is to be observed, Monteverdi must outdo previous settings of the text: his cruel dissonance illustrating 'Cruda . . .' must be more cruel than those of his predecessors. His setting of 'ahi lasso' must therefore give more vivid expression to this cry of anguish than had Wert, Marenzio or Pallavicino – or, indeed, any other composer who had previously set this very common exclamation in other texts. He has every intention of 'offending the ear' (as Artusi put it) in order to give a more pungently powerful emphasis to the grief expressed. Two ways – basically – are open to Monteverdi in the pursuit of progress in expressive writing: the road of chromaticism, and the road of dissonance. A combination of extreme dissonance and extreme chromaticism seems only rarely to have been contemplated – one finds such things in Gesualdo's last madrigal books.[58] On the whole, though, composers writing extremely dissonantly do not also use

Example 62   Monteverdi: *Cruda Amarilli*

chromaticism, and those who use extreme chromaticism are generally conservative in their treatment of dissonance. It is almost as if musicians feared that the whole fabric of music would be torn asunder if both elements were to be pushed to extremes simultaneously. Chromaticism, by 1600, already had a venerable half-century of history in the madrigal (and also to a lesser extent in the motet). Gesualdo had still to publish his most extreme examples, though it seems that he may already have written them: but it must have been plain to most people that the extent to which chromaticism could be developed had clear limits: limits which were not altered by the kind of tuning in use, and not really extended by the researches into micro-intervals indulged in by theorists like Vicentino. We may suspect that Monteverdi recognized that chromatic language did not carry within itself the seeds of any further development, and that the way forward for music must lie elsewhere. Dissonance must, for him, have seemed a much more fruitful field.[59]

By not including the text in his discussion of Monteverdi's piece, Artusi denies Monteverdi's place in the tradition, not only of *Cruda Amarilli* settings, but also of settings of 'ahi lasso': he clearly denies, too, any purpose that might have been accorded to expression and rhetoric. But there is another element of text setting which is vital here – the solmization of 'ahi lasso'. We may note the classical 'la sol' shape in the quinto of Example 62, preceded by the note la–mi or la–mi–re (for 'ahi'),[60] and joined by the kind of coloratura runs that had been in vogue since the days of the *Concerto della Donne* at Ferrara. 'Ahi' is in fact sounded simultaneously as 'FA' moving down to 'mi' (and passing through 'MI' and 'fa') in the bass and la–mi in the quinto, so setting both vowels of the word. The soprano entry on an unprepared ninth at 'ahi' is similarly logical, for this A is none other than the note la–mi: the dissonance provides the required cruelty of sound, while the solmization helps the singer to pitch the unusual ninth entry accurately.[61] The alto uses *inganno* within the 'la sol' shape, so making a leap upwards.[62] The cross-relation between F natural and F♯ is the logical result of the use of 'fa mi' in the naturale hexachord at the same time as 'mi fa' in the hexachord on D. This clash is symptomatic of the frequent dichotomy between the keys of C and G in the piece as a whole.

The overall primacy of the text in producing dissonant music, as in the passage just discussed, is plain enough to us: but to Artusi, who thought of music as pure music, whatever text might be involved, such new-fangled dissonance as occurs here was iconoclastic. He makes an attempt to understand the canto's 'ahi lasso' dissonances by trying to see them as a shorthand version of a much more common cadential formula: he supplies a crotchet G in place of the rest which precedes 'ahi' and G and F in the rhythm ♩ ♪ in place of the long dominant seventh (F) as mentioned above. This makes the A a returning note (on a weak pulse), quite within the classical style. He then points out that the G which replaces the rest is present at that place in the quinto, but in the wrong octave: he maintains, however, that the ear does not hear what is not there. Naturally the same thing applies to the neutralization of the dominant seventh by making it simply a passing-note. We may be sure that Monteverdi himself would not have advanced such arguments, since it would remove the element of cruelty ('*Cruda* Amarilli'). Artusi does not mention the close solmization, and would probably not have regarded it as a viable excuse for dissonant writing: it is, after all, quite possible to set the textual vowels to their corresponding hexachord sounds without breaking the rules of the classical style.[63]

The subsequent setting of the exclamation 'ahi lasso' extends the use of the dominant seventh chord (and the triad on the leading-note of C major) to virtually consonant status, for not only is F in this chord used as a preparation for suspensions, but B natural (in the bass) is introduced after a rest. Therefore, although the music for this second 'ahi lasso' sounds less extreme than that of the first, the techniques involved are pushed further, since the acceptance of the unprepared ninth and the dominant seventh in Example 62 – for reasons of close text illustration and solmization – presupposes the possibility of those sounds being acceptable as (relatively) consonant for the next exclamation. Artusi's objection to the passage has already been quoted in the discussion of Wert's music shown in Example 45: the tritone, he implies, makes the singer imagine that he has sung a wrong note, and that the interval should have been a perfect fifth, supplied by *musica ficta*. He admits that composers have used the tritone widely, but insists that it should be preceded by a consonance and not a rest.[64] He makes no comment on Monteverdi's preparation of a suspension over a tritone. Yet again, then, we have an instance of 'mi fa' – in its tritone form on this occasion – being used for vivid expression.

The gorgeous expansion of 'Amarilli' shown in Example 63 is a break with the emulative tradition, for both Marenzio and Pallavicino had copied Wert's rhythm for this line of poetry (though after the word 'Amarilli' Monteverdi does revert to Wert's rhythm).

Example 63   Monteverdi: *Cruda Amarilli*

The expansion of 'Amarilli' at the repetition of that word raises three points of interest. Firstly, the shift from C major into D minor involves mentally changing from the naturale hexachord to the molle – a shift of a fourth upwards which parallels that applied to the opening phrase of the madrigal.

This is the more effective since it provides the only touch of molle hexachord in the piece. Secondly, the move towards the molle hexachord illustrates a growing feeling of softness or tenderness towards Amarilli as her name is repeated. By setting the solmization syllables closely, Monteverdi helps the mind to focus on the hexachord system, perhaps so that the listener may be the more aware of the processes at work. (The major thirds which set the syllables of 'Amarilli' to the major third 'mi' recall Marenzio's processes shown in Examples 50 and 51). The third point of interest is that Monteverdi has again integrated the material thematically with its surroundings, with 'x' and its inversion clearly stated in the canto. The seventh on A in the canto is not resolved, for purely musical reasons: the second 'Amarilli' (in that voice) is an ornamented version of the first – just such as might have resulted from improvisation. These accidents of improvisation were accepted – so why should they not be written down? This is one of those places in the madrigal that Artusi would describe as 'accented' singing – a term he in fact uses about the 'ahi lasso' shown in Example 62 rather than this one. Monteverdi's written canto part includes notated ornaments which, while slightly obscuring 'x',[65] have the advantage of including its inversion.

The durum hexachord (used to illustrate hardness at the opening) has by now shifted through the naturale towards (if not quite into) the sweeter molle: modulation[66] is clearly being used for the illustration of the ideas in the poem. Such a use of tonality for structural purposes is not at all typical of Renaissance music: on the contrary, it points the way forwards to the major–minor tonal system which characterizes Baroque and later music. The seeds of the later tonality can be found in the hexachord system, for the balance between chords and tonalities on the sharp and flat sides of the key-note in the tonal system can be traced back to such a piece as this, since the naturale hexachord holds in balance the hard (sharp-side) and soft (flat-side) hexachords. Even the oft-mentioned (but never explained) subconscious feeling that many have about later tonal writing – that movement towards the sharp side is dynamic, and that movement towards the flat side is relaxing – has its roots in the hexachord system and its treatment in pieces like Monteverdi's *Cruda Amarilli*.[67]

At 'Ma de l'Aspido sordo' (see Example 64) – another passage roundly criticized by Artusi – it is not true that every voice is consonant with the tenore, though it is true that every voice is consonant if one omits the bass. In a sense, then, the procedure is a logical outcome of that shown in Example 61 (and of processes already seen in Wert and Pallavicino), where also it is the bass part that causes the dissonances: in both Examples 61 and 64 the classical rules are observed if one omits the bass. The basso of Example 64 provides a pedal against which the tenore and canto sing unprepared major sevenths which 'resolve' upwards by step. The dissonances are a means of illustrating the text in a more vivid fashion than Marenzio had done with his double-leading-note, or Pallavicino with his cross-relations and suspensions resolving in an unconventional place. Palisca[68] shows that the passage might be a decoration of a simpler harmonic framework: he shows, too, that Christoph Bernard in a manuscript treatise of as much as sixty years later refers to the use of the *subsemitonum* in Monteverdi's manner as an embellishing figure called a 'searching note'. Neither of these ideas helps us very much. (The solmization of the text may offer another angle: one cannot use it to account for the dissonant pedal, but a singer imagining the solmization sounds would certainly find it easier to pitch the dissonant note accurately). There is, however, yet another aspect to take into account: if the bass were omitted, the result would be a conventional pedal (in the tenore) with chords of G and C (the normal I and IV from the pedal note) revolving around it – a very common device in the Renaissance, particularly at the end of a piece. The C in the bass constitutes a second pedal; C and G are, indeed, the fundamental notes of the two hexachords around which most of the madrigal is built, and between which Monteverdi continually moves.[69]

The imitative parts in Example 64 twice drop down a fourth giving in outline the descending tetrachord 'x' as well as reversing the mutation up a fourth from durum to naturale which Monteverdi has already used. The next phrase capitalizes upon this point: 'E piu sorda' first occurs in G major, and is immediately repeated in C to the words 'e piu fera', with an unprepared dominant seventh on the first syllable of 'fera' – a feature also used by Pallavicino at precisely this place.[70] The transposition process is reversed in the following phrase 'e piu fugace', for the C-major opening moves to a close in G (see Example 65).

This phrase was one of those criticized by Artusi: the quickness of the note-values is given (by 'Luca') as a reason for the acceptance of the dissonances.[71] But, again, there is a more important reason for them. As Palisca points out,[72] the lower three voices and upper three voices make *prima prattica* sense when heard alone: this is another way of saying that the parts were probably written around the tenore rather than the bass. The three lower voices provide a choral 'continuo' for the upper two voices, giving the underlying chordal background.[73] The clashes made by the two upper voices against this three-voice 'continuo' help draw attention to the parallel thirds in canto and alto – and thus to the fact that 'x' is being used in diminution, though still in parallel thirds. We may go so far as to suggest that the trio texture so beloved of Baroque composers – one, indeed, that often occurs in the Villanella too[74] – is being employed in the extract quoted in Example 65: that is, the texture consists of two melodic upper voices with (choral) continuo support. The repetition of 'x' a fourth lower, naturally, helps to draw attention to the modulation down a fourth. Looked at in this way, the processes are no different from those in the initial setting of the words 'Cruda Amarilli', for

Example 64   Monteverdi: *Cruda Amarilli*

there, too, it is clear that the function of the three lower voices is to provide a 'continuo' which throws the parallel thirds version of 'x' into relief. One of the functions of dissonance in this piece has been to separate the harmonic activity from the melodic: the dissonances help to throw a spotlight onto the balance between tonal and melodic elements throughout the madrigal.

Monteverdi, who sets only the *prima parte* of the speech, ends with a double point for 'Poi che col dir t'offendo / I'mi morò tacendo'. All the previous settings had likewise set this passage to a double point. Monteverdi, still keen to integrate the material with the rest of the work, uses the descending tetrachord (in fact, a diminution of the opening 'x') for 'Poi che col dir' and – just as Marenzio does (see Example 53) – a rising version of the same line in crotchets for 'I'mi morò'. A dominant seventh, which is virtually identical to one in Pallavicino's setting (see 'Piu fera' in Example 57) occurs twice during this final couplet (see Example 66). The second crotchet beat of Example 66 probably results from Monteverdi's knowledge of Wert's use of the device of 'expanding' the consonant fourth idiom, shown in Example 48 and discussed above. The idea recurs in the final cadence, and has already been foreshadowed in the three-voice passage shown in Example 67: in this last Example, the elements of the first bar of Example 66 are present, but in invertible counterpoint. In other words, in Example 67, a different voice

Example 65

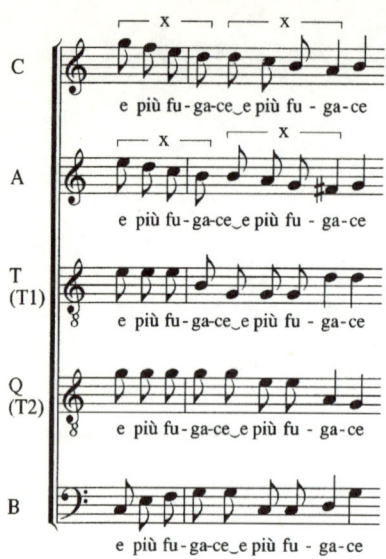

Monteverdi: *Cruda Amarilli*

Example 66   Monteverdi: *Cruda Amarilli*

serves as the bass from the voice which would be expected were the classical
rules of dissonance treatment to be observed: the expected sound occurs later

Example 67

Monteverdi: *Cruda Amarilli*

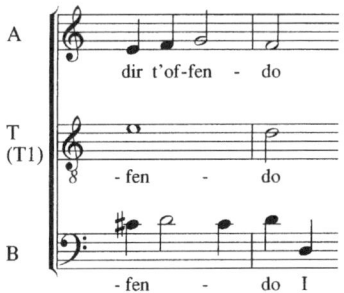

(in Example 66). The unusual dissonances in this later cadence are partially explained by having already occurred in a simpler form. Moreover, the device looks back to previous settings: it was just such an inversion of the expected ordering of voices that caused the dissonant effect at the start of Wert's setting, and Marenzio adopted a similar procedure. The alto G in Example 66, introduced as an unprepared fourth, is yet another development of the consonant fourth idiom, and one also foreshadowed in Wert's opening. Monteverdi twice inverts the 'I'mi morrò' phrase, so making it conform to Pallavicino's setting, and changing it to the original 'x' shape. More to the point, however, is his shift from naturale to durum in the final bars: the inevitable result of this shift of a fourth downwards when applied to a melodic figure of a rising fourth is a leap of a minor seventh downwards. This 'forbidden' interval is thus, in canto and basso, the logical result of the purely musical process of reversing the initial movement from durum up to naturale hexachords.[75] Melodic and tonal materials interact with one another here. Indeed, the seventh leaps help to draw attention to the process, just as the dissonances do elsewhere in the piece, and just as the major sixth leaps had done in Rore's *Mia benigna fortuna/Crudele acerba*. This is a more likely reason for its use than the desire to emulate Pallavicino's major seventh shown in the bass of Example 58.

We are now in a position to understand Monteverdi's musical logic more thoroughly. Much of the *prima parte* of the soliloquy derives, in one way or another, from the name Amarillis: it is cast in language full of words similar to, or suggested by, her name (amar, amaramente, sordo, sorda). This close organization is given a musical parallel in that much of the material also derives, in some way, from the opening words, set to 'x'; Monteverdi's setting thus constitutes an attempt to outdo Wert's rudimentary use of thematic integration for the same purpose. The processes, in both composers, demonstrate an awareness of the conceits and literary purpose behind Guarini's poem.

Monteverdi begins by adopting the phrase 'x', already known because of its association with the preceding settings: he sets it, however, in the key of G so as to make the hard hexachord more prominent than it had been in the preceding settings. The descending tetrachord is nicely balanced by being set twice to the opening words 'Cruda Amarilli', once in G, and once in C, so that the rising fourth of the tonal scheme balances the falling melodic one of 'x' (see Example 61). The process is then reversed at the following 'Che col nome ancora D'amar', for the bass takes over 'x' so that its line moves melodically from C down to G: meanwhile the upper parts modulate from C back to G. The result is an opening of perfect balance between tonal and melodic elements, and one in which the dissonances serve to draw attention to the division into two elements – the melodic tetrachords 'x' and the purely harmonic support. There is thus a clear musical process at work, as well as that involved with setting the word 'Cruda' more vividly than anyone had previously done.

At 'ahi lasso' (Example 62) the double vowel sound of the initial word is set as 'fa mi', 'mi fa', and the pitches la–mi and la–mi–re. This not only gives rise to pungent dissonances which vividly illustrate the anguish of the text, but a cross-relation occurs between F natural and F#: in this context F natural is 'fa' and F# is 'mi?'. This combination of 'mi' and 'fa' is a transposition, by one degree round the circle of fifths, of the combination of durum ('MI' = B natural) and molle ('*fa*' = B♭). There are two advantages in this. Firstly, the combination – particularly in view of the suspicion in which combinations of durum and molle were held – recalls the mnemonic rhyme *mi contra fa diabolus est in musica*: the combination of syllables in 'ahi' therefore in theory gives rise to 'diabolical' dissonance, though in this instance the result is not a tritone but a chromatic semitone. Secondly, the transposition makes the combination of F–E and F#–G a relationship that emphasizes on a small scale the C major/G major polarity of the overall scheme – a scheme that prefigures the tonic–dominant polarity of tonal music, even though Monteverdi (from the *tonal* point of view) ends on the dominant.

The shift from the naturale towards the molle hexachord (even though it is D minor rather than F major) at the repetition of the name Amarillis (see Example 63) takes the opening tonal shift a stage further round the hexachord system, though this time the two versions of the balancing melodic 'x' do not change in pitch. In Example 64 the two main centres are held in equilibrium – as a double pedal: of this double pedal, C fits the surrounding counterpoint less smoothly, for dissonances continually sound against it. G, the pedal that fits the other voices much more smoothly, does, indeed, take over as the ultimate tonic at the end of the piece. The imitative voices state 'x', though the filling-in of passing-notes has now been omitted, leaving only a leap of a fourth down. 'E più sorda, e più fera' omits the melodic element of the argument completely, simply moving up from G to C. As shown in Example

65, 'e più fugace' moves back from C to G (rising rather than falling, in fact), while the parallel thirds version of 'x' also makes the same point, in descending versions. Again the dissonances draw attention to the two fundamental elements, melodic activity and tonal direction, by making them cause friction rather than harmony with one another. The final point, of which a portion can be seen in Example 66, uses the melodic versions of 'x' in both ascending and descending forms, and the two are again held in a nice equilibrium: the overall balance is achieved when the final tonal progression down a fourth from C to G reverses the shift at the opening of the madrigal.

One further objection of Artusi's must be mentioned here: an objection made in reply to 'l'Ottuso' rather than in the 1600 discourse. Monteverdi, he says, breaks modal purity by writing more cadences in the twelfth mode than in the seventh – or, to put it in modern terms, he writes a piece ostensibly in G, but cadences more frequently on C. Monteverdi would not wish to deny this. In Artusi's view, to cadence more frequently on C than on G in a mixolydian piece was to mix up the modes: Artusi would have held to the *prima prattica* view that each mode had its own particular quality and was suited to a certain type of expression.[76] Giulio Cesare, replying in his glosses to his brother's letter, quite correctly draws attention to the practice of using mixed modes.[77] He does not point out that this practice is the exception rather than the rule among composers, but he does imply that Artusi ought to have been aware of this and – by implication – ought to have directed his criticisms elsewhere. Another argument might have been that, although there was general agreement about what each mode expressed, the matter was subjective, and occasionally theorists disagreed on the matter: more persuasive might have been the argument that for years pieces in the phrygian mode had cadenced more often on A than on E; or that the lydian mode, by the large-scale inclusion of B♭s, had ceased to be modally pure and turned into ionian transposed. Moreover, Monteverdi himself might have shown how he mirrors the harshness of Amarillis by using the durum hexachord, and how the hexachords soften gradually as her name is repeated: and he might very well have indicated that the clashing of tonalities (and thus of semitones) could be thought of as resulting from a conflict between hardness and softness.

Conservative theorists may lament the loss of classical balance in the music of this madrigal;[78] but there is no denying that a completely new type of balance has taken its place – and, as we know from our studies of later music, one which has within itself the seeds of considerable development. The procedures later used by Beethoven inevitably spring to mind – as they did to Alfred Einstein when he treated the same madrigal in comparison with Marenzio's and Pallavicino's settings. Einstein's conclusion is

> But Monteverdi carries the procedures of his colleagues to such extremes that stylistic unity is threatened. The urge to outdo his predecessors sweeps him onwards, just as it does Beethoven when he measures himself against Haydn and

Mozart, except that Monteverdi lacks Beethoven's exuberance. There is something demonic in him, something bent on destruction; he is a man of destiny in the history of music, in an even more fatal sense than Beethoven is.[79]

This overstates the case somewhat, for such was not Monteverdi's aim at all. He was by no means the first Italian madrigalist to attempt to outdo the composers who had previously set the text he chose. As Artusi's dialogue puts it:

> Luca . . . everyone is occupied with new things; musicians too should expand their art, for making all compositions after one fashion sickens and disgusts the ear.
> Vario . . . I do not deny that discovering new things is not merely good but necessary.[80]

These new things were sought in order to set texts ever more faithfully. As we have seen, it had been an unfailing quest in the Renaissance to communicate feelings vividly to the listener. Those who read about the music of classical Greece tried to recover its supposedly marvellous effects; the Council of Trent made provision for the careful setting of texts in church music so that the divine message should be the more clearly communicated; and the interest in Humanism focused attention on man and his emotions. It is scarcely to be wondered at that both Artusi and the Monteverdi camp made reference back to classical authors – indeed, it had been part of the human mentality since the Middle Ages to do so, whether writing music or theoretical treatises. It was considered right to improve upon any borrowed material: and we have seen how Marenzio went beyond Wert in his setting of *Cruda Amarilli* by increasing the amount of chromaticism and the amount of dissonance, and how Pallavicino, trying to outdo Marenzio and yet remain – as far as one can judge his intentions – within the *prima prattica*, resorted to a high density of dissonance: even so, he had on occasions to go beyond the rules laid down for the strict style. Monteverdi, if he was to outdo this setting which pushed the *prima prattica* style to the absolute limit (and occasionally beyond), was bound to forge a new style.

The cry 'The words are mistress of the harmony'[81] became a well-known slogan of the new music. Indeed, it was the primacy of the text that gave rise to most of the advances in musical language during the late Renaissance. Passionate music was needed to express passionate texts: cruel dissonance illustrated cruelty. Artusi did not object to dissonance, but he did want dissonances to be treated 'so that they seem properly to lose some of their harshness and acquire sweetness'.[82] A treatment that tempered and sweetened the cruelty of Amarillis would have failed to express adequately the text we have been considering; and one imagines that Monteverdi would have made this criticism of Pallavicino's setting. Monteverdi could, and did, sweeten dissonance and use the *prima prattica* style when the words did not require the sharpness of dissonance for the full realization of the ideas in the text.

The rift between the classical Renaissance style and that of the *avant-garde* madrigal was emphasized by Artusi in a way that had not previously obtained to quite the same extent.[83] Artusi was lucky in that, like all traditional theorists, he had a ready-made theoretical language – a jargon – with which to elucidate his own point of view; and he does this with some skill. Monteverdi may well, in his early life, not have known where his writing would lead him, and neither he nor his brother yet had any firm foundation of theoretical principles for the new style from which they could argue. In particular, major/minor tonality had not yet taken over from the modes, though the process was under way; and the principles governing tonality had yet to be established. We can see, by hindsight, that the new texture of trio sonata or of solo and continuo led towards Baroque practice. Monteverdi cannot have foreseen this in the closing years of the sixteenth century. If, as is likely, his writing was mainly intuitive, he may not even have recognized the interplay between tonal shifts and melodic outlines which provides *Cruda Amarilli* with a sense of balance; a balance that, while being undeniably present, is yet utterly different from that found in the great masters of the *prima prattica*.

We are left with the question, 'Why Monteverdi?' Gesualdo, Marenzio, and Luzzaschi would surely have served Artusi's purpose just as well. Gesualdo, as one of a group of nobleman composers, held a privileged position. He had no need to satisfy patrons, or anything other than his own whims. Pallavicino only rarely treats his suspensions other than correctly: Marenzio was an absolute master of counterpoint in the Renaissance style, though one who could use quite extreme chromaticism. Like many chromatic composers, however, only on very rare occasions does he at the same time use unconventional treatments of dissonance. Both he and Wert – the latter another very fine contrapuntist, as well as a writer of *avant-garde* madrigals – were revered in their time: both were already dead when Artusi's first discourse appeared:[84] both, in fact, came in for criticism in Artusi's reply to 'l'Ottuso'. In both, the ideals and techniques of the Renaissance were still alive, though they may be considerably stretched at times, particularly in Pallavicino's setting: Wert's piece, which seems to have been intended for a stage production, did not break very much new ground. It can scarcely be Monteverdi's youthfulness that caused him to be singled out; the battle is not really one of the generations, *pace* Palisca.[85] There is a newness about Monteverdi which is quite outside the newness which stretched the great Renaissance traditions but yet remained, basically, Renaissance. In Monteverdi, dissonance helps to illustrate the text; but it also helps the mind to understand the new structural logic. There is counterpoint; but rather than the equality of all the voices Monteverdi establishes a situation in which the performers at times function in two groups – solo and 'continuo'. The tonal scheme, which (despite Artusi's criticism of it) is one of the more conservative elements, interacts with the melodic ideas. There is balance; but it is certainly not of the type that stems from careful handling of dissonance, establishing of an equilibrium between rising and falling lines, and restraint in the choice of note-values. Artusi may not have liked what he heard – he may even have feared it; certainly he did not understand it. But he was aware that here was something that had crossed the Rubicon, that could no longer fit into his theoretical notions.[86]

Notes

1. Palisca 1968. Other controversies of the time are discussed in Tomlinson 1987, pp. 18 and 22–30.
2. Palisca 1968, p. 134. See also Chater 1981, p. 124.
3. Strunk 1950, p. 400.
4. See Chater 1981, p. 124.
5. One imagines that he had not encountered *Ohimè, se tanto amate*, discussed in Chapter 1, for surely he would have found much to criticize there.
6. Gesualdo spent much time in Ferrara, and seems to have written his fourth and fifth books there in the 1590s. See Watkins 1973, pp. 149, 167f.
7. Meier 1974 maintains that the important Renaissance treatises 'did not invariably lag behind compositional practice ... the writers were usually very much in touch with the latest styles, either as composers or performers or both' (quoted from Perkins 1978, p. 136). Berger 1976 takes the traditional view that most theorists are bound to be behind the times.
8. *Prima* and *seconda prattica* are used here as convenient labels, even though the terms had not been coined when Artusi was writing his 1600 discourse.
9. Not all the editions include this Preface.
10. Reproduced in Rowen 1979, p. 153ff; and Strunk 1950, p. 405ff.
11. Strunk 1950, p. 407.
12. Strunk 1950, p. 408. Rore is usually called 'Cipriano'. Artusi does make some criticism of Rore in Artusi 1603.
13. Strunk 1950, p. 409.
14. As Selfridge-Field 1990, p. 54. says, 'This divergence of opinion about licence is fundamental to the metamorphosis of the Italian Renaissance into the Italian Baroque'.
15. Strunk 1950, p. 402.
16. Palisca 1968, p. 150, notes that the first use of the term *seconda prattica* is in the correspondence between 'L'Ottuso' and Artusi which followed the latter's attack on the new music.
17. Palisca 1968, p. 150: Palisca discusses the identity of 'L'Ottuso Academico' on pp. 142f.
18. Maniates 1979, *passim*. The large amount of excellent sixteenth-century music in the *prima prattica* style makes one question Maniates' designation of the period – largely on the basis of the Italian madrigal alone – as 'Mannerist'.
19. Strunk 1950, p. 407.
20. Strunk 1950, p. 396.
21. Ibid.
22. Strunk 1950, pp. 400f. Cf. also p. 403: 'And it is truly marvellous that the ancients, with their great industry and diligence, have taught the way, not to make consonant those intervals which nature herself created dissonant, but so to use them that they seem properly to lose some of their harshness and to acquire

sweetness. But when, by a departure from the manner taught by the ancients, they are used and taken absolutely, they cannot have a good effect'.

23. Strunk 1950, p. 379.
24. Strunk 1950, p. 407.
25. The later settings need not detain us. Sigismondo d'India's and Paolo Petti's settings are mentioned below, and the monody version (which Willetts 1962, pp. 329ff, tentatively suggests is in the hand of Walter Porter) in British Library Additional 31440 uses only the opening phrase of the Wert–Marenzio–Pallavicino–Monteverdi settings. Some obvious rhythmic cross-references between the Wert, Marenzio, Pallavicino and Monteverdi settings help to prove that each composer is in some way indebted to his predecessor. In the *prima parte*, both Marenzio and Monteverdi use a similar rhythm in homophony at 'che col nome ancora'; all four use similar rhythms in homophony for 'Amarilli del candido ligustro Più candida e più bella' (though Monteverdi is individual in his setting of 'Amarilli'); and Pallavicino and Marenzio use the same rhythmic pattern for an imitative point at 'Poiche col dir t'offendo'. In the *Seconda parte* (only partially set by Wert, and not set by Monteverdi), Pallavicino and Marenzio both write homophonic passages in similar rhythms at the following places: 'Si spesso il tuo bel nome Di risonare insegno'; 'E mormorando'; 'Parlera nel mio volto la pietade'; and 'E, se fia muta ogn'altra'. These copyings are, however, not 'emulative' in that they do not attempt to improve upon or develop the material of the model (the exception to this is noted below).
    There is a setting by Monte (see Mann 1983, p. 60): Mann states that Monte was not involved in emulation (see ibid, p. 103).
26. See Maniates 1979, p. 77.
27. The amar–Amarillis pun is picked up nicely by Marenzio in *Comè dolce il gioire* (1595) – also a setting of part of Guarini's *Il pastor fido*: at the words 'amarissima Amarilli' the bitter harmony – an augmented triad – occurs during the name 'Amarilli' rather than on the word 'amar' ('bitter').
28. See Haar 1986, p. 133. See also the discussion of the various styles of the madrigal earlier in the century in Haar 1986, pp. 116 and 118.
29. Arnold 1983.
30. Taken from James Chater's edition of the Marenzio setting. Monte's *O d'aspido* is a corrupt text of *Cruda Amarilli* (see Mann 1983, p. 381).
31. See MacClintock 1966, pp. 127 and 178; also Chater 1975. The difficulties over the projected performance are treated in Fenlon 1980, Chapter 4.
32. Strunk 1950, p. 379.
33. Strunk 1950, p. 403.
34. Strunk 1950, p. 401.
35. See bar 29 of the edition by Carol MacClintock and Melvin Bernstein, *CMM* 24, no. 12.
36. See pp. 138–40 above.
37. Strunk 1950, p. 401.
38. Marenzio and Pallavicino set more of the poem than this.
39. At bar 21 of the *seconda parte*.
40. See Berger 1987, p. 152.
41. A third example occurs later, in the *prima parte*, at 'aspido sordo'. One can also find double-leading-notes in Reggio's *O beata colei*, bar 36; Coma, *Come tutto m'ardete* (bar 39 – there is no solmization here); Monte, *Per aspre horride*, bar 23. For an instance of a double-leading-note being possible (because of its use of

solmization syllables) yet evidently not being intended, see the opening of Verdelot's *Italia mia*.

42. Strunk 1950, p. 383: Caccini was not the first to use the shape, as I have pointed out above.

43. We have encountered a similar instance at the start of the *seconda parte* of Rore's *Mia benigna/Crudele acerba* (see above).

44. As Chater 1981, (p. 125) says, '. . . the imitation of the meaning of the words becomes discretionary instead of obligatory. This is well illustrated in . . . *Cruda Amarilli*, where musical imitation is admitted only when it reinforces the central mood of pathos. This inevitably means that such poetic images as "white jasmine" in the *prima parte*, or the "valleys", "hills", "streams", and "woods" in the *seconda parte*, receive little or no attention'.

45. Transposition of this type is not peculiar to Marenzio, being found in several other composers.

46. See Monteath 1980.

47. With the few exceptions noted below.

48. The position of Pallavicino as a member of either the *prima* or *seconda prattica* camp is mentioned briefly in Fenlon 1980, p. 143. Incidentally, the second C♯ in the tenore part of Example 56 might illustrate the way in which solmization could act as an indicator of accidentals and their cancellation. Example 56 could be compared with Example 51. If one argues that the third note of the quinto in Example 51 has to be C natural (cancelling the sharp added two notes earlier) because the syllables '– so la –' indicate *sol* and FA (as well as ut), then the second C in Example 56 should also be C natural, paralleling '– so! a –' (of 'lasso! amaramente'). The additional sharp in Example 56 guards against the singer changing back to C natural on account of solmization (or on account of the temptation to sing a perfect fourth rather than a diminished one between that note and the following F). In Example 51 the second C would in any case normally revert to its natural form, since the line continues to descend afterwards.

49. See Palisca 1968, p. 155: and Chater 1981, p. 124f.

50. The II–I cadences are sometimes called *semiperfectae*: see Meier 1974, p. 80.

51. Artusi recommended sustaining the dissonant note over to the point of suspension: see the discussion in Palisca 1968, pp. 153f. He cannot, however, have been unaware that as strict a *prima prattica* technician as Palestrina sometimes sounds a note again at the point of dissonance.

52. As mentioned above, it is known that Monteverdi did not have a very high opinion of Pallavicino (see Monteath 1980), and was not so likely to have chosen him as a model. The relationship between Wert and Monteverdi is treated in MacClintock 1966, p. 228, and Einstein 1949, p. 845.

53. See Palisca 1968, pp. 139f.

54. Palisca 1968, p. 135.

55. Unprepared and unresolved dissonances are also found in *Ohimè, se tanto* (1603) discussed above – not to mention the unresolved dissonances to be found in earlier Renaissance music like Morales's *O sacrum convivium* (dissonances which Palestrina 'corrected' in his Parody mass based on Morales's material).

56. Strunk 1950, pp. 396f.

57. See Burke 1974, especially p. 194. 'L'Ottuso', in his correspondence with Artusi, maintains that 'there are also those who esteem invention more than imitation' (see Palisca 1968, p. 157: also Strunk 1950, p. 400).

58. And the six-voice *O vos omnes*, perhaps.

59. Monteverdi does, nevertheless, occasionally write chromatic music; *Vattene pur crudel* (1592) and *Piagn'e sospira* (1603) are good examples.

60. Compare the setting of 'Ahi' in Monteverdi's *Si ch'io vorrei morire* (1603); and also the first 'Ahi' of Messaggiera in Act II of *l'Orfeo*.

61. Entries on a dissonance that cannot be explained in hexachord terms are found in *Ohime se tanto*, and in Orfeo's lament in Act V of Monteverdi's opera.

62. This process is discussed in Chapter 1.

63. We have already seen that dissonances which could not be explained by solmization were also written.

64. Strunk 1950, p. 403. This was not the first time that Monteverdi had used the tritone: *Luci serene e chiare* (1603) has one at 'Si strugg'e'; and *Ohimè, se tanto amate* (1603) marks an E natural at a cantus entry above a bass B♭ just after the opening to ensure that the singer does not attempt to avoid the tritone.

65. Though it is still clearly audible as the skeleton background, especially since it follows a plain statement at the same pitch.

66. 'Modulation' in the modern sense: see Bent 1984, footnote 26.

67. In view of the modern treatments of the seventh already noted, the secondary seventh (of a crotchet's length) on the first syllable of 'ligustro' is relatively mild: a similar occurrence is in Pallavicino's setting, at 'fugace'. Monteverdi ends the *seconda parte* of *Anima mia perdona* (1603) with a cadence that includes an unprepared dominant seventh: Artusi criticized this in his 1600 discourse: this piece must therefore also have been available in manuscript copies for some years before publication.

68. Palisca 1968, pp. 138f.

69. Another double pedal causing dissonances is found in Monteverdi's *Anima mia, perdona*, at 'non tuoi tormenti'.

70. 'L'Ottuso's' defence of the chord is discussed above.

71. Strunk 1950, p. 401.

72. Palisca 1968, p. 141.

73. The trio texture becomes even more obvious at the beginning of the next book, at the opening of the *Lament of Arianna*.

74. Newcomb 1980, p. 74.

75. There are melodic sevenths also in *Voi pur da me partite* (1603) at 'gioite e voi': and they are relatively frequent in *Ohimè se tanto* (1603).

76. See the discussion in Palisca 1968, p. 151.

77. Strunk 1950, pp. 411f.

78. As Levy 1975 says (p. 236), 'few arts at any time . . . have advanced by respecting the "rules"'.

79. Einstein 1949, p. 853.

80. Strunk 1950, p. 400.

81. *Ut oratio sit Domina Harmoniae* is therefore used as the sub-title for this section of the book.

82. Strunk 1950, p. 403.

83. Palisca points out that struggles between theorists of the old and new styles go back to Vicentino and Lusitano in 1551. See Palisca 1968, p. 134.

84. Arnold 1963 (p. 104) maintains that Wert's madrigals had ceased to be popular by 1600.

85. Palisca 1968, p. 133.

86. Some later imitations of the *Cruda Amarilli* material deserve brief notice. Sigismondo d'India's setting of the poem (in his first book of five-voice madrigals, 1610) does not belong within the tradition of parodied melodic

material with which we have been mostly concerned. The five-voice setting by Paolo Petti (British Library Add MS 31412 fol. 32, olim 59r) also belongs outside this tradition. The monodic setting, possibly by Walter Porter (British Library Add MS 31440 fol. 33v), opens with a close approximation to Monteverdi's first two phrases. Wilbye's three-voice *Ah, cruel Amarillis* (*Second Book of Madrigals*, 1609) uses the descending tetrachord 'x' with considerable frequency, but without any of the 'shock tactics' employed by the Italians. Wilbye has shown his knowledge of the tradition by using the material; yet the poem is only very loosely related to the Italian (*pace* the remarks in Brown 1974, p. 33, and Einstein 1944, p. 72f), and does not necessitate such extreme treatments as Monteverdi and his forebears used. One other composer seems to have been concerned to show his awareness of the Italian parody tradition as it concerned *Cruda Amarilli*; Philips, in making his keyboard version of Caccini's *Amarilli* (*FWVB* 82: the title is *Amarilli di Julio Romano*) filled in Caccini's downward leaps of a fourth at the opening so that the melodic phrase 'x' resulted. Indeed, we may well reflect on the similarity of the incipit of Caccini's *Amarilli* with Monteverdi's passage quoted in Example 65. Frescobaldi, in *Se la doglia e'l martire* seems to have learned from Monteverdi: see also the opening of *Se lontano voi sete*.

5 Sorrow and Secularism

Games with hexachords are particularly a mark of secular music written in Italy in the period covered by this book; brilliant witticisms of the kind described above are found much more rarely in church music: indeed, they are rather out of place there, even though not entirely absent. The matching of solmization syllables to sounds in the text is rarer outside Italy (indeed, it is Italian and Latin words that most readily match the hexachord sounds, though the hexachord joke at the start of Dowland's 'Me, me, and none but me' is one of the exceptions), and such examples as do occur tend to be isolated ones: the *fa* (B♭) chord at 'walk–' in Weelkes's *Three Virgin Nymphs were walking all alone*, the fa–mi at 'Mariae' in the tenor of Byrd's *Ave verum corpus*, the sudden F-major chord at 'sweet' in Dowland's *An heart that's broken and contrite*, and the opening of Morley's *Laboravi in gemitu meo* are all single, isolated examples. The first part of this chapter, however, examines a set of interconnected English sacred pieces whose structure, in one case, is very clearly influenced by the solmization sounds that mirror part of its text.

Instrumental music does not use solmization syllables, though a knowledge of them helps in the understanding of *inganno*, as I have shown above. But instrumental pieces using the hexachord as their basis can be found, and a number of English examples are considered in the second section of this chapter.

Tallis and the Lamentation style

This section will deal with three closely-related penitential works by Thomas Tallis: they are two Lamentation settings (*Incipit lamentatio Ieremiae prophetae*, which, following the Tudor Church Music edition, I shall refer to as 'Lamentations I', and *De lamentatione Ieremiae prophetae*, which I shall refer to as 'Lamentations II'); and the Lenten motet *In ieiunio et fletu*. All three are

181

specifically Catholic pieces, and they date from the last years of Tallis's life, when Elizabeth was on the throne of England and the Catholic liturgy was officially banned. All three bear certain similarities as to style and content.

The Lamentations of Jeremiah form part of the liturgy of Holy Week, and are sung at the three Nocturns of Matins on Maundy Thursday, Good Friday, and Holy Saturday. Tallis's Lamentations, however, do not fit into the liturgical pattern. The two sets together make up one single reading – the first *Lectio* of the first Nocturn of Matins on Maundy Thursday. But clearly Tallis's two Lamentations are not meant to be sung together as that *Lectio*, for the refrain *Jerusalem, Jerusalem . . .* would be redundant after Lamentations I if sung liturgically, the two sets are incompatible because their modes are very different, and there are changes in the text – some of them small, but one of them involving the omission of the evoctive phrase *Viae Syon lugent* ('The ways of Sion do mourn').[1] It seems most likely that Tallis wrote these pieces as devotional music to be used outside the liturgy, perhaps even in the homes of Catholics.[2] If that is so – and it seems quite likely that it is so – then it follows that the texts were chosen for their appropriateness to that Catholic community: the texts must have sounded 'like an almost literal description of the ruin which had befallen the ancient church'.[3] The omission of 'The ways of Sion do mourn' is significant: by avoiding association of the text with Sion, Tallis makes it easier for his contemporaries to see the pieces as referring to the troubles of the sixteenth-century English Catholics attempting to worship in a way that was banned by the Protestant authorities: Catholic worship – even the possession of Catholic books – could lead to the most dire penalties. This applies no less to *In ieiunio et fletu* (a Respond for the First Sunday in Lent, but also part of a lesson at the Ash Wednesday Mass), which appeared in the *Cantiones Sacrae* published jointly by Byrd and Tallis in 1575.

Lamentations, as used in the liturgy, include settings of the Hebrew letters that initiate the verses; and the Lamentations for each Nocturn are framed by material not taken from Jeremiah. They begin with an invocation ('Here begins the Lamentation of the prophet Jeremiah') and end with an exhortation to the faithful ('Jerusalem, Jerusalem, turn again to the Lord your God'). Tallis, though apparently not intending his music for the liturgy, nevertheless follows this pattern. The remainder of Lamentations I is:

> Aleph. Quomodo sedet sola civitas plena populo? Facta est quasi vidua domina gentium: princeps provinciarum facta est sub tributo.
> Beth. Plorans ploravit in nocte, et lacrimae eius in maxillis eius: non est qui consoletur eam ex omnibus caris eius. Omnes amici eius speverunt eam, et facti sunt ei inimici.
> Jerusalem, Jerusalem . . .

> (Aleph. How solitary lies the city, that was once so full of people! she has become as a widow, who was once great among the nations! she that was a princess among the provinces, how is she put to forced labour!

Beth. She weeps bitterly in the night, and her tears run down her cheeks: among all her lovers she has none to comfort her: all her friends have dealt treacherously with her, and have become her enemies.

Jerusalem, Jerusalem . . .)   (Lamentations 1, 1–2)

Lamentations II takes up Chapter 1 of the Lamentations of Jeremiah from the point where Lamentations I leaves off:

Gimel. Migravit Iuda propter afflictionem ac multitudinem servitutis: habitavit inter gentes, nec invenit requiem.

Daleth. Omnes persecutores eius apprehenderunt eam inter angustias: luget eo quod non sunt qui veniant ad solemnitatem. Omnes portae eius destructae, sacerdotes eius gementes, virgines eius squalidae, et ipsa oppresa amaritudine.

Heth.[4] Facti sunt hostes eius in capite, inimici illis locupletati sunt: quia Dominus locutus est super eam propter multitudinem iniquitatum eius. Parvuli eius ducti sunt captivi ante faciem tribulantis.

Jerusalem, Jerusalem . . .

(Gimel. Judah has gone into exile and endless servitude because of affliction: she dwells among the heathen, finding no rest.

Daleth. All her persecutors fell upon her in her sore straits: there is mourning, for none attends her solemn feasts: all her gates are destroyed, her priests sigh, her virgins are afflicted, and she is treated cruelly.

Heth. Her adversaries have become her masters, and her enemies prosper; for the Lord has punished her because of the great number of her misdeeds: her children have gone into captivity, driven away by the enemy.

Jerusalem, Jerusalem . . .)   (Lamentations 1, 3–5)

Of Tallis's two sets of Lamentations, one – *Incipit lamentatio Ieremiae prophetae* – exhibits strong signs of being composed with solmization syllables in mind. The entry of the first voice on B (with the second entry following on E) is a sure indicator of phrygian intent (see Example 68). As mentioned above, the phrygian is a highly appropriate mode for penitential music. The entry on B is, however, the only one on that note in the whole of the opening section. The line is cast in the hard hexachord, and for some time carefully follows the solmization syllables suggested by the text: MI MI MI LA re FA MI mirror the first seven syllables, for instance. The setting of the opening word and the subsequent leap up a fourth to LA alert the performer to the hexachord basis of Tallis's music: performers who realize this are the more likely to be aware of the subsequent development of the argument.

The second voice enters on E: by being in imitation this line also mirrors the hexachord syllables, but it does so in the natural hexachord, so causing a move in a flatwards direction (see Example 68). Tallis could have countered this flatwards tendency by bringing the following (third) voice in on B, but he does not do so. The third entry is, in fact, on A, confirming the flatwards tendency, though the leap of a fifth rather than a fourth ensures that only the first three syllables of the text are set in the *molle* hexachord.[5] Further entries are on E and A, so it is hardly surprising that the opening section ends on a chord of A; phrygian pieces had often cadenced on A, but here the feeling is

Example 68   Tallis: *Lamentations I*

much more aeolian than phrygian. Indeed, despite the opening suggestion of the phrygian mode, there have been no phrygian cadences – and no cadences on E – in this opening section.

   The opening discussed above contrasts markedly with that of Tallis's other Lamentation set, *De lamentatione Ieremiae prophetae*. This is cast in G dorian, a mode that in its pure form contains E natural, but which can also use E♭ under certain conditions. Tallis is at pains to maintain the modal purity of his opening by using E natural throughout the first section: indeed, E♭ appears only once in that section (see Example 69).

Example 69   Tallis: *Lamentations II*

The opening point is largely constructed without reference to solmization syllables (there is a little correlation between pitches and hexachord sounds, but one feels that it is less deliberate than in the other setting). The entries on G and D – the final and fifth of G dorian – carefully emphasize the mode, but the entry of two voices on A strengthens the E natural (especially as the imitative point moves up by step from the root to the fifth). The following setting of the Hebrew letter *Gimel* contrasts with the foregoing purely modal emphasis by using E flat and avoiding E natural completely (see Example 70). Tallis thus colours the setting of the Hebrew letter quite differently from the introductory announcement. The letter becomes like an illuminated capital in a manuscript, set off from the rest of the text by its colourful treatment.

This, indeed, is also the case in *Incipit lamentatio. . . .* In this set the first Hebrew letter is *Aleph*. As one might expect in view of the solmization of the opening of Lamentations I, the 'ah' vowel of this word is carefully matched to hexachord sounds – at first LA rather than fa (see Example 71). The first two entries are on E and A, a combination set up by the preceding cadence on A. Tallis does not confine himself to LA, but also sets *Aleph* as fa; this move from LA to fa results in the phrygian second (E–F) in the uppermost part, a part whose opening line in this section begins firmly in the E-phrygian mode even if it veers towards aeolian at its end.[6] The entries on A, however, contradict E phrygian by dint of following the rise of a semitone accurately:[7] the B♭ (*fa*) that results is as far from E phrygian as can possibly be, and throughout the *Aleph* section B♭s alternate with cadences on A as if the music is in A phrygian. The E phrygian of the opening has moved to A phrygian under the influence of the solmization of *Aleph*, the flatwards tendency of the opening being carried a stage farther.

To move from E phrygian to A phrygian must perforce mean moving from B natural to B♭; and it is a discussion between the two aspects of B that lies behind the beginning of Tallis's setting of the Lamentation text itself (*Quomodo sedet sola civitas plena populo? Facta est quasi vidua domina gentium: princeps provinciarum facta est sub tributo*). The word *sola* in this passage – a word that very often attracted solmization among composers in Italy at that time – is not set to the obvious hexachord syllables;[8] E phrygian is not actually in evidence at all, despite the occurrence of the first real cadence on E (at 'gentium'): and the section ends with a D-major chord that acts as a half-close in G minor.

The next Hebrew letter, *Beth*, is – like the first – set apart from the surrounding music by its colouring. It begins in F – a key not in any way prepared – and cadences in B♭. The long F in the topmost part makes an important point: it is a prolongation of the phrygian second of the 'home' tonality. The F major that provides this large-scale phrygian relationship is composed-out by using an imitative double-subject in parallel thirds which rises up through a fourth and then falls back through the same interval: the imitative voices, taken as pairs, between them delineate the *molle* hexachord (F–D) with the utmost clarity (see Example 72).

Example 70

Example 71   Tallis: *Lamentations I*

The Bb cadence at the end of *Beth* marks the farthest point of tonal travel in the work: Bb is not at this stage governed by solmization, though the following section, *Plorans ploravit in nocte*, begins on Bb, and by solmizing the 'ah' vowels of the first two words as fa and *fa* – and the flatter *fa* and *fa* (Bb and Eb) in the bass – produces a line that is quite similar to that used in imitation

Example 72 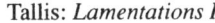 Tallis: *Lamentations I*

Example 73   Tallis: *Lamentations I*

at the opening of the piece (see Example 73). This, whether the similarity was
created consciously or not, produces a fascinating link between the tonal B♭ at
Plorans ploravit and the far distant E phrygian of *Incipit lamentatio* (compare
Example 68).

De Lamentatione . . . does not go to such extremes, remaining much more
closely within its chosen G dorian modality: it does, however, include a
discussion between E natural and E♭ that reaches a point where, in order to
emphasize E♭ strongly, Tallis sets the Hebrew word *Heth*[9] in a clear C minor.
It is in the Lenten motet *In ieiunio et fletu* – a piece cast in a musical language
very similar to that of *Incipit lamentatio* . . . – that the procedures of the
Lamentations I set are most closely echoed.[10] Here is a piece that also
modulates around the tonal universe in order to illustrate the profound
penitence and grief of the text. This text is:

> In ieiunio et fletu orabant sacerdotes, Parce, Domine, parce populo tuo, et ne des
> hereditatem tuam in perditionem: inter vestibulum et altare plorabant sacerdotes,
> dicentes, parce populo tuo.

> (Sighing and weeping the priests pray: Spare thy people, Lord, and do not cast your
> heritage into perdition. Between the porch and the altar the priests cry, saying:
> Spare thy people.) [from Joel 2, 17]

Phrygian relationships are at the heart of this motet: the E♭ opening moves to
a cadence on D before returning; a short A♭ section cadences in G; at *parce
Domine* (see Example 74) these two phrygian progressions are repeated on a

Example 74   Tallis: *In ieiunio et fletu*

smaller scale, with a B♭–A phrygian cadence that leads on to a setting of *parce populo tuo, et ne des hereditatem tuam* that juxtaposes E and F. The central *Inter vestibulum et altare plorabant sacerdotes dicentes ...* prolongs A♭ – a somewhat extreme area to English ears at this time: the passage forms a striking parallel to the setting of *Plorans ploravit* in Lamentations I not only because of its prolongation of the flat area, but also because both sections use a technique favoured by Englishmen in which all the voices except one move homophonically, shadowing a single voice that is detached by being 'out of phase' with the rest, though closely related to it in outline and rhythm. A♭ cadences on G, furthering the phrygian relationship. At *parce populo tuo* a B♭ entry in the upper voice is followed by an A entry in the same voice, forming a parallel to the echoing of the opening of Lamentations I at *Plorans ploravit in nocte*. *In ieiunio et fletu* finally cadences on G as if the piece had been in G aeolian.

Such a concentration of phrygian elements also informs Lamentations I, for the B♭ of *Plorans ploravit* eventually cadences on F, the phrygian second above the main tonic. *Non est qui consoletur eam* then begins to reintroduce the B naturals which – if E phrygian is ever to be regained – must replace the now strong B♭s. B♭s remain strong until the F cadence at *inimici* (with *fa* – B♭ – rather than the closer solmization that would have resulted from using B natural). This cadence is in a phrygian relationship with the home tonic. The final passage, *Jerusalem, Jerusalem, convertere ad Dominum Deum tuum*, must replace B♭ with B natural and return to E phrygian; and this it does, starting in F (with the use of only two B♭s) and moving to A before cadencing several times in E. The return of B natural is nowhere more obvious than in the unusual final cadence, where the topmost voice uses the highest note of the whole piece – a B natural (see Example 75).[11]

Example 75   Tallis: *Lamentations I*

The whole *Jerusalem* section has the phrygian relationship writ large, in a way similar to that of *In ieiunio et fletu*.

Lamentations I provides an English parallel to Monteverdi's *Cruda Amarilli*, discussed above. In both there is a 'hard' opening that gives way to flatter music before returning to the point of departure; both are in some way the result of solmization – but there the comparison ends. Tallis considers the flat areas to be 'doleful', while Monteverdi – at least, in *Cruda Amarilli* – considers them 'sweet'. The two approaches nicely illustrate the difficulty which results from the fact that flats had two possible interpretations in the sixteenth and early seventeenth centuries.

Hexachord Games

Composers as different as Palestrina and Avery Burton used the hexachord to provide the basic melodic material of masses: and English composers in particular seem to have regarded the writing of fantasias on certain kinds of *cantus firmus* as part of their technical preparation as composers, or as a means of proving their worth. Thus we find many settings of the *In nomine* –

a long-note *cantus firmus* derived from the Benedictus of John Taverner's mass *Gloria tibi Trinitas* – stretching from Taverner's time as far as Purcell. *In nomine* fantasias were a particular mark of English instrumental music, and the plainsong *Miserere* (a compline antiphon) was also popular. Though there are fewer examples of fantasias based on the hexachord, Englishmen also turned to the *Ut, re, mi, fa, sol, la* shape for a scaffolding on which to build as skilfully-contrived a contrapuntal edifice as they could manage.

Among the Englishmen we must include the two Alfonso Ferraboscos, father and son; though of Italian extraction, they worked in England and were highly regarded by native English composers. Alfonso Ferrabosco I did much to introduce the style of the Italian madrigal – and the style of Lasso – to England, and was greatly admired for his 'deep skill':[12] he vied with William Byrd by exchanging settings of a *cantus firmus*, settings made 'in a virtuous contention in love betwixt themselves'.[13] Such a friendly rivalry shows the importance attached by composers to practising their skill in writing against a *cantus firmus*. But there is a factor to consider beyond the understandable honing of a composer's contrapuntal art: with the reformation in England, many of the texts which had previously provided opportunities for writing music against a *cantus firmus* had vanished from the liturgy. Protestantism no longer called for intricate polyphonic music in church, and the plainsong of the old liturgy was no longer part of the normal services. The transference to instrumental music of the skills required to write the old *cantus firmus* settings was understandable in a Protestant country: indeed, many composers seem to have felt that they could not manage without attempting to write in this way, and thus did so for instruments rather than for voices. This helps to explain why, despite the experiments in tonality discussed below, the basic musical language remained polyphonic, looking back to the great days of the classical contrapuntal tradition. Even the Italians Alfonso Ferrabosco I and II demonstrate the deepest contrapuntal skills, while the younger Alfonso – a composer who was one of the most forward-looking in the use of chromatic and enharmonic music – rejects influences from the *seconda prattica* of Italy.

The use of the most basic material in the hexachord fantasias – the six notes which were fundamental to the learning of music – is interesting, for it juxtaposes the beginner's initial building-blocks with music of the most demanding kind. Indeed, the absolute basicity and lack of inherent musical interest in the scale itself was a challenge to composers to put their best skill into producing gold from base metal. Morley's definition of the fantasia is well known,[14] and identifies the form as the one in which it is most possible to demonstrate compositional skill:

> The most principal and chiefest kind of music which is made without a ditty is the Fantasy, that is when a musician taketh a point at his pleasure and wresteth and turneth it as he list, making either much or little of it according as shall seem best in his own conceit. In this may more art be shown than in any other music because the

composer is tied to nothing, but that he may add, diminish, and alter at his pleasure. And this kind will bear any allowances whatsoever tolerable in other music except changing the air and leaving the key, which in Fantasie may never be suffered. Other things you may use at your pleasure, as bindings with discords, quick motions, slow motions, Proportions, and what you list. Likewise this kind of music is, with them who practise instruments of parts, in greatest use, but for voices it is but seldom used.

Many of the hexachord fantasias discussed below may have been written 'in virtuous contention', but since they survive in manuscript and are difficult to date, one cannot always be sure who was influenced by whom. I shall therefore consider a collection of such works in ascending order of complication, starting – as a beginner in the art of music would have done – with the most basic quotations of the hexachord as a *cantus firmus* and tracing its development upwards.

The hexachord, when laid out as a long-note *cantus firmus*, suggests its own quite obvious harmonization. Example 76 gives this in its most basic

Example 76

form for durum, the hexachord most often used in these fantasias. (The alternative central cadence in Example 76 is common: the reader may easily transpose this example to see how the chords relate to the naturale and molle hexachords.) The implied change of key from G to C and back could account for the use of the six-note scale rather than the – to us – more obvious five notes between tonic and dominant: but the continual use of such a basic harmonic pattern as that shown in Example 76 will result in monotony and a four-square feeling. It is not the use of the harmonic scheme shown that is of interest, but the ways in which composers avoided that obvious scheme.

The Basic Hexachords

Before beginning the investigation proper, it will be as well to take a particular example as a starting-point, so as to see the ways in which composers played games with the hexachord in order to frustrate the hearer's expectations. The keyboard duet *Ut, re, mi, fa, sol, la*[15] by William Byrd uses an extraordinary series of tricks of this kind. One player – presumably in the early stages of learning – plays simply the notes of the hexachord which move very slowly up and down. Meanwhile a second player performs more intricate music, some of it full of runs, some of it using involved imitation of which each subject grows from some feature of its predecessor, and some of it embodying quotations of popular songs (*The Woods so wild* and *The Shaking of the sheets*[16]). More interesting still is Byrd's choice of the naturale hexachord for the 'pupil' and his decision to harmonize it as if it is molle (i.e., the hexachord is on C, but Byrd sets it in F major). In these circumstances mi fa (notes 3–4) suggest a perfect cadence in F, though normally the leading-note (E in this case) would not remain stationary throughout the dominant chord; and sol la will also suggest a perfect cadence in F or an A-phrygian cadence. These expectations are quite different from those shown in Example 76. There are five statements of the *cantus firmus*: in only the first two are notes 3–4 made into a perfect cadence on F, and in only the first statement are notes 5–6 so treated: in only one place does Byrd use an A-phrygian cadence beneath G–A, and there the bass part also uses G–A (with a leap of a ninth to disguise the consecutive octaves): in all other places the 'obvious' harmonization is avoided. The normal durum colour of hexachord fantasias is mostly eschewed in the harmony, but the F♯s that would logically result from the presence of durum crop up in Byrd's own harmony from time to time, sometimes clashing with the *cantus firmus* played by the 'pupil' (see Example 77). This is a clear case of Byrd using the three basic hexachords almost simultaneously: the 'pupil' plays

Example 77   Byrd: *Ut, re, mi, fa, sol, la*

in naturale; but the harmonization starts in molle and moves straight to durum (a change forbidden by the normal rules of hexachord usage). Clearly, when a composer can use all three hexachords at virtually the same time, the connotations of 'sweetness' and 'hardness' can no longer be relevant in that passage.

Byrd has one last joke to offer. Having given a convincing perfect cadence in F for notes 8–9 (G–F) of the final variation, he then ends with a quite unprepared perfect cadence – left to the very end of the penultimate bar – in C (the key of the naturale hexachord used by the 'pupil'). The whole is a brilliant witticism of a kind that parallels those found in John Donne's poetry. In no way is the piece controlled by the hexachord shape: on the contrary, it plays games with it as if to make the listener feel, at times, that the *cantus firmus* is a distracting irrelevance. In the series of fantasias discussed below we shall encounter some works which are hide-bound by the presence of the hexachord, seemingly unable to escape from its limiting presence; and others that take wing with a brilliance matching that shown by Byrd in his hexachord duet.

In its simplest form the hexachord fantasia comprised a piece of music written around a long-note *cantus firmus* consisting of the six notes rising from G to E and then falling again. Several hexachord fantasias are intended for beginners. Thomas Tomkins (1572–1658)[17] wrote one with a durum *cantus firmus* in the bass first, and then in the treble, the hand without the *cantus firmus* having mostly scalic runs (there is no attempt at invertible counterpoint, despite the fact that the changing over of hands would seem to call for it). There are also two settings of a single hexachord statement by Tomkins,[18] which were possibly sketches for variations that might have been included in a larger fantasia.

An example of the basic type, one that uses only the durum hexachord ascending and descending, is provided by John Bull:[19] the title, as so often in pieces of this nature, is *Ut, re, mi, fa, sol, la* rather than *Hexachord fantasia*. This example nevertheless starts like a fantasia, for it uses the hexachord as the basis of an imitative point; after the initial two-part imitation, however, Bull simply repeats the hexachord continuously in the right hand: beneath it he provides a series of technical keyboard excercises, first of all for the left hand and then for both hands. The technical devices explored include parallel thirds and sixths, parallel 6–3 chords, scales and rapid passage-work, rhythmic devices such as triplets co-existing with duplets, and intricate polyphonic webs. For the player it is a *tour de force*; but for the composer, too, the fantasia – at least, in this form – presents problems which only the gifted could solve.

In Bull's piece the compositional problems are posed by the repetition of the hexachord rising and falling regularly in one position 23 times without a break. (Tregian, who copied the manuscript between 1609 and 1619,[20] helpfully numbers the appearances: I shall refer to the statements of the hexachord as 'variations' in the following discussion.) Some variety is provided by the invention of characteristic keyboard figures which test the player's skill; but some skill is needed from the composer, too, if monotony is to be avoided. As I have said above, to use the obvious cadence in G at the end of each descending hexachord would lead to monotony and a four-square rhythmic feeling; so Bull sometimes omits the cadence altogether at that point (in variations 1 and 2, for instance), or he treats the A–G as belonging to some other key (G minor or modal E flat in variation 3, C major in variations 10, 11, 13, 14, 20, 22 and 23, modal E minor in variation 16, and mixolydian in variations 15, 19 and 21).

Similarly, the composer needs to provide a variety of treatments at the last two notes of the rising hexachord (D–E). As Example 76 shows, the two most obvious cadences here would be a full close in C and an E-phrygian cadence. Bull entirely avoids a cadence at this juncture in variations 1, 2 and 3; he uses a modal E-major cadence in variation 8, a G-major half-close in variations 4 and 13, and an A-minor cadence in variation 7; but he never uses the E-phrygian cadence. Within the hexachords, too, Bull contrives to use some accidentals (B♭ and E♭ in variation 3, for instance); and this can sometimes be combined with intricate cross-rhythms (see Example 78).

Example 78   Bull: *Ut, re, mi, fa, sol, la*

The start of a new type of accompanying material does not always coincide with the start of a new statement of the hexachord: this, too, helps to break down the four-squareness that would inevitably result if new material invariably coincided with a new variation. Thus triple time, introduced at the beginning of variation 8, reverts to duple time in the middle of variation 15; parallel thirds in the left hand begin in the middle of variation 11; and the juxtaposition of duplets and triplets begins in the middle of variation 12. The gradually increasing rhythmic complexities of the triple-time section go far towards helping provide a sense of growing excitement in anticipation of a climax:[21] such devices are highly necessary on an instrument in which the volume cannot be varied by touch. The whole piece is a scintillating display of brilliance for the composer no less than for the performer.

The *Ut, re, mi, fa, sol, la*[22] by Robert Parsons is written for four-part consort: it likewise repeats the durum hexachord rising and falling in regular fashion in the top part throughout the piece. Being for four melodic instruments, this fantasia is perforce treated differently from the one discussed above, and the result is much more like the conventional fantasia – at least in the first part – in that imitative points are continually invented to fit the *cantus firmus*. There is less obvious brilliance about this more 'scholarly' treatment in the opening part, though the severe style is tempered by a *secunda pars* cast in triple time, during which rhythmic tricks of enormous complexity are used. Various prolation signs complicate the matter, resulting in a set of syncopations that are both exhilarating and taxing for the players (see Example 79).

Example 79   Parsons: *Ut, re, mi, fa, sol, la*

Parsons makes duple and triple times co-exist, as Bull had done in the piece discussed above: and, like Bull, Parsons is careful to avoid regular perfect cadences in G. At the mid-point of each rising and falling hexachord, too, there is variety: D–E produces both an E-phrygian cadence (not used by Bull) and an A-phrygian cadence. The result is a pyrotechnic display of virtuosity for both composer and performer.

Variations on this basic pattern occur. William Daman and Alfonso Ferrabosco senior[23] wrote imitative pieces based around the rising and falling hexachord shape, without using it as a long-note *cantus firmus*. Since imitation is employed, the hexachord is used on degrees other than G, so that naturale and durum both occur: the two hexachords sometimes overlap in both Daman and Ferrabosco I. Neither composer uses the molle hexachord in their *Ut, re, mi, fa, sol, la* fantasias.

John Bull transcends these non-*cantus firmus* examples in a keyboard fantasia that is so full of such intricacy that one suspects that he had the continental *Ricerar* in mind; since Bull spent much of his working life abroad, this is highly likely. The *Ut, re, mi, fa, sol, la* fantasia for keyboard[24] uses as many devices as Bull can imagine: there is inversion (in the opening imitations); there is the beginning of an augmentation (at bar 159) which starts like a long-note *cantus firmus* and proceeds as far as FA, leaving the listener to supply SOL and LA mentally (the notes fit the harmony, but are not actually sounded); there is overlapping of neighbouring hexachords so as to form a scale of more than six notes; there are mixings of various hexachords; the outline of a sixth formed by the hexachord becomes a leap of a sixth; the descending notes LA SOL FA MI are used to prepare more complete entries of the descending hexachord; F hexachords make the player ponder whether to use a B♭ instead of the notated B natural, by *musica recta* (see bars 48–9, 142–3 and 156–7); the notes of the hexachord are occasionally rearranged (in bars 182–4, for example); hexachords start on a normal note for ut (G, C or F), but descend rather than ascend; hexachords migrate between parts; and there is *inganno* on several occasions (the treble G–A–B–C–G–A at bars 30–2 is UT RE MI FA sol la). Example 80 shows a series of these statements that

Example 80   Bull: *Ut, re, mi, fa, sol, la*

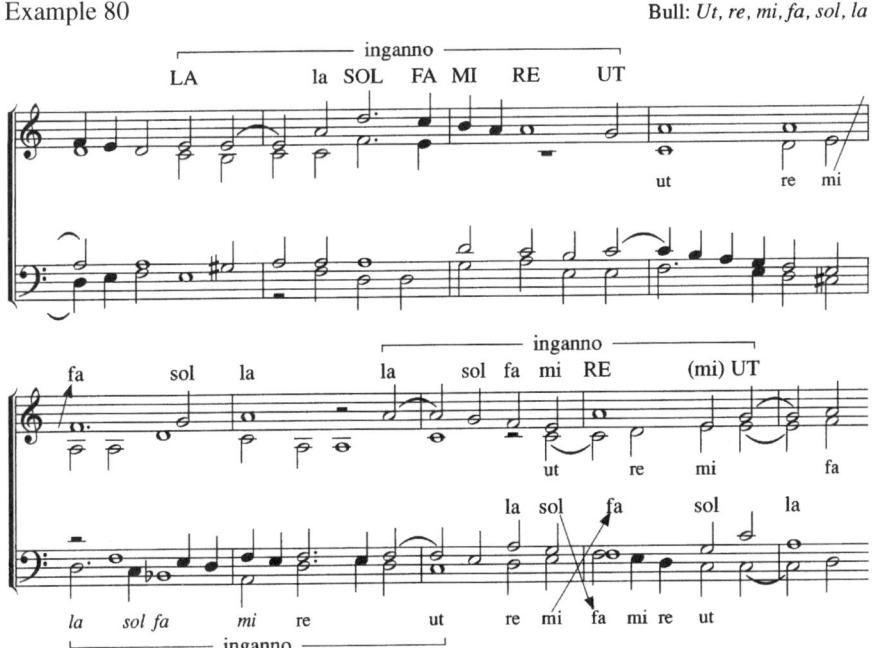

migrate from one hexachord to another ('*Inganno*'). Furthermore, there is an attempt – perhaps suggested by Byrd's hexachord duet, mentioned above – to combine all three of the basic hexachords in one single passage: to achieve such a combination was a considerable feat, given the constraints of musical language at the time (see Example 81). For once, Bull shows no interest in brilliant keyboard technique: here he produces a piece of the utmost compositional skill, full of learned devices, in which scarcely a beat passes by – in a very large piece – which is not in one way or another connected with the hexachord.

New directions

The fantasias so far examined have not gone beyond the three basic hexachords, durum, naturale, and molle. Such reticence in using the hexachord at various pitches is not shared by the composers of the examples discussed below: the remaining pieces, in fact, break Morley's rule that fantasias should not leave the key (indeed, the combinations of the three basic hexachords in the pieces described above could also be construed as 'leaving the key'). The *Ut, re, mi, fa, sol, la* fantasia for keyboard[25] by William Byrd uses the hexachord in rising and falling form, but the two are bisected with a rest. Byrd separates the various statements of the hexachord by rests as well, and uses the hexachord on many more finals than do the examples so far discussed. G, as usual, is the starting-point (though the first statement – again the variations are carefully numbered by Tregian – is preceded by an imitative introduction on hexachord-derived material): but thereafter entries occur on D, C, C (harmonized in F), C (but preparing the following F hexachord), F, G[26], A, Bb, C, G (3 times), D, and G (3 times). The tonal variety in the piece as a whole is enormous: the remote chord of B major occurs in variation 14 (which is based on D), and the entries on F and Bb are tonally far distant from that chord: but there is no recourse to enharmonic modulation, and Byrd is careful about his handling of chromaticism.[27] The wide harmonic range means that there is not the same necessity for Byrd to avoid continual perfect cadences at the end of the statements of the descending hexachord, but he is nevertheless keen to provide variety. He certainly avoids the obvious harmonizations (see Example 82, which is part of the Bb variation): furthermore, the cadence to variation 5 (a C hexachord harmonized in F) occurs only under the first three notes of the subsequent variation (which is on an F hexachord). In addition, he lets the statements of the hexachord migrate among the voices. Indeed, much of the piece is more-or-less conceived in 'voices', for the fantasia style has led Byrd to write in a contrapuntal manner full of imitations, the subjects of some of them deriving from the hexachord itself.

This fantasia forms a pair with the one that follows it in the *Fitzwilliam Virginal Book*, as is shown by the direction 'Perge' ('link to the following piece') which occurs at the end. The second fantasia of the pair has the title *Ut, mi, re*.[28] Here the hexachord is re-arranged rather than being presented 'straight': the result, for durum, is G–B–A–C–B–D–C–E E–C–D–B–C–A–B–G

Example 81   Bull: *Ut, re, mi, fa, sol, la*

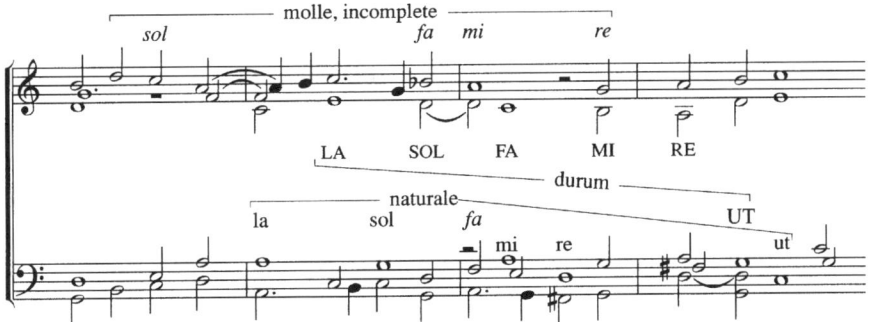

Example 82   Byrd: *Ut, re, mi, fa, sol, la*

(A–G is added at the close, since an ending on the notes B–G makes it difficult to arrange a perfect cadence in G). This is a much more spacious *cantus firmus* than the 'straight' hexachord, and the reversals of direction within both rising and falling shapes, along with the greater repetition of pitches, gives the composer more harmonic scope: the larger canvas makes it less likely that monotony will result from a regular use of the 'obvious' cadences. There are other dangers, though: the start of the descent (E–C–D–B) suggests a perfect cadence on A followed by another on G: a composer's success in avoiding the overuse of the obvious will be a test of his skill.

In the *Ut, mi, re* form the hexachord is itself no longer the simple basic shape known to all beginners, but has become something of more interest, something more 'artistic'. Perhaps because of this there is no necessity to use a wide variety of pitches for the hexachords, and 'ut' appears only on G, D and C: these are not the three basic hexachords, for D (which in fact has only one appearance in this piece) replaces the F that one might reasonably expect. There is an added complication here in that the C and G hexachords twice appear in canon with each other. Indeed, the *Ut, mi, re* shape is one of the easiest to manage in imitation, and is found throughout the late Renaissance as the basis of imitative points. Byrd makes full use of this quality of the shape, building it into his fugal themes (especially in the first half of the piece).[29] Only once does he use the most obvious A minor–G major formula at the E–C–D–B passage. Neither of Byrd's pieces discussed here makes such phenomenal demands on the player as does Bull, but in the matter of learnedness and contrapuntal skill Byrd yields to none.

Two fantasias for keyboard by Thomas Tomkins (*Ut, re, mi, fa, sol, la* and *Ut, mi, re*)[30] may belong together, and were probably written in imitation of Byrd's set just discussed. The *Ut, re, mi* fantasia is massive (with 38, or in shorter form 32, variations), and it has very few hexachords other than durum; Tomkins attempts to achieve variety by moving the *cantus firmus* around the voices. The piece is strongly governed by the *cantus firmus*: most changes of material coincide with UT or LA, and there is continual cadencing in C major at LA (except when the *cantus firmus* is in the bass) and in G major at UT. MI in the ascending hexachord sometimes avoids being the obvious third at a V–I cadence.

Tomkins's *Ut, mi, re* is smaller (there are 11 variations), and is also strongly governed by the hexachord shape: durum is used except where a canon at the fifth leads to a C or D hexachord alongside the G statement. Variations tend to start with new material: it is as if they have been written separately and subsequently stitched together. Diminutions and ornamentations of the *cantus firmus* are original touches, but the cadences are predictable, and the E–C–D–B part of the *cantus firmus* only avoids V–I in A minor followed by V–I in G when imitation forces some other treatment.[31]

If Byrd's *Ut, re, mi* and *Ut, mi, re* are extraordinary pieces, there is a keyboard fantasia by Bull which is even more extraordinary. This is the chromatic *Ut, re, mi, fa, sol, la*.[32] In this piece Bull starts, as is normal, with durum (rising and falling), but – without repeating the hexachord at any pitch – proceeds to use the shape on A, B, Db, Eb and F. Variation 7 should therefore logically be on G (Tregian numbers the variations, as usual), but instead Bull uses Ab, and proceeds to Bb, C, D, E and F#. Logically Ab (= G#) should follow, but Bull returns instead to G, a hexachord he uses four times at the end in order to anchor the tonality – for he has of necessity gone right round the tonal universe during the piece. The hexachords are themselves arranged in a set of interlocking 'hexachords' which omit the semitone: Bull first uses the six notes from G up to F (moving by whole tones), then he uses the six notes from Ab up to F# (also moving by whole tones). Two features of Bull's treatment of the various hexachords help him to handle this enormous range of keys. Firstly, the final 'ut' of each descending hexachord is repeated,[33] so that it sounds like the start of the subsequent variation, there being no gap between the statements. Secondly, since each variation (with the two exceptions noted above) is a tone above its predecessor, the first five notes of each hexachord are the same as notes 2–6 of the preceding one, except for a change from minor ('fa' of one hexachord) to major ('mi' of the subsequent hexachord). Given that Bull repeats the last 'ut' of each variation, this in fact stretches to six the number of notes that coincide (starting with the one *before* each new variation), except for the single change of accidental. Example 83 makes this clear.

Example 83   Bull: *Ut, re, mi, fa, sol, la*

The writing is for four contrapuntal parts throughout: indeed, the four-part texture (except for the final chord) is maintained more thoroughly than in Byrd's fantasia of this type, though Bull's interest is in harmonic experiment rather than in imitative device. He, too, shifts to triple time, and the intricacies found in the section before the eventual return to duple may well be influenced by those evident in Parsons's hexachord fantasia.

The use of all twelve semitones in a keyboard piece is rare at this time, but is not unknown; there is an example, for instance, by Nicholas Carleton: but the kind of equal temperament tuning that is clearly required for such pieces was more readily obtainable on the lute and viols, for these instruments, having frets, necessarily gave similar-sized semitones for each string covered by a particular fret. Given this, and given the severely four-part writing of Bull's piece, one may well wonder whether the fantasia just discussed is a keyboard version of a consort piece.[34]

The chromatic and enharmonic writing, using the hexachord on all twelve semitones, which we have seen in Bull's fantasia is also the basis of a pair of four-part consort fantasias by Alfonso Ferrabosco II.[35] One half of the pair treats only the rising hexachord, the other piece only the descending one, and in them the games played around the hexachord are even more extraordinary. All twelve semitones are again covered by the notes of the hexachords: in the fantasia based on *La, sol, fa, mi, re, ut* the shapes are organized in a sequence of descending semitones, so that 'ut' is heard in G (the conventional starting-point), F#, F natural, E, Eb, D, Db and C. This segment of the complete chromatic scale contains all the basic hexachords (durum at the opening and naturale at the close, with molle as the third variation). There is no need to use 'ut' on all twelve semitones, for the complete chromatic scale has already been covered by the time the natural hexachord is reached.

Ferrabosco II appears to be at pains to set himself a task which is more demanding than that faced in the most *avant-garde* piece of enharmonic writing we have so far encountered – the chromatic hexachord fantasia by Bull discussed above. Whereas Bull is content to make a convenient overlap between neighbouring hexachords, Ferrabosco in the *La, sol, fa, mi, re, ut* fantasia moves directly from any given hexachord to the one a semitone lower with only a rest of a breve's length between them. Each new statement will therefore begin on the minor sixth above the foregoing 'ut'; but Ferrabosco II never takes the superficially obvious path by which, for example, the durum hexachord will cadence on G, that pitch becoming the dominant of the chord containing the new 'la' (Eb), whose hexachord could then start in C minor. To do so would have posed problems for the second and subsequent notes of the hexachord, for Eb (the third of C minor) would have to proceed downwards to Db and Cb – notes inconsistent with C minor.

Much more enharmonic modulation must therefore be achieved at each change of hexachord, so the music continually veers between tonalities close (or relatively close) to the fundamental durum, naturale and molle hexachords and those far away from them tonally. The transition from the end of the G hexachord to the beginning of the F# one is shown in Example 84. Throughout the fantasia the *cantus firmus* is in the top part: the other instruments maintain an imitative texture more like that of Byrd than the freely-polyphonic web of Bull. Some of the points of imitation derive from the scalic material of the hexachord itself; and sometimes the result of this is to provide six-note scales that do not conform to the tone–tone–semitone–tone–tone shape of the conventional hexachord. Moreover, as if to draw attention to his severely polyphonic approach, Ferrabosco II starts the piece with a set of

Example 84

imitations, with one of the parts being presented in inversion. As in the other pieces discussed in this section, changes of imitative point by no means always coincide with the advent of a new hexachord; and Ferrabosco never uses the obvious V–I cadence beneath 're' and 'ut' (the nearest in the fantasia on *La, sol, fa, mi, re, ut* is in the naturale hexachord, which comes last, where a G-minor chord beneath D moves to a C-minor chord beneath C – and this despite the fact that hexachords are major). It is as if Ferrabosco has deliberately set out to demonstrate his superior skill, outdoing the native Englishmen on their own ground in every facet (except that he does not use triple time).

But that is not the end of the story. Splendid as the four-part fantasias are, and fully satisfying as their harmonic language sounds, Ferrabosco succeeds in adding a further part (a second treble) without any sense of strain to provide a pair of five-part works.[36] The passage that corresponds to the one shown in Example 84 is given in Example 85.

Example 85   Alfonso Ferrabosco II: *Fantasia*

The apparent contention between composers over the treatment of the hexachord forms a parallel to the idea of emulation in the Italian madrigal: and it may seem that Ferrabosco's treatment of the hexachord could not be possibly be surpassed. If it were possible to go farther, the next stage might be to treat the six stepwise notes rising and falling as chromatic notes; this would result in the line conventionally known today as the chromatic tetrachord. Some composers, indeed, did exactly this. Just as Ferrabosco II writes individual fantasias on rising and falling tetrachords, so John Dowland writes two fantasias for the lute, one treating six chromatic notes rising stepwise, the other six chromatic notes falling stepwise. Given the chromaticism, these cannot be called *Ut, re, mi, fa, sol, la* (or its inversion) or *Hexachord fantasia*:[37] but it is symptomatic of the growth in expression that accompanies the wider use of chromaticism and accidentals that Dowland uses programmatic titles for these two pieces: they are called *Forlorn Hope Fancy*[38] for the falling six-note theme, and *Farewell*[39] for the rising six-note theme. This kind of expression is clearly beginning to replace the connotations of the old hexachords: the descending chromatic tetrachord in particular became an illustrator of profound emotion throughout the baroque period.

Both fantasias are monothematic, but they are like fugues rather than ostinato pieces that keep reiterating long-note versions of the theme. In both pieces Dowland occasionally relaxes the chromatic style by writing a more tonal interlude. Stretto and diminution occur in both pieces, making them rather like a prototype of the chromatic fugue; and *Forlorn Hope Fancy* moves from its basic G into very remote keys in one of the interludes between the statements of the main subject. The opening of *Forlorn Hope Fancy* is shown in Example 86.

Example 86   Dowland: *Forlorn Hope Fantasy*

Although the Amsterdam composer Jan Pieterzoon Sweelinck cannot be regarded as central to the issues of this chapter, his keyboard music is so clearly influenced by that of his English contemporaries that he has to be regarded as an 'honorary Englishman' as far as music for the virginals is concerned.[40] Moreover, his imitative fantasias contain chromatic subjects very like those of Dowland discussed above. Through his connections with ex-patriate Englishmen such as Bull and Philips he forms a connection between the English virginalists of the late sixteenth and early seventeenth centuries and the later German baroque – for many of his pupils were important links between Sweelinck himself and such composers as J.S. Bach.

The link between the English virginalists and Sweelinck is quite clear in the latter's *Ut, re, mi, fa, sol, la. a 4 voci* which Tregian included in the *Fitzwilliam Virginal Book*, dating the piece (or perhaps his copying of it) 1612.[41] This builds upon the features of English works, though there is no attempt at chromatic or enharmonic writing. Unusually, Sweelinck bases the piece around the F hexachord (F major), though a number of statements move to naturale. He casts the opening as an imitative fantasia on a subject that includes a descending hexachord, but not as part of its head. The opening imitations extend throughout the first five statements of the hexachord (as usual, the variations are numbered by Tregian, at least at the beginning), and it is sometimes used in inversion so as to include the rising hexachord. By inventing a point whose head – the portion most likely to be involved in imitation – is not scalic, Sweelinck demonstrates a contrapuntal skill that does not rely on the conventional imitations that are so easy to apply when the scale alone is the basis of the material.

In order to create a sense of build to a final climax – a flight of scalic runs over the last cadence and the final chord – Sweelinck gradually quickens the statements of the hexachord, first halving them (at variation 9), then quartering them (at variation 15), and finally stating them in a series of canonic stretti with the hexachords in notes an eighth of their original length. By this time – near the end – Tregian has given up trying to number the variations, for there has been such a complex set of stretti after variation 20 that it is virtually impossible to keep track of the statements. It is in these stretti that Sweelinck uses the obvious imitative devices that are so readily available when scales are the main material – the kind of imitation with which many Englishmen had begun their hexachord fantasias. Sweelinck, however, includes within this set of stretti his own attempt – no doubt suggested by those of Byrd and Bull discussed above – at combining the three basic hexachords. Example 87 shows this: the passage preceding the stretto shows one of the conventional ways of using the scale in imitation. The responsibility for deciding whether the last hexachord in the middle part of Example 87 should be made into a real durum shape by turning the B♭ into B natural (and presumably in the left hand, too) rests with the player. It may be that, as sometimes happened in the Italian madrigal, such puzzles are deliberately set for the performers, who will be able to demonstrate their musicality by the way in which they react to the conundrum.

One other device is quite original. Variation 19 consists of the rising F hexachord, but at first there is no corresponding descent, for Sweelinck follows it with a rising B♭ hexachord, and then a rising C hexachord. By so doing he increases the tension as the final climax approaches, since the listener's expectations are not fulfilled, and the pitch of the hexachords rises unexpectedly. The expected descents are at first omitted in each of these hexachords: but once the rising C hexachord has been reached, the process is

Example 87   Sweelinck: *Ut, re, me, fa, sol, la a 4 voci*

given in reverse, so that the falling C hexachord is immediately followed by a descending B♭ and a falling F hexachord (the end of this process is shown in Example 87). The complications here no doubt suggested to Tregian that he should abandon his numbering of the variations.

Treatments such as we have seen in this section stretch the old system of three basic hexachords to the limit – indeed, beyond the limit. When the hexachord can appear on any degree, clearly a new system is evolving. The contrapuntal skill and inventiveness of the majority of composers who wrote hexachord fantasias – to look no further than those pieces – are firm evidence that Roger North was right when he wrote so glowingly about English instrumental music:

. . . all so full and industriously woven that the forreigners themselves use to owne that the English in the instrumentall and the Itallians in the vocall music excelled.[42]

The works discussed above – some clinging tenaciously to the old classical polyphonic style, some exhibiting an extraordinary desire to experiment harmonically and tonally – lead quite naturally to the many examples of chromatic fantasias of the later seventeenth century, and they culminate in the chromatic fugues of J.S. Bach.

Notes

1. The other 'English' Lamentations (the anonymous set in the British Library Royal Appendix 12–16 – from Nonsuch Palace – and those by Alfonso Ferrabosco I) that include the 'Daleth' verse contain settings of the words 'Viae Syon lugent'. However, as Joseph Kerman points out (Kerman 1981, p. 93), Byrd also omitted some portions of the liturgical text in his Lamentations.
2. See Doe 1968, p. 39. See also Milsom 1995, pp. 161–79.
3. Collins 1929, p. 163. This cannot be dismissed as a 'romantic notion', as Doe does (op. cit., p. 39): it is true that many composers wrote Lamentations during the sixteenth century; but it is also true that the Catholic church was beset by problems, facing a rising tide of reformation theology, and Lamentation sets may have been set with a hidden political agenda in mind by other composers than Tallis. In this context, see Bray 1995, p. 91.
4. Given as *He* in some sources, and in the liturgy itself (see note 9 below).
5. If the resulting solmization *mi mi* LA re FA MI be accepted, it breaks one of the rules of the system by moving directly from molle to durum: but, as is clearly evident almost throughout this book, that rule was more often honoured in the breach than in the observance, especially towards the end of the period with which I have concerned myself.
6. The line includes the clear tritone F–B natural, the B natural in no way a solmization of the 'ah' sound. Kerman, op. cit., p. 97, remarks on the small number of imitative points in the English repertoire that use affective semitones. Byrd's own Lamentations – clearly influenced by Tallis – provide some examples dependent on solmization (see Kerman's Example 8, for instance).
7. The difficulty posed by imitating E–F–E at the fifth below is one of the central tenets of Palestrina's motet and mass *Sicut lilium inter spinas*. Many continental *De Beata Virgine* pieces address the same problem.
8. 'Facta', however, seems to be carefully set to la la and FA FA.
9. It is given as 'He' in some sources.
10. Or pre-echoed: one cannot be sure about the dates of composition.
11. Byrd copied this cadence at the end of *De lamentatione*.
12. Morley 1597, p. 294.
13. Ibid, p. 202.
14. Ibid, p. 296. The definition is echoed much later by Christopher Simpson: see Field 1992, p. 202.
15. *MB* XXVIII 58. Apel 1972, p. 307, comes to a different conclusion. Caldwell 1973, p. 77, suggests that 'Mr Whight's' hexachord setting is the earliest and most primitive example: he reproduces the complete piece (which consists of a single hexachord rising and falling).

16. See Neighbour 1978, p. 116.
17. *MB* V 34.
18. *MB* V 36 and 37.
19. *FWVB* vol. II 215.
20. See Field, op. cit., p. 206.
21. Caldwell 1973, pp. 77–81, discusses the Bull hexachord fantasias in detail, and points out that there are errors in the *MB* transcription of the proportions in this particular piece.
22. *MB* XLIV 12.
23. *MB* XLIV 2.
24. *MB* XIV 19.
25. *FWVB* vol. I 101.
26. The move from molle to durum was forbidden by theorists.
27. Neighbour, op. cit., p. 228, points out that Byrd avoids hexachords that include A♭ and G#.
28. There is another pair of such fantasias, one by Parsons and the other attributed to Byrd, in BL Add MS 32377 (a single part-book): see Neighbour, op. cit., p. 90. Frescobaldi, in *Recercari et Canzoni* (1615) writes a number of recercars with the solmization syllables of the main subject in the title: they include *Recercar Quarto sopra mi, re, fa, mi* and *Recercar Sesto sopra fa, fa, sol, la, fa*. Such things occurred in England, too, as witness the *Uppon la mi re* attributed to Preston.
29. Neighbour, op. cit., p. 230, finds *Ut, mi, re* disappointing as a sequel to *Ut, re, mi*. He suggests (p. 231) an early date of composition, partially on the basis of the modal harmonic touches.
30. *MB* V 35 and 38.
31. Tomkins's *Ut, re, mi, fa, sol, la* for four viols (*MB* LIX 18) starts as a version of the first seven variations of this keyboard piece. The remainder of the fantasia has a great many short imitative sections; it rather regularly cadences on G.
32. *FWVB*, vol. I 51. Field 1996 equates chromatic movement round the complete harmonic circle, such as is found in this piece by Bull and in those by Ferrabosco II discussed below, with contemporary exploration.
33. So is the top note on most occasions.
34. Another *Ut, re, mi* attributed to Bull is actually transcribed from a fantasia by Caurroy. See Elcombe 1995, p. 240; Field 1996, p. 22.
35. The fantasia on the descending hexachord is printed in *MB* IX 23. See the remarks in Field 1996, pp. 24–9.
36. The fantasia on the descending hexachord is printed in *MB* IX 39.
37. Two anonymous lute pieces based around the descending chromatic tetrachord (a scale of six notes descending chromatically by step) may be by Dowland: see Poulton and Lam 1974, nos 71 and 72. They share many features with the two fantasias known to be by Dowland and discussed here, though no. 72 uses material other than the opening chromatic theme.
38. Ibid. no. 2.
39. Ibid. no. 3.
40. See Curtis 1972, *passim*.
41. *FWVB* vol. II 118.
42. North 1959, p. 200.

Bibliography

A: Music

The following is a list of the music to which reference is made in this book. The abbreviations are:

A	Arnold, *Marenzio*. See Bibliography B: Literature, Arnold 1965
b.c.	basso continuo
BL	British Library
CMM	*Corpus Mensurabilis Musicae*
CW	Collected Works/Complete Works
d.	died
EECM	*Early English Church Music*
Ein	Einstein, Volume 3. See Bibliography B: Literature, Einstein 1949
EMS	*English Madrigal School*
Ex.	Example
F	Fenlon, Volume 2. See Bibliography B: Literature, Fenlon 1980
fl.	flourished
fol.	folio
FWVB	*Fitzwilliam Virginal Book*
GA	*Golden Age of the Madrigal*. See Bibliography B: Literature Einstein 1942
L	Lera, *Arcadelt*. See Bibliography B: Literature, Lera 1989
Ma	Mann, *Monte*. See Bibliography B: Literature, Mann 1983
MB	*Musica Britannica*
ME	Modern Edition
MS	Manuscript
N	Newcomb, Volume 2. See Bibliography B: Literature, Newcomb 1980

OBFC	*Oxford Book of French Chansons.* See Bibliography B: Literature, Dobbins 1987
OBIM	*Oxford Book of Italian Madrigals.* See Bibliography B: Literature, Harman 1983
O.O.	*Opera Omnia*
OUP	Oxford University Press
PBIM	*Penguin Book of Italian Madrigals.* See Bibliography B: Literature, Roche 1974. Two volumes, given as I and II in the list below
PIM	*Popular Italian Madrigals.* See Bibliography B: Literature, Harman 1976
RF	Roche, *Flower of the Italian Madrigal.* See Bibliography B: Literature, Roche 1988
TCM	*Tudor Church Music.*
SW	Sämtliche Werke (complete works)

In addition, madrigal collections are referred to by the number of the volume (in Roman numerals) and the number of voices (in Arabic numbers): thus 'II *a* 5' means 'The Second Book of Madrigals for Five Voices'.

ANIMUCCIA, Giovanni (*c.* 1500–1571).
    Infinita beltà, a 5. I *a* 4, 5 and 6, 1547. ME: RF, I 1.

ANONYMOUS.
    Lamentations, a 5. BL Royal Appendix 12–16.
    Mia Benigna fortuna, a 4, or *a* 1 plus lute, *c.* 1508. ME: *An Anthology of Early Renaissance Music*, eds Greenberg and Maynard, Dent, London, 1975, 25.

ARCADELT, Jacques (*c.* 1505–1568). ME: CMM, 31. See also Bibliography B: (Literature), Lera: 1989.
    Chi potrà dir, a 4. I *a* 4, *c.* 1538. ME: L, 4.
    Crudele acerba, a 5. In *Di Verdelot le dotte et eccelente compositioni de i madrigali a cinque voci*, 1538.
    Dormendo un giorno, a 3. I *a* 1, 1542. ME: *OBIM*: 8.
    Il bianco e dolce cigno, a 4, 1539. ME: *PBIM*, 5; *OBIM*, 6; *PIM* 2, L, 1.
    Io mi rivolgo indietro, a 4. II *a* 4, 1539. ME: *PBIM*, 6; Ein, 22.
    Ma quell'in un momento, see *Qualor m'assal'Amore.*
    Nova donna m'apparve, a 4. I *a* 4, *c.* 1538. ME: L 18.
    Qualor m'assal'Amore/Ma quell'in un momento, a 5. *Le dotte . . . c.* 1538. ME: RF, I:2.
    S'infinita bellezza, a 5. II *a* 5, 1544. ME: *GA* 1.

AVE MARIS STELLA *Liber Usualis* (q.v.), p. 1259.

BLITHEMAN, John (*c.* 1525–1591).
 Gloria tibi Trinitas [I], keyboard. ME: *MB* I 91.

BULL, John (*c.* 1562–1628).
 Almighty God, who by the leading of a starre, a 2–5 plus organ. (The 'Starre Anthem'). ME: OUP 1937, 1962.
 Ut, re, mi, fa, sol, la. ME: *FWVB* II 115.
 Ut, re, mi, fa, sol, la. ME: *MB* XIV 19.
 Ut, re, mi, fa, sol, la. (Chromatic) ME: *FWVB* I 51.

BURTON, Avery (*c.* 1470–*c.* 1543).
 Mass *Ut re mi fa sol la*, a 6 (incomplete, lacking second bass). Bodleian Library, Oxford, MS Mus Sch 376–81.

BYRD, William (1543–1623). ME: CW ed. Fellowes 1937–50, rev. Dart etc, 1962–, Stainer and Bell.
 Ave, verum corpus, a 4, 1605.
 De lamentatione Hieremiae prophetae, a 5.
 Gradualia, 1605 and 1607.
 Laudibus in sanctis, a 5, 1591.
 O quam suavis est, a 4, 1607.
 Peccavi, a 5, ME: *TCM*.
 Ut, re, mi, fa, sol, la. ME: *FWVB*, I:101.
 Ut, re, mi, fa, sol, la. (Keyboard duet) ME: *MB* XVIII 58.
 Ut, mi, re. ME: *FWVB* I 102.

CACCINI, Giulio [Giulio Romano] (*c.* 1545–1618).
 Amarilli, a 1 plus b.c. *Nuove musiche*, 1602. ME: ed. Perinello, Istitutio Editorale Italiano, 1919: ed. Hitchcock, A–R Editions, Madison, 1970.

CAIMO, Gioseppe (1545–1584).
 Piangete valli, a 4. I a 4, 1564. ME: Ein 67; *PBIM* 21.

CARLETON, Nicholas (*c.* 1570/5–1630).
 A verse of 4 pts: and *Upon the sharpe*. ME: *Schott's Anthology of Early Keyboard Music*, IV, London, 1951.

CASIMIRI (ed.).
 G. P. da Palestrina: Le opere complete, Rome 1939–.

COMA, Annibale (*c.* 1550–after 1598).
 Come tutto m'ardete, a 5, 1588. ME: F 12.

CORTECCIA, Francesco di Bernardo (1502–1571).
   Se per onesti Preghi, a 4. Madrigale II a misura di breve, Gardane, 1543.
      ME: *PBIM* 7.

CROCE, Giovanni (*c.* 1557–1609)
   Erme campagne, see *Valli profonde.*
   Valli profonde/Erme campagne (*a* 6), I *a* 6, 1590. ME: RF I 6.

DAMAN, William (*c.* 1540–1591).
   Ut, re, mi, fa, sol, la, a 3. ME: *MB* XLIV 1.

d'INDIA, Sigismondo (*c.* 1582–1629).
   Cruda Amarilli, a. 5, 1610.

DOWLAND, John (1563–1626). ME *Lute songs*, ed. E.H. Fellowes, Stainer
and Bell, rev. T. Dart, 1968: *Lute music*, eds Poulton and Lam, Faber, 1974
and 1978.
   An heart that's broken and contrite. ME: *EECM* XI 9.
   Farewell. Poulton and Lam 1974, 3.
   Flow my tears. Second Book of Songs, 1600.
   Forlorn Hope Fancy. Poulton and Lam 1974, 2.
   Lachrimae, or Seaven Teares figured in Seaven Passionate pavans . . .
      1605.
   Lasso vita mia. A Pilgrim's Solace, 1612.
   Me, me, and none but me. Third Booke of Songes, 1603.
   A Pilgrime's Solace. 1612.
   Stay, sorrow, stay. Second Book of Songs, 1600.

FERRABOSCO I, Alfonso (1543–1588). ME: Sacred music, *CMM*, XCVI.
   Lamentations (Incipit lamentatio Jeremiae Prophetae), *a* 5. No. 3.
   Lamentations (Incipit lamentatio Jeremiae Prophetae), *a* 6. No. 4.
   Ut, re, mi, fa, sol, la, a 3. ME: *MB* XLIV 2.

FERRABOSCO II, Alfonso (1575–1628).
   Ut, re, mi, fa, sol, la. a 4. ME: *MB* IX 23.
   Ut, re, mi, fa, sol, la. a 5. ME: *MB* IX 39.

FEVIN, Antoine de (*c.* 1470–late 1511 or early 1512).
   Petite camusette, a 3. ME: A–R Editions, Inc., Madison, 1985. *OBFC*
      3.

FRESCOBALDI, Girolamo (1583–1643), ME of I *a* 5, ed. Jacobs, Pennsylva-
nia State Press, 1983.
   Lasso io languisc'e moro, a 5. I *a* 5, 1608.
   Recercari et Canzoni. 1615.

Se la doglia e'l martire, a 5. I *a* 5, 1608.
Se lontano voi sete, a 5. I *a* 5, 1608.

GABRIELI, Andrea (*c.* 1510–1586). ME: *Complete madrigals*, ed. Merritt, A–R Editions, Madison, 1983.
   Caro dolce ben mio, a 5. Musica divina, Antwerp, 1583. RF, I:10.
   I'vo piangendo/Si che s'io vissi, a 5. III *a* 5, posth. 1589. ME: *OBIM*, 40; Arnold, Andrea Gabrieli, *Ten madrigals*, OUP 1970.
   Non vedi o sacr'Apollo, a 5, 1570. ME: Arnold, Andrea Gabrieli, *Ten Madrigals*, OUP, 1970.
   S'io che s'io vissi, see *I'vo piangendo*

GAGLIANO, Marco da (1582–1643).
   O sonno/Ov'è'il silenzio, a 5, 1602. ME: RF, I:13.

GESUALDO DI VENOSA, Carlo (*c.* 1561–1613). ME: SW, eds Weismann and Watkins, Hamburg, 1957–1967.
   Ahi, già mi discoloro, see *Ecco, morirò dunque.*
   Dalle odorate spoglie/E quella Arpa, a 5. II *a* 5, 1594.
   Ecco, morirò dunque/Ahi, grà mi discoloro, a 5, IV *a* 5, 1596. ME: RF, I:18.
   E quella Arpa, see *Dalle odorate spoglie.*
   Languisce al fin, a 5. V *a* 5, 1611.
   Moro lasso, a 5. VI *a* 5, 1611.
   O vos omnes, a 6. Responsoria, 1611.
   Se per lieve/Che sentir, a 5. II *a* 5, 1594.

GUERRERO, Francisco (1528–1599).
   Beata Dei genitrix, a 6, 1589. ME: Mapa Mundi series A, 69.
   Duo Seraphim, a 12, 1597. ME: Mapa Mundi series A, 6.

HABERL, F.X., and others (ed.). *G.P. da Palestrina, Werke,* Leipzig, 1862–1907.

JOSQUIN des Prez (*c.* 1440–1521). ME: *Werken,* ed. Smijers and others, Amsterdam, 1921–.
   Absolon fili mi, a 4.
   Missa Hercules Dux Ferrariae, a 4.
   Missa La sol fa re mi, a 4.

LAMBE, Walter (1450 or 1451–after Michaelmas 1499).
   Nesciens Mater, a 5. Eton Choirbook. ME: *MB*, XII.

LASSO, Orlando di (*c.* 1532–1594), ME: SW, eds Haberl and Sandberger, Leipzig, 1894–1926: and SW, neue Reihe, eds Hermelink and others, Kassel, 1956–.

> *Alma Nemes, a* 4, 1555.
> *Alme Deus,* (sacred contrafactum of *Alma Nemes*).
> *Bonjour mon coeur, a* 4. 1564.
> *Cantai, hor piango/Tengan dunque, a* 5. I *a* 5, 1555.
> *Crudele acerba, a* 5. I *a* 5, 1555.
> *Deh, lascia, anima, a* 4. Madrigali novamente composti, *a* 4–6, 1587.
> *La nuit froide et sombre, a* 4. 1576.
> *Mia benigna fortuna/Crudele acerba, a* 5. I *a* 5. 1555.
> *Quanto il mio duol, a* 4. I *a* 4, 1560.
> *Queste non son piu lagrime, a* 4. I *a* 4, 1555. ME: Arnold, *Lassus, Ten madrigals for mixed voices,* OUP, 1977.
> *Tengan dunque,* see *Cantai, hor piango.*
> *Tristis est anima mea, a* 5, 1565.

LIBER USUALIS, The. Desclée Company, Tournai and New York, 1961.

LUZZASCHI, Luzzasco (?1545–1607).

> *De le odorate spoglie/E quell'Arpa, a* 5. III *a* 5, 1582. ME: N, 25.
> *Dhe, se pur secco,* see *Se il Lauro.*
> *Dolorosi martir, a* 5. IV *a* 5, 1594. ME: Ein 81.
> *E quell'Arpa,* see *Da le odorate spoglie.*
> *Quando io miro, a* 5. IV *a* 5, 1594. ME: N 26.
> *Quivi sospiri, a* 5. II *a* 5, 1576. ME: GA 7.
> *Se il lauro e sempre verde/Dhe, se pur secco, a* 5. Il lauro secco, 1582. ME: N, 10.

MARENZIO, Luca (1553–1599). ME: SW, ed Einstein, Leipzig, 1929–31; O. O. eds Meier and Jackson, *CMM,* LXXII, 1976–. Other modern editions listed below.

> *Affliger chi per voi/Nulla da voi, a* 4. Madrigali libro primo, *a* 4, 5, 6, 1588. ME: *PBIM,* 28.
> *Baci soave e cari, a* 6. V *a* 6, 1591.
> *Come è dolce gioire, a* 5. VII *a* 5, 1595. ME: RF, 27.
> *Come fuggir per selva ombrosa, a* 6. V *a* 6, 1591.
> *Cosi nel mio parlar, a* 5. IX *a* 5, 1599.
> *Cruda Amarilli/Ma grideran per me, a* 5. VII *a* 5, 1595. ME: ed. Chater, Novello, 1975: *OBIM,* 46.
> *Crudele acerba, a* 5. IX *a* 5, 1599. ME: A 10.
> *Dolorosi martir, a* 5, I *a* 5, 1580. ME: RF I:23.
> *E cosi nel mio parlare*: see *Cosi nel mio parlar.*

E so come in un punto, a 5. IX *a 5*, 1599.
Fieri silvestri, a 5. Madrigali libro primo *a 4, 5, 6*, 1588. ME: *GA*, 9.
Fuggito è'l sonno, a 5. Madrigali *a 4, 5 e 6*, 1588.
Leggiadre Ninfe e Pastorelli, a 6. V *a 6*, 1591. ME: *PIM*, 10.
Ma grideran per me, see *Cruda Amarilli.*
Mi fa lasso languisce, a 5. II *a 5*, 1581.
Nulla da voi, see *Affliger chi per voi.*
O dolcezze amarissime, a 5. VII *a 5*, 1595.
O fere stelle, a 6. I *a 6*, 1588. ME: Ein, 80.
Pur mi, see *Se la mia vita.*
Se la mia vita/Pur mi, a 4. Madrigali libro primo *a 4, 5, 6*, 1588. ME: A,
    6.
Vezzosi augelli, a 4. I *a 4*, 1585. ME: *PBIM*, 27.

MASNELLI, Paolo (fl. 1578–1609).
Non puo, dolce mia vita, a 4. I *a 4*, 1582. ME: *PBIM*, 25.

MERULO, Claudio (1533–1604).
Quando'io pens'al martire, I *a 5*, 1566. ME: *GA*, 3.

METALLO, Grammatio (1539/40–after 1615).
del Metallo Ricercari a due voci per sonare et cantare, Venice, 1614.
*Del Metallo . . . Magnificat a quattro, et a quinque . . . In Venetia
    MDCIII.* (Magnificat Quinti Toni, ME: Collyer 1987, pp. 239–49.)

MONTE, Filippo de (1521–1604). ME Opera, eds van den Borren and van
Doorslaer, Bruges, 1927–1939; New Complete edition, ed. Lenaerts and
others, Louvain, 1975–.
Ahi, chi mi rompe il sonno, a 5. III *a 5*, 1570. ME: *PIM*, 6; *OBIM*,
    30.
Bonjour mon coeur, a 6, 1575.
Cruda Amarilli, a 5. XIV *a 5*, 1590.
Crudele acerba, see *Mia benigna fortuna.*
Dolorosi martir, a 4. Barre, Libro II delle Muse, 1558. ME: *PBIM*, 17.
Fui preso fui ferito, arsi e gelai, a 5. XVI *a 5*, 1595. ME: Ma, Ex. 61.
I'piansi, hor canto/Si profo'era, a 5. III *a 5*, 1570. ME: Ma, Ex. 26.
La dolce Vista, a 4. II *a 4*, 1569. ME: Ma, p. 151.
Lasso, Amor/Ma lagrimosa, a 4. 1595. ME: Ma, Ex. 27.
Ma lagrimosa, see *Lasso, Amor.*
Mia benigna fortuna/Crudele acerba, etc a 4. I *a 4*, 1562 (setting of the
    whole sestina).
O voi c'havete, a 5. VII *a 5*, 1578. (18 stanzas of ottavas).
Per aspre horride vie, a 5. XIV *a 5*, 1590. ME: Ma, Ex. 56.

Si profon'era, see *I'piansi, hor canto.*

Solingo in selve e'n in boschi, a 5. XVI *a* 5, 1595. ME: Ma, Ex. 60.

Vergine pura, a 6. I *a* 6, 1583. ME: RF, II:2.

Zefiro torna, a 5. I *a* 5, 1554.

MONTEVERDI, Claudio, (1567–1643). ME: Tutte le opere, ed. Malipiero, Asola, 1926–1942, with revisions; and O.O., ed. Fondazione Claudio Monteverdi, 1970–.

Anima mia, perdona/Chi se tu se'il cor mio, a 5. IV *a* 5, 1603.

Ch'io t'ami, a 5. V *a* 5, 1605.

Chi se tu se'il cor mio, see *Anima mia, perdona.*

Cruda Amarilli, a 5. V *a* 5, 1605.

Crudel, perche mi fuggi, a 5. II *a* 5, 1590.

Lagrime d'amante, in 6 *partes, a* 5 plus b.c. VI *a* 5, 1614.

Lament of Arianna, see *Lasciatemi morire.*

La piaga c'ho nel core, a 5. IV *a* 5, 1603. ME: RF II 6.

Lasciatemi morire, a 5. VI *a* 5, 1614.

Longe da te cor mio, a 5. VI *a* 5, 1603.

L'Orfeo, 1609 (first performed in 1607).

Luci serene e chiare, a 5. IV *a* 5, 1603.

Mentr'io mirava fiso, a 5. II *a* 5, 1590.

O come è gran martire, a 5. III *a* 5, 1592. ME: F 14.

Ohimè, il bel viso, a 5. VI *a* 5, 1614.

Ohimè, se tanto amate, a 5. IV *a* 5, 1603.

O Mirtillo, Mirtillo anima mia, a 5. V *a* 5, 1606.

Piagne e sospira, a 5. IV *a* 5, 1603.

Si ch'io vorrei morire, a 5. IV *a* 5, 1603.

Vattene pur crudel, a 5. III *a* 5, 1592.

Vespers ('Sanctissimae virgini missa senis vocibus ad ecclesiarum choros ac Vespere pluribus decantandae cum nonnullis sacris concentibus ad sacella sive Principum cubicula accomodata'), *a* 1–10 plus instruments, 1610.

Voi pur da me partite, a 5. IV *a* 5, 1603.

Zefiro torna, a 5. VI *a* 5 and 7, plus b.c., 1614.

MORALES, Cristobal de (*c.* 1500–1553), ME: O.O. ed. Angles, Monumentos de la Musica Espanola, 1952–.

O sacrum convivium, a 5.

MORLEY, Thomas (1557/8–1602). *Thomas Morley, Collected Motets*, eds Andrews and Dart, Stainer and Bell, London, 1959.

Laboravi in gemitu meo.

MOUTON, Jean (*c.* 1460–1522).
  En venant de Lyon, a 4. OBFC, 6.

NASCO, Giovanni (*c.* 1510–1561).
  Madonna, quand'io penso, a 5. Il terzo libro della Muse, 1561. ME: RF,
  II:9.

OCKEGHEM, Johannes (*c.* 1410–1497). ME: SW, ed. Plamenac, Leipzig,
1927.
  Missa Mi–mi, a 4.

PALESTRINA, Giovanni Pierluigi da (1525 or 1526–1594). ME: see Casimiri,
and Haberl.
  Dies sanctificatus, a 4. Motecta Festorum Totius Anni, 1563.
  Io son ferito, ahi lasso, a 5. 1561.
  La ver l'Aurora, a 4. I *a* 4, 1568.
  Missa de Beata Virgine, a 4. 1567.
  Missa Dies sanctificatus, a 4, 1594.
  Missa Sicut lilium inter spinas, a 5. 1590.
  Missa Ut, re, mi, fa, sol, la, a 6. 1570.
  Sicut lilium inter spinas, a 5. 1569.
  Stabat Mater, a 8. 1588 or 1589.
  Vestiva i colli, a 5. 1566.
  Voi mi poneste in foco/Pero che da l'ardore, a 5. 1558.

PALLAVICINO, Benedetto (1551–1601).
  Cruda Amarilli, VI *a* 5, 1600. ME: ed. Arnold, *Das Chorwerk,* LXIII.
  O dolorosa sorte, a 5. VII *a* 5, 1604. ME: RF II 13.

PARSLEY, Osbert (*c.* 1511–1585).
  Lamentations, a 5. ME: *TCM.*

PARSONS, Robert (d. 1570).
  Ut, re, mi, fa, sol, la. ME: *MB* XLIV 12.

PERI, Jacopo (1561–1633).
  L'Euridice, 1601 (first performed 1600).

PETTI, Paolo (d. 1678).
  Cruda Amarilli, BL Add MS 31412 fol 32, olim 59r.

PHILIPS, Peter (1560 or 1561–1628).
  Amarilli di Julio Romano, keyboard. ME: *FWVB* 82.
  Chiesi un guardo, a 6. II *a* 6, 1603.

Correa vezzosamente, a 6. II *a* 6, 1603. ME: *MB*, XXIX:19.
Gaude Maria virgo/ Virgo prudentissima, a 5. 1612. ME: *Peter Philips, Cantiones sacrae quinis vocibus*, ed. John Steele, University of Otago Press, 1992.
Tocca la vista mia, a 6. II *a* 6, 1603. ME: *MB* XXIX 23.
Ut re mi fa sol la, a 6. I *a* 6, 1596. ME: *MB* XXIX 11.
Virgo prudentissima, a 5, see *Gaude Maria virgo*
Virgo prudentissima, a 2 plus b.c, 1628.

PORTER, Walter (*c.* ?1587 or ?1595–1659).
Cruda Amarilli, BL Add MS 31440 fol. 33v.

attrib. PRESTON, Thomas (fl. early 16th century).
Uppon la re mi. BL Add MS 29996/i.

RAMSEY, Robert (fl. 1612–1644).
Sleep, fleshly birth, a 6. ME: *Oxford Book of English Madrigals*, 1978, 43.

REGGIO, Hoste da (fl. 1540–1560).
O beata colei, a 4. 1547. ME: F 2.

REGNARD, Francois (fl. *c.* 1579).
Las, je me plains, a 4. ME: *OBFC* 70.

RORE, Cipriano de (1515 or 1516–1565). O.O. ed. B. Meier, *CMM*, 1959–.
A guisa d'hom che da, see *Strane ruppi*.
Ancor che col partire, a 4. 1547. ME: *PBIM* 11; *OBIM* 13; Ein, 47; *PIM*, 4.
Crudele acerba, see *Mia benigna fortuna*.
Dalle belle contrade, a 5. V *a* 5, 1566. ME: RF II 15.
Mia benigna fortuna/Crudele acerba, a 4. II *a* 4, 1557. ME: *PBIM* 12; *OBIM*, 20; Ein, 48 (*seconda parte* only).
O sonno/Ov'e'l silentio, a 4. 1557. ME: *OBIM* 18.
Ov'e'l silentio, see *O sonno*
Parmi d'udirla, see *Per mezz'l bosch' inhospiti*.
Per mezz'l bosch' inhospiti/Parmi d'udirla, a 5. I *a* 5, 1542. ME: Ein, 45.
Strane ruppi/A giusa d'hom che da, a 5. I *a* 5, 1542. *OBIM* 10.

SHEPPARD, John (*c.* 1515–*c.* 1559).
Gaude gaude gaude Maria virgo, ed. David Chadd, *EECM* XVII; *John Sheppard, Collected Works*, I, ed. David Wulstan, Oxford, 1978.

SWEELINCK, Jan Pieterszoon (1560–1575). ME: *Werken*, ed. Seiffert, The Hague and Leipzig, 1894–1901: *Werken voor orgel en clavicembel*, ed. Seiffert, Amsterdam: *Werken*, ed. Annegarn, Amsterdam, 1958: *O.O.*, editio altera, ed. Lagas and others, Amsterdam, 1957–.
> *Qui vult venire post me, a 5* plus b.c., 1619.
> *Ut re mi a 4 voc.* ME: *FWVB* II 118.

TAGLIA, Pietro (fl. second half of 16th century).
> *Come 'esser puo che si contrari effeti, a 4.* I *a 4*, 1555. ME: *PBIM* 16: Ein, 50.

TALLIS, Thomas (*c.* 1505–1585).
> *De lamentatione Ieremiae prophetae, a 5.* ME: *TCM.*
> *Incipit lamentatio Ieremiae prophetae, a 5.* ME: *TCM.*
> *In ieiunio et fletu, a 5.* 1575. ME: *TCM.*
> *Sancte Deus, a 4.* ME: *TCM.*

TAVERNER, John (*c.* 1495–1545)
> *Ave Dei Patris filia, a 5* and 6. ME: *EECM*, XXV.
> *Gloria tibi Trinitas* Mass, *a 6.* ME: *TCM.*

TOMKINS, Thomas (1572–1656).
> *Ut, mi, re.* ME: *MB* V 38.
> *Ut, re, mi, fa, sol, la.* Various settings, ME: *MB* V: 34–7.

TYE, Christopher (*c.* 1505–?1572).
> *Cantate Domino, a 6.* ME: *EECM* XXXIII.
> *Miserere mei Deus, a 5.* ME: *EECM* XXXIII.
> *Omnes gentes plaudite, a 5.* ME: *EECM* XXXIII.

UT QUEANT LAXIS.
> Liber Usualis (q.v.), p. 1504.

VECCHI, Oratio (1550–1605).
> *S'udia un pastor, a 3.* Il convito musicale, *a 3–8vv*, 1597. ME: *OBIM* 49.

VERDELOT, Philippe (between 1470 and 1480–before 1552).
> *Dormendo un giorno, a 5.* I *a 5, c.* 1538. ME: *OBIM* 1.
> *Italia mia, a 5*, 1538. ME: *OBIM* 3; and Jeppesen, Italia Sacra Musica, vol. I.

VICENTINO, Nicola (1511–*c.* 1576).
> *Hierusalem convertere, a 5*, 1555. ME: Maniates 1979, p. 190f.

VICTORIA, Tomas Luis da (1548–1611). ME: *O.O.* ed. Pedrell, 1902–; *O.O..* ed. Angles, 1965–8.

> *Gaude Maria virgo, a 5.* 1572.

WEELKES, Thomas (1576–1623).

> *My flocks feed not/In black mourn I/Clear wells spring not, a 3. a 3, 4, 5* and 6, 1597. ME: *EMS* IX.
> *O Jonathan, a 6.* ME: *MB* XXIII.
> *O Lord arise, a 7.* ME: *MB* XXIII.
> *Three Virgin Nymphs, a 4.* 1597. ME: *EMS* XI.
> *When David heard that Absolom was slain, a 6.* 1600. ME: *MB* XXIII.
> *When Thoralis delights to walk, a 6.* 1600. ME: *EMS,* XII.

WERT, Giaches de (1535–1596). ME: CW eds MacClintock and Bernstein, *CMM,* XXIV.

> *Amen, amen dico vobis, a 5.* 1581. ME: Mapa Mundi Series B, 11.
> *Amor, io fallo/Pero, s'oltra suo stile, a 5.* II *a 5.* ME: RF II 23.
> *Ascendente Iesus in naviculum, a 6.* 1581. ME: Mapa Mundi Series B, 16.
> *Ben rinosco in voi,* see *Valle, che de'lamenti meie.*
> *Cruda Amarilli, a 5.* XI *a 5,* 1595.
> *Crudele acerba,* see *Mia benigna fortuna.*
> *Egressus Iesus, a 7.* 1581. ME: Mapa Mundi Series B, 16.
> *Giunto alla tomba/Non di morte sei tu, a 5.* VII *a 5,* 1581. ME: RF II 24.
> *Mia benigna fortuna/Crudele acerba, a 5.* IX *a 5,* 1588.
> *Non di morte sei tu,* see *Giunto alla tomba*
> *Pero, s'oltra stile,* see *Amor, io fallo.*
> *Valle, che de'lamenti miei/Ben riconosco in voi, a 5.* I *a 5,* 1588. ME: RF II 25.
> *Vezzosi augelli, a 5.* VIII *a 5,* 1586.

WHITE, Robert (*c.* 1538–1574).

> Hexachord setting (by 'Mr Whight'), ME: Caldwell 1973, p. 77.
> *Lamentations, a 5* and *a 6.* ME: *TCM.*

WILBYE, John (1574–1638).

> *Adieu sweet Amaryllis, a 4.* I *a 3–6,* 1598. ME: *EMS* VI.
> *Ah, cruel Amarillis, a 3.* II *a 3–6,* 1609. ME: *EMS* VII.
> *Draw on, sweet night, a 6.* II *a 3–6,* 1609. ME: *EMS* VII.

WILLAERT, Adrian (*c.* 1490–1562). ME: eds Zenck and Gerstenberg, *CMM*, 3.

> *Alla dolce armonia*, see *Qual dolcezza giamai*.
> *Amor mi fa morire*, *a* 4. 1536. ME: *PIM* I; Ein, 31.
> *Cantai, or piango*, *a* 6. 1559. ME: *OBIM* 22.
> *Passa la nave/Pioggia di lagrimar*, *a* 6. Musica Nova, 1559. ME: RF II 27.
> *Pioggia di lagrimar*, see *Passa la nave*.
> *Qual dolcezza giamai/Alla dolce armonia*, *a* 5. In Verdelot, Le dotte . . . *c.* 1538. ME: RF II 26.
> *Quanto piu m'arde/Non e ghiacciol*, *a* 5. *c.* 1538. ME: *OBIM* 4.

B: Literature

The following is a list of the books and articles to which reference is made in the notes. The abbreviations used in this bibliography are:

CUP	Cambridge University Press, Cambridge
EM	*Early Music*
EMH	*Early Music History*, ed. Iain Fenlon, Cambridge University Press, Cambridge
JRMA	*Journal of the Royal Musical Association*
MD	*Musica Disciplina*
ML	*Music and Letters*
MQ	*Musical Quarterly*
MT	*The Musical Times*
NG	*The New Grove Dictionary of Music and Musicians*, ed. Stanley Sadie, Macmillan, London, 1980
n.p.	No place of publication given
OUP	Oxford University Press, London etc.
PRMA	*Proceedings of the Royal Musical Association*
RMA	Royal Musical Association

In all journals that are listed below, the volume number is given in Roman numerals, the page numbers in Arabic numerals.

Allaire, Gaston G. (1972). *The Theory of Hexachords, Solmization and the Modal System*. Musicological Studies and Documents, XXIV, American Institute of Musicology, n.p.

Andrews, Herbert Kennedy (1958). *An Introduction to the Technique of Palestrina*. Novello and Company Ltd, London.

———(1966). *The Technique of Byrd's Vocal Polyphony*, OUP.

Andrews, H.K., and Dart, Thurston (1959). *Thomas Morley, Collected Motets*, Stainer and Bell, London.

Apel, Willi (1972). *The History of Keyboard Music to 1700*, tr. and rev. Hans Tischler, Indiana University Press, Bloomington/London.

Arnold, Denis (1963). *Monteverdi*, The Master Musicians Series, J.M. Dent and Sons Ltd, London.

———(1965). *Marenzio*, Oxford Studies of Composers (2), Oxford University Press, London.

———(1983). Record sleeve-note to UEA recording, *Madrigals by Luca Marenzio*, University of East Anglia B2126, issued in 1983.

Artusi, Giovanni Maria (1603). *Seconda parte dell Artusi dovera Delle imperfettione della moderna musica*, Venice.

Beebe, Ellen S. (1983). 'Text and Mode as Generators of Musical Structure in Clemens non Papa's "Accesserunt ad Jesum"', in *Music and Language*, Studies in the History of Music, I, Broude Brothers Limited, New York, pp. 79–94.

Bent, Margaret (1972). 'Musica Recta and Musica Ficta', *MD* XXVI, pp. 73–100.

———(1984). 'Diatonic ficta' in *EMH* IV, pp. 1–48.

Bentmann, Von Reinhard, and Lickes, Heinrich (1979). *Churches of the Middle Ages*, (transl. Anthony Lloyd), Cassell, London.

Berger, Karol (1976). 'Theories of Chromatic and Enharmonic Music in Late 16th century Italy', Studies in Musicology X, UMI Press, Ann Arbor, 1976, 1980.

———(1987). *Musica ficta: Theories of Accidental Inflections in Vocal Polyphony from Marchetto da Padova to Gioseffo Zarlino*, CUP.

Bianconi, Lorenzo (1973). 'The Caccinian Workshop of Pietro Maria Marsolo', in his edition of Marsolo's four-voice madrigals of 1614, *Musiche Rinascimentali Siciliani*, IV, Rome.

Blackburn, Bonnie J. (1987). *Music for Treviso Cathedral in the late Sixteenth Century*, RMA Monograph, III, London.

Boorman, Stanley (1990), 'False relations and the Cadence', in Richard Charteris (ed.) *Essays on Italian Music in the Cinquecento*, Altro Polo series, Frederick May Foundation for Italian Studies, University of Sydney.

Bray, Roger (1995). 'Sacred Music to Latin Texts', in *The Blackwell History of Music in Britain, The Sixteenth Century*, ed. Roger Bray, Blackwell, Oxford, pp. 46–93.

Brown, David (1974). *Wilbye*, Oxford Studies of Composers XI, OUP.

Buelow, George J. (1980). 'Rhetoric and Music', in *NG*.

Burke, Peter (1974) *Tradition and Innovation in Renaissance Italy: A Sociological Approach*, Fontana/Collins, London.

Byrd, William (1606 and 1607). *Gradualia*, Thomas Este, London.

Caldwell, John (1973). *English Keyboard Music before the Nineteenth Century*, Basil Blackwell, Oxford.

Carter, Tim (1988). Review of Tomlinson 1987, in *EMH* VIII, pp. 245–60.

——(1988a). 'Caccini's *Amarilli, mia bella*: some Questions, and a Few Answers', *JRMA* CXVIII part 2, pp. 250–73.

Chater, James (1975). '*Cruda Amarilli*: a cross-section of the Italian madrigal', *MT* March 1975, pp. 231–4.

——(1981). *Luca Marenzio and the Italian Madrigal 1557–1593*, UMI Research Press, Ann Arbor.

Chew, Geoffrey (1989). 'The Perfections of Modern Music: Consecutive Fifths and Tonal Coherence in Monteverdi', *Music Analysis* VIII No 3, October, pp. 247–73.

Collins, H.B. (1929). 'Thomas Tallis', *ML* X, pp. 152–66.

Collyer, Joanna (1987). 'The Church Music of Grammatio Metallo, 1602–1613'. M. Litt. thesis, University of Oxford.

Curtis, Alan (1972). *Sweelinck's Keyboard Music*, published for the Sir Thomas Browne Society, Leiden and Oxford.

Dobbins, Frank (1969). 'Doulce Memoire: A study of the Parody Chanson', *PRMA* XCVI, 1969–70, pp. 85–101.

——(ed.) (1987). *The Oxford Book of French Chansons*, OUP.

Doe, Paul (1968). *Tallis*, Oxford Studies of Composers, OUP.

Doughtie, Edward (1986). *English Renaissance Song*, Twayne Publishers, Boston, 1986.

Einstein, Alfred (1944). 'The Elizabethan Madrigal and "*Musica Transalpina*"', *ML* XXV, pp. 66–77.

——(1949). *The Italian Madrigal* (tr. by Alexander H. Krappe, Roger H. Sessions, and Oliver Strunk), Princeton University Press, Princeton.

Elcombe, Keith (1995). 'Keyboard Music', in *The Blackwell History of Music in Britain, The Sixteenth Century*, ed. Roger Bray, Blackwell, Oxford pp. 210–62.

Falk, Robert (1979). 'Parody and Contrafactum: A Terminological Clarification', *MQ* LXV, pp. 1–21.

Fanning, David (1988). *The Breath of the Symphonist: Shostakovich's Tenth*. RMA Monographs IV, RMA, London.

Fellowes, Edmund H. (1936). *William Byrd*, OUP.

Fenlon, Iain (1980). *Music and Patronage in sixteenth-century Mantua*, Cambridge Studies in Music, CUP.

——(1989). 'Music and Society', in Iain Fenlon (ed.), *Man and Music: The Renaissance*, Macmillan, Basingstoke and London, pp. 1–62.

Fenlon, Iain, and Haar, James (1988). *The Italian madrigal in the early sixteenth century. Sources and Interpretation*, CUP.

Field, Christopher (1992). 'Consort Music I: up to 1660', in *The Blackwell History of Music: The Seventeenth Century*, ed. Ian Spink, Blackwell, Oxford, pp. 197–244.

Field, Christopher D.S. (1996), 'Jenkins and the Cosmography of Harmony', in Andrew Ashbee and Peter Holman, *John Jenkins and his Time*, Clarendon Press, Oxford, pp. 1–74.

Finscher, Ludwig (1972). 'Gesualdo's "*Atonalitat*" und das Problem des musikalishen Manierismus', *Archiv fur Musikwisseschaft* XXIX, p. 7.

Geyl, Peter (1961). *The Netherlands in the Seventeenth Century*, London.

Glarean, Heinrich (1547). *Dodecacordon*, Basel 1547, tr. Clement Miller, Musicological Studies and Documents VI, n.p., 1965.

Godwin, Joscelyn (1987). *Harmonies of Heaven and Earth: The Spiritual Dimension of Music from Antiquity to the Avant-Garde*. Thames and Hudson, London.

Haar, James (1966). 'Pace non trovo: A study in Literary and Musical Parody', MD XX, pp. 95–149.

——(1976). 'Remarks on the Missa La sol fa re mi', in Lowinsky and Blackburn (eds), *Josquin des Prez*, OUP.

——(1986). *Essays on Italian Poetry and Music in the Renaissance, 1350–1600*, University of California Press, Berkeley, Los Angeles and London.

——(1989). 'Munich at the Time of Orlande de Lassus', in Iain Fenlon (ed.), *Man and Music: The Renaissance*, Macmillan, Basingstoke and London, pp. 243–62.

——(1990). 'Lessons in Theory from a Sixteenth-Century Composer', in Richard Charteris (ed.), *Essays on Italian Music in the Cinquecento*, Altro Polo series, Frederick May Foundation for Italian Studies, University of Sydney.

Harman, Alec (1976). *Popular Italian Madrigals of the Sixteenth Century for Mixed Voices*, OUP.

——(1983). *The Oxford Book of Italian Madrigals*, OUP.

Harper, John (1978). 'Frescobaldi's Early *Inganni* and their Background', *PRMA* CV, 1978–9, pp. 1–12.

——(1980). *Inganno*, in NG.

Hughes, Andrew (1980). 'Solmization', in NG.

Hulme, Edward (1976). *Symbolism in Christian Art*, Blandford Press, Poole.

Jeppesen, Knud (1946). *The style of Palestrina and the dissonance*, Munksgaard, Copenhagen, and OUP.

Kerman, Joseph (1981). *The Masses and Motets of William Byrd*, Faber and Faber, London.

La Rue, Jan (ed.) (1967). *Aspects of Medieval and Renaissance Music: a Birthday tribute to Gustave Reese*, OUP.

Lera, Luigi (1989). *Jacques Arcadelt (1504ca.–1568), VENTI MADRIGALI dal 1 Libro*. Pizzicato Editioni Musicali, Udine.

Levy, Michael (1975). *High Renaissance*, Penguin Books, Harmondsworth.

Lockwood, Lewis (1967). *On 'Parody' as a Term and Concept in 16th-century Music: a Birthday offering to Gustave Reese*, OUP.

———(1985). 'Adrian Willaert and Cardinal Ippolito I d'Este: new light on Willaert's early career in Italy', 1515–21, *EMH* V, pp. 85–112.

Lowinsky, Edward E. (1967). *Secret Chromatic Art in the Netherlands motet*, (tr. Carl Buchman), Columbia University Studies in Musicology VI, New York, reprinted 1967.

MacClintock, Carol (1966). 'Giaches de Wert (1535–1596): Life and Works', Musicological Studies and Documents XVII, American Institute of Musicology, Bloomington.

Mace, Dean T. (1983). 'Tasso, La Gerusalemme liberata, and Monteverdi', in *Music and Language*, Studies in the History of Music I, Broude Brothers Limited, New York, pp. 118–56.

Maniates, Maria Rika (1979). *Mannerism in Italian Music and Culture, 1530–1630*, University of North Carolina Press and Manchester University Press, Manchester.

Mann, Brian (1983). *The Secular Madrigals of Filippo di Monte, 1521–1603*, Studies in Musicology LXIV, UMI Research Press, Ann Arbor.

Martin, John Rupert (ed.) (1981). *The Antwerp Altarpieces*, Thames and Hudson, London.

Meier, Bernhard (1974). *Die Tonarten der Klassischen Vokalpolyphonie*, Oosthoek, Scheltema and Holkema, Utrecht.

Merritt, Arthur Tillman (1939). *Sixteenth-century Polyphony: A Basis for the Study of Counterpoint*, Harvard University Press, Cambridge, Massachusetts.

Milsom, John (1995). 'Sacred Songs in the Chamber', *in English Choral Practice 1400–1659*, ed. John Morehen, CUP, pp. 161–97.

Monteath, K. Bosi (1980). 'Benedetto Pallavicino', in *NG*.

Morley, Thomas (1597). *A Plain and Easy Introduction to Practical Music*, Peter Short, London; ed. Alec Harman, Dent and Sons Ltd., London, 1952.

Neighbour, Oliver (1978). *The Consort and Keyboard Music of William Byrd*, Faber and Faber, London.

Newcomb, Anthony (1980). *The Madrigal at Ferrara, 1579–1597*, Princeton University Press, Princeton, 1980.

North, Roger (1959). *Roger North on Music*, ed. John Wilson, Novello, London.

Novack, Saul (1983). 'The Analysis of Pre-Baroque Music', in *Aspects of Schenkerian Theory*, ed. David Beach, Yale University Press, New Haven, pp. 113–34.

Owens, Jessie Ann (1990). 'Mode in the Madrigals of Cipriano de Rore', in Richard Charteris (ed.), *Essays on Italian Music in the Cinquecento*, Altro Polo series, Frederick May Foundation for Italian Studies, University of Sydney.

Palisca, Claude V. (1968). 'The Artusi–Monteverdi Controversy', in *The Monteverdi Companion*, ed. Denis Arnold and Nigel Fortune, Faber and Faber, London.

———(1977). *Girolamo Mei (1519–1594), Letters on Ancient and Modern Music to Vincenzo Galilei and Giovanni Bardi*, Musicological Studies and Documents III, American Institute of Musicology, n.p.

———(1985). *Humanism in Italian Renaissance Musical Thought*, Yale University Press, New Haven and London.

Parrish, Carl (1958). *A Treasury of Early Music*, Faber and Faber, London.

Perkins, Leeman (1978). Review of Meier 1974 in *MQ* XXXI.

Petrobelli, Pierluigi (1968). '"*Ah dolente*": Marenzio, Wert, Monteverdi', in *Congresso internazionale sul tema Claudio Monteverdi et il suo tempo*: Venice, Mantua and Cremona.

Picker, Martin (1989). 'The Habsburg Courts in the Netherlands and Austria, 1477–1560', in Iain Fenlon (ed.), *Man and Music: The Renaissance*, Macmillan, Basingstoke and London, pp. 216–42.

Pike, Lionel (1969). '*Gaude Maria Virgo*: Morley or Phillips?', *ML* L, pp. 127–35.

———(1984). 'Marian Symbolism in Phillips', *MT* August, pp. 461–5, with corrections in *MT*, October, p. 596.

———(1986). 'The opening of Palestrina's *Stabat Mater*', *The Consort* XLII, 1986.

———(1993). Review of Peter Phillips's 'English Sacred Music 1549–1649', in *ML* Vol 74 No 1, September, pp. 68–71.

Pirrotta, Nino, and Povoledo, Elena (1982). *Music and Theatre from Poliziano to Monteverdi* (tr. Karen Eales), Cambridge Studies in Music, CUP.

Poulton, Diana (1972). *John Dowland*, Faber and Faber, London.

Poulton, Diana, and Lam, Basil (1974). *The Collected Lute Music of John Dowland*, Faber Music Limited, London, 1974, 1978.

Powers, Harold S. (1974). 'The Modality of "*Vestiva i Colli*"', in *Studies in Renaissance and Baroque Music in Honor of Arthur Mendel*, Barenreiter, Kassel.

Praetorius, Michael (1615). *Syntagma Musicum*, 1615 and other dates.

Rainbow, Bernarr (1982). *English Psalmody Prefaces: Popular methods of teaching, 1562–1835*, Boethius Press, Kilkenny.

Reardon, Bernard M.G. (1981). *Religious Thought in the Reformation*, Longman, London and New York.

Reynolds, Christopher A. (1989). 'Sacred Polyphony', in Howard Mayer Brown and Stanley Sadie, *Performance Practice before 1600*, New Grove Handbooks on Music, Macmillan, Basingstoke and London, pp. 185–200.

Roche, Jerome (ed.) (1974). *The Penguin Book of Italian Madrigals for four voices*, Penguin, Harmondsworth.

———(ed.) (1984). *North Italian Church Music in the Age of Monteverdi*, Clarendon Press, Oxford.

———(ed.) (1988). *The Flower of the Italian Madrigal* (2 vols), Galaxy Music Corporation, New York.

Rowen, Ruth Halle (1979). *Music through sources and documents*, Prentice Hall, Englewood Cliffs.

Rubio, P. Samuel (1972). *Classical Polyphony* (tr. Thomas Rive). Basil Blackwell, Oxford.

Salzer, Felix (1983). 'Heinrich Schenker and Historical Research: Monteverdi's Madrigal *Oimè, se tanto amate*', in David Beach (ed.), *Aspects of Schenkerian Theory*, Yale University Press, New Haven and London.

Sandon, Nick (1984). 'F G A B flat A; Thoughts on a Tudor motif', *EM* XII, No. 1, pp. 56–63.

Schrade, Leo (1964). *Monteverdi, Creator of Modern Music*, Victor Gollancz Ltd, London.

Selfridge-Field, Eleanor (1990). 'Three Practices, Three Styles: Reflections on Sacred Music and the *Seconda Prattica*', in John Caldwell, Edward Olleson, and Susan Wollenberg (eds), *The Well Enchanting Skill. Music, Poetry and Drama in the Culture of the Renaissance. Essays in Honour of F.W. Sternfeld*, OUP, pp. 53–63.

Stevenson, Robert (1961). *Spanish Cathedral Music in the Golden Age*, University of California Press, Berkeley and Los Angeles.

Strainchamps, Edmond (1985). 'The Life and Death of Caterina Martelli: New Light on Monteverdi's "Arianna"', *EMH* V, pp. 155–86.

Strunk, Oliver (1950). *Source Readings in Music History*, W.W. Norton and Company Ltd., New York.

Tilmouth, Michael (1980). 'Parody (i)' in *NG*.

Tomlinson, Gary (1987). *Monteverdi and the end of the Renaissance*, Clarendon Press, Stocksfield, Oxford.

Trowell, Brian (1980). 'Faburden – New Sources, New Evidence: a Preliminary Survey', in Edward Olleson (ed.), *Modern Musical Scholarship*, Oriel Press Ltd, pp. 28–78.

Watkins, Glenn (1973). *Gesualdo: The Man and his Music*, OUP.

Wells, Robin Headlam (1984). 'The ladder of love: verbal and musical rhetoric in the Elizabethan lute-song', *EM* May, pp. 173–89.

Whenham, John (1986). *Claudio Monteverdi: Orfeo*, CUP.

Willetts, Pamela (1962). 'A Neglected Source of Monody and Madrigals', *ML* xliii, pp. 329–39.

Zager, Daniel (1987). 'From the Singer's Point of View: A Case Study in Hexachordal Solmization as a Guide to *Musica Recta* and *Musica Ficta* in Fifteenth-Century Vocal Music', *Current Musicology*, XLIII, pp. 7–21.

Zarlino, Gioseffo (1558). *Le Istitutioni Harmoniche*, Venice. Part III tr. Guy A. Marco and Claude V. Palisca as *The Art of Counterpoint*, Yale University Press, New Haven and London, 1968. Part IV tr. Vered Cohen as *On the Modes*, Yale University Press, New Haven and London, 1983.

Index

233